Environment

Promoting Meaningful Access, Participation, and Inclusion

DEC Recommended Practices Monograph Series

Division for Early Childhood
of the Council for Exceptional Children

Washington, DC

ISBN: 978-0-9905128-1-3

Disclaimer

The opinions and information contained in the articles of this monograph are those of the authors of the respective articles and not necessarily those of the Division for Early Childhood (DEC) of the Council for Exceptional Children. Accordingly, DEC assumes no liability or risk that may be incurred as a consequence, directly or indirectly, or the use and application of any of the contents of this monograph.

Published and Distributed by:

of the Council for Exceptional Children

E-mail: dec@dec-sped.org
Website: http://www.dec-sped.org/

The Division for Early Childhood (DEC), a division of the Council for Exceptional Children, is an international membership organization for individuals who work with or on behalf of young children with disabilities and other special needs. Founded in 1973, DEC's mission is to promote policies and advance evidence-based practices that support families and enhance the optimal development of young children who have or are at risk for developmental delays and disabilities. Information about membership and other resources available can be found at www.dec-sped.org

Editors: Tricia Catalino, *Touro University Nevada*, and Lori E. Meyer, *University of Vermont*
Copy editor: Kevin Dolan
Cover and interior design: Kevin Dolan
Indexer: Jean Jesensky, *Endswell Indexing*
Typeset in Warnock Pro, Myriad Pro, and Calibri
Photos provided by iStock except those provided by authors on pages 94, 97, 138, 141, and 144

Suggested Citation

Catalino, T., & Meyer, L. E. (Eds.). (2016). *Environment: Promoting meaningful access, participation, and inclusion* (DEC Recommended Practices Monograph Series No. 2). Washington, DC: Division for Early Childhood.

TABLE OF CONTENTS

Division for Early Childhood

of the Council for Exceptional Children

Download the DEC Recommended Practices
www.dec-sped.org/recommendedpractices

Environment: A Key Intersection for the DEC Recommended Practices

TRICIA CATALINO
Touro University Nevada

LORI E. MEYER
University of Vermont

ENVIRONMENT AFFECTS CHILDREN'S HEALTH AND DEVELOPMENT AND is integral to every interaction a child might have with people, built space, materials, and even time. Practitioners, families, and leaders can influence and advocate for positive changes to environments that in turn improve child outcomes. In this issue, the second release in the DEC Recommended Practices Monograph Series, we focus on environment as an essential area of attention for practitioners who support young children with disabilities and their families. As one of the eight topic areas in the DEC Recommended Practices, Environment intersects with several other topic areas, and decisions made here can impact the quality of care and education we provide while showing measurable influence on expected outcomes.

Our look at the Environment recommended practices includes 10 articles outlining the best available evidence supporting these practices as a way to promote access and encourage participation within various settings. We selected articles that featured a variety of environments and considered multiple perspectives to offer strategies for implementation by practitioners and families. In editing the monograph, we had also hoped to include images that reflect the beautiful diversity we see in our homes, communities, and classrooms. We scoured photograph collections available to us; however, we realized the representation of children, families, and adults would not be as diverse as we had hoped. We hope that you find the monograph not only helpful in implementing the Environment recommended practices but also in reinforcing the importance of the environment to optimize outcomes for children with or at risk for disabilities and their families.

This monograph opens with two articles that speak broadly about the Environment practices and explain how they can help promote or constrain a child's access to and participation in everyday learning experiences. Barton, Steed, and Smith provide an overview of the current state of inclusion for young children with disabilities and address the ongoing need to support high-quality services in natural and inclusive environments. The authors summarize evidence supporting inclusion and present several strategies that practitioners can use to create quality inclusive environments for all children. Jeffries and Fiss add to this outlook by connecting the Environment recommended practices to the World Health

For Your Reference

The Environment recommended practices are presented on the next page as a reference while you read these articles. We encourage you to access the entire set of DEC Recommended Practices at …

www.dec-sped.org/
recommendedpractices

Organization's International Classification of Functioning, Disability, and Health (ICF). They use a case vignette of a child using assistive technology to show how the ICF environmental factors apply to the DEC Recommended Practices.

A significant portion of this monograph explores Universal Design for Learning (UDL), a set of principles for curriculum development that give all people equal opportunities to learn. Fundamentally, UDL strives to provide all young children with access to learning opportunities within their environments. De Arment, Xu, and Coleman describe these principles in children's natural environments, such as the home, classroom, and the community more broadly. These authors also emphasize how UDL can facilitate collaboration among members of interdisciplinary teams and help empower families. Horn and her colleagues present a planning process for teachers to use that includes UDL and differentiation as they design curricula to promote children's engagement and learning. Pisha and Spencer similarly offer strategies and self-monitoring tools informed by UDL principles to encourage physical activity among young children with disabilities. Stanton-Chapman and Schmidt conclude the section by outlining a collaborative process that applies Universal Design concepts to creating inclusive playgrounds.

The final four articles provide specific examples of how to implement the Environment recommended practices, and these examples provide further insight on how improving natural environments to facilitate more participation can have positive benefits for young children with disabilities. Hallam and Hooper bring attention to Environment recommended practices in home-based child care. They argue that the introduction of the Environment recommended practices in such settings potentially increases access to high-quality, inclusive educational experiences for young children with or at risk for disabilities. Across classroom environments, Yu, Ostrosky, Favazza, and Meyer ask us to consider how materials, curriculum, and language can impact the acceptance of young children with disabilities. They illustrate how increasing the representation of disability in an environment can enhance children's sense of belonging. Meadan and Angell meanwhile offer strategies for arranging children's environments to increase their opportunities for communication through the use of a naturalistic teaching strategy called "Pick, Present, Play." Lastly, Gagnon and colleagues describe how modifying readily available ride-on toy cars can increase self-initiated mobility for young children with physical disabilities. These authors also show how moving from place to place on their own can improve children's development and how communities can work together to create this type of technology for any young child who might benefit from it.

The monograph ends with Catlett's ever popular and valuable Resources Within Reason article where you will find many free resources to help implement the Environment recommended practices.

The influence of the environment on the health and development of children with or at risk for disabilities cannot be overstated. We hope that practitioners, families, caregivers, professional development providers, and educators alike will use the information in these articles on the Environment recommended practices to help guide decisions about the environment in their worlds, particularly as they affect a child's ability to access and participate in all learning experiences.

Environment

Young children who have or are at risk for developmental delays/disabilities learn, play, and engage with adults and peers within a multitude of environments such as home, school, child care, and the neighborhood. Environmental practices refer to aspects of the space, materials (toys, books, etc.), equipment, routines, and activities that practitioners and families can intentionally alter to support each child's learning across developmental domains. The environmental practices we address in this section encompass the physical environment (e.g., space, equipment, and materials), the social environment (e.g., interactions with peers, siblings, family members), and the temporal environment (e.g., sequence and length of routines and activities). They relate not only to supporting the child's access to learning opportunities but also ensuring their safety. It is important for practitioners to remember that these environmental dimensions are inextricably intertwined for young children who have or are at risk for developmental delays/disabilities and their families. Through implementation of the environmental practices, practitioners and families can promote nurturing and responsive caregiving and learning environments that can foster each child's overall health and development.

We recommend the following practices associated with the child's environment:

E1 Practitioners provide services and supports in natural and inclusive environments during daily routines and activities to promote the child's access to and participation in learning experiences.

E2 Practitioners consider Universal Design for Learning principles to create accessible environments.

E3 Practitioners work with the family and other adults to modify and adapt the physical, social, and temporal environments to promote each child's access to and participation in learning experiences.

E4 Practitioners work with families and other adults to identify each child's needs for assistive technology to promote access to and participation in learning experiences.

E5 Practitioners work with families and other adults to acquire or create appropriate assistive technology to promote each child's access to and participation in learning experiences.

E6 Practitioners create environments that provide opportunities for movement and regular physical activity to maintain or improve fitness, wellness, and development across domains.

Organization's International Classification of Functioning, Disability, and Health (ICF). They use a case vignette of a child using assistive technology to show how the ICF environmental factors apply to the DEC Recommended Practices.

A significant portion of this monograph explores Universal Design for Learning (UDL), a set of principles for curriculum development that give all people equal opportunities to learn. Fundamentally, UDL strives to provide all young children with access to learning opportunities within their environments. De Arment, Xu, and Coleman describe these principles in children's natural environments, such as the home, classroom, and the community more broadly. These authors also emphasize how UDL can facilitate collaboration among members of interdisciplinary teams and help empower families. Horn and her colleagues present a planning process for teachers to use that includes UDL and differentiation as they design curricula to promote children's engagement and learning. Pisha and Spencer similarly offer strategies and self-monitoring tools informed by UDL principles to encourage physical activity among young children with disabilities. Stanton-Chapman and Schmidt conclude the section by outlining a collaborative process that applies Universal Design concepts to creating inclusive playgrounds.

The final four articles provide specific examples of how to implement the Environment recommended practices, and these examples provide further insight on how improving natural environments to facilitate more participation can have positive benefits for young children with disabilities. Hallam and Hooper bring attention to Environment recommended practices in home-based child care. They argue that the introduction of the Environment recommended practices in such settings potentially increases access to high-quality, inclusive educational experiences for young children with or at risk for disabilities. Across classroom environments, Yu, Ostrosky, Favazza, and Meyer ask us to consider how materials, curriculum, and language can impact the acceptance of young children with disabilities. They illustrate how increasing the representation of disability in an environment can enhance children's sense of belonging. Meadan and Angell meanwhile offer strategies for arranging children's environments to increase their opportunities for communication through the use of a naturalistic teaching strategy called "Pick, Present, Play." Lastly, Gagnon and colleagues describe how modifying readily available ride-on toy cars can increase self-initiated mobility for young children with physical disabilities. These authors also show how moving from place to place on their own can improve children's development and how communities can work together to create this type of technology for any young child who might benefit from it.

The monograph ends with Catlett's ever popular and valuable Resources Within Reason article where you will find many free resources to help implement the Environment recommended practices.

The influence of the environment on the health and development of children with or at risk for disabilities cannot be overstated. We hope that practitioners, families, caregivers, professional development providers, and educators alike will use the information in these articles on the Environment recommended practices to help guide decisions about the environment in their worlds, particularly as they affect a child's ability to access and participate in all learning experiences.

For Your Reference

The Environment recommended practices are presented on the next page as a reference while you read these articles. We encourage you to access the entire set of DEC Recommended Practices at …

www.dec-sped.org/recommendedpractices

Environment

Young children who have or are at risk for developmental delays/disabilities learn, play, and engage with adults and peers within a multitude of environments such as home, school, child care, and the neighborhood. Environmental practices refer to aspects of the space, materials (toys, books, etc.), equipment, routines, and activities that practitioners and families can intentionally alter to support each child's learning across developmental domains. The environmental practices we address in this section encompass the physical environment (e.g., space, equipment, and materials), the social environment (e.g., interactions with peers, siblings, family members), and the temporal environment (e.g., sequence and length of routines and activities). They relate not only to supporting the child's access to learning opportunities but also ensuring their safety. It is important for practitioners to remember that these environmental dimensions are inextricably intertwined for young children who have or are at risk for developmental delays/disabilities and their families. Through implementation of the environmental practices, practitioners and families can promote nurturing and responsive caregiving and learning environments that can foster each child's overall health and development.

We recommend the following practices associated with the child's environment:

E1 Practitioners provide services and supports in natural and inclusive environments during daily routines and activities to promote the child's access to and participation in learning experiences.

E2 Practitioners consider Universal Design for Learning principles to create accessible environments.

E3 Practitioners work with the family and other adults to modify and adapt the physical, social, and temporal environments to promote each child's access to and participation in learning experiences.

E4 Practitioners work with families and other adults to identify each child's needs for assistive technology to promote access to and participation in learning experiences.

E5 Practitioners work with families and other adults to acquire or create appropriate assistive technology to promote each child's access to and participation in learning experiences.

E6 Practitioners create environments that provide opportunities for movement and regular physical activity to maintain or improve fitness, wellness, and development across domains.

Solutions and Strategies to Support Access to Natural and Inclusive Environments for All Children

Erin E. Barton
Vanderbilt University

Elizabeth A. Steed
Barbara J. Smith
University of Colorado Denver

INCLUSION HAS BEEN AT THE HEART OF POLICY, PROFESSIONAL STAN-dards, and research for decades. Early childhood (EC) inclusion is compelling for three main reasons: (a) research supports inclusion of all young children in natural environments where their peers with typical development are found, (b) current education laws and regulations support EC inclusion, and (c) national EC professional organizations support inclusion of all children. For example, re-search consistently demonstrates that high-quality and responsive environments such as those promoted in the Division for Early Childhood's (DEC) Environ-ment recommended practices (2014) are associated with positive outcomes for young children, including for children with disabilities (Camilli, Vargas, Ryan, & Barnett, 2010; Espinosa, 2002; Pianta, Barnett, Burchinal, & Thornburg, 2009). Also, the Individuals With Disabilities Education Act (2004) has encouraged that educational services for children with disabilities be delivered where those services are delivered for typically developing children (Musgrove, 2012). A key component of this effort includes using the DEC Recommended Practices (DEC, 2014) to increase young children's access to and participation in natural and in-clusive environments. Inclusive environments are "settings where the values, policies, and practices support the right of every infant and young child and his or her family, regardless of ability, to participate in a broad range of activities and contexts as full members of families, communities, and society" (DEC, 2015, p. 8). Natural environments are

> settings in which children without disabilities spend time. Common
> places include the home, child care programs, family daycare homes,

and community settings (e.g., stores, barber shops, doctor's offices, parks, etc.) and programs (e.g., children's hour at the library, gymnastics classes, etc.) available to all children in society. Activities and routines may need to be adapted to ensure that children with disabilities are able to participate and be integral members. (DEC, 2015, p. 11)

The purpose of this manuscript is to outline the current state of inclusion and highlight common strategies and solutions that support DEC Environment recommended practice E1: "Practitioners provide services and supports in natural and inclusive environments during daily routines and activities to promote the child's access to and participation in learning experiences." The authors used the aforementioned definitions of inclusive and natural environments to guide the development of solutions and strategies to ensure children with disabilities participate with typically developing children with supports that lead to positive social relationships, learning, and a sense of community for all involved (Odom, Buysse, & Soukakou, 2011).

> Over the past two decades, the term *preschool inclusion* has replaced the term *preschool mainstreaming* to promote the full acceptance of the child as an engaged and participating member of his/her family, classroom, and community.

Research Supports for EC Inclusion

High-quality inclusive environments are correlated with positive outcomes for children, including children with disabilities (Camilli et al., 2010; Guralnick, 2001; Pianta et al., 2009; Strain, 1990; Strain & Bovey, 2011). The research on EC inclusion has evolved, and several effective components of preschool inclusion have emerged (Barton & Smith, 2015a; Soukakou, 2012; Wills, Darragh-Ernst, & Presley, 2012). For example, high-quality inclusive classrooms with higher ratios of more competent peers, in particular, are related to positive outcomes for children with disabilities (Justice, Logan, Lin, & Kaderavek, 2014; Strain & Bovey, 2011). Additional components include high-quality adult-child interactions, specialized instruction, and individualized goals focused on positive social relationships and friendships between classmates with and without disabilities. In fact, over the past two decades, the term *preschool inclusion* has replaced the term *preschool mainstreaming* to promote the full acceptance of the child as an engaged and participating member of his/her family, classroom, and community. Further, research has shown that placement alone is ineffective (Strain, McGee, & Kohler, 2001). Children need multiple supported opportunities to participate in the environment and with socially competent peers; children with and without disabilities benefit from high-quality inclusive EC settings (Strain & Hoyson, 2000).

Laws Support Preschool Inclusion

In addition to the research findings on the efficacy of inclusive service delivery for preschoolers with disabilities, special education placement options are driven by the "least restrictive environment" (LRE) requirement of Part B of IDEA. In fact, there has been federal commitment for inclusion for many years. For more than 35 years, IDEA and federal EC programs (e.g., Head Start) have encouraged educational services for preschool children with disabilities to be delivered in general education classrooms with typically developing peers. IDEA has a strong preference for the placement of young children with disabilities in settings with typically developing children (Musgrove, 2012). The exact wording of IDEA (2004) asserts that school districts must ensure that all children with disabilities are educated with children without disabilities to the maximum extent appropriate (34 CFR § 300.114). Indeed, IDEA states that the "removal" of children from the regular educational setting can be done only if the regular education placement is not satisfactory even with the provision of supplementary aids and services (34 CFR § 300.114) and training and technical assistance for administrators and teachers (34 CFR § 300.119).

Recent years have seen increased political commitment as well. For example, a 2012 policy letter from the U.S. Department of Education's Office of Special Education Programs (OSEP) clarified that IDEA's LRE provisions also apply to preschool children with disabilities. According to the policy letter, "These requirements state IDEA's strong preference for educating students with disabilities in regular classes with appropriate aids and supports" (Musgrove, 2012, p. 1). In 2015, the U.S. Departments of Education (DOE) and Health and Human Services (HHS) released a policy statement on inclusion of children with disabilities in EC programs. The policy statement set a vision and provided recommendations for increasing the inclusion of infants, toddlers, and preschool children with disabilities in high-quality EC programs. This policy statement gave the broader EC community an opportunity to advocate and facilitate high-quality inclusion for all children; set a high expectation regarding the quality of inclusive programs and the numbers of children with disabilities included in those programs; and highlighted the research, laws, resources and strategies that support high-quality EC inclusion.

National Professional Organizations Support Inclusion

In 2009, two professional EC organizations, the Division for Early Childhood and the National Association for the Education of Young Children (NAEYC), developed and published a joint position statement on EC inclusion (DEC/NAEYC, 2009). The collaboration between DEC and NAEYC provided new opportunities at the state and local levels to engage in meaningful dialogue around critical issues for children with disabilities within broader EC systems (Odom et al., 2011). This was especially important given the fragmented nature of EC (e.g., child care, Head Start, community preschools, ECSE; Odom et al., 2011). Diverse EC systems (e.g., Head Start, child care, public school) need to work together to ensure sufficient supports for children with disabilities, their families, and the practitioners who work with them (Hayden, Frederick, & Smith, 2003).

With this position statement, these organizations partnered to advocate for and support EC inclusion. This statement offered a definition of EC inclusion and provided recommendations for developing high-quality inclusive settings. With this statement, the organizations collectively defined EC inclusion by access, participation, and supports and emphasized that all children should be participating members of both the physical and social environment. DEC/NAEYC recommended that the broad field of EC revise program and professional standards, create

and integrate EC professional development systems, and adapt federal and state accountability systems to support collaboration around the shared goal of providing services for all children in natural and inclusive settings.

However, in 28 years, the practice of providing special education and related services in regular EC settings to preschoolers with disabilities has increased only about 6%, and many young children with disabilities continue to be educated in separate settings (Barton & Smith, 2015a). While the definitions of settings and reporting methods by states have changed over time, data from 2013, which is reported in the 37th annual report to Congress on IDEA, indicated that 43% of children with disabilities received most of their services in regular EC settings as their primary education setting (U.S. HHS & DOE, 2015). The practice of providing special education and related services to children with disabilities in regular EC settings increased just marginally over the last three decades (U.S. HHS & DOE, 2015). This suggests that school districts need more support for making inclusive placement decisions, designing services, implementing systems, and crafting policies and procedures that result in the full inclusion of young children with disabilities into high-quality natural and inclusive settings.

EC Inclusion Surveys

In an effort to understand the lack of progress in EC inclusion, Barton and Smith (2015a) conducted an online survey of preschool and special education administrators (e.g., 619 coordinators). The survey instrument was developed to gain descriptive information from a national sample of administrators to identify current challenges to preschool inclusion and solutions or strategies to address those challenges. The survey asked respondents to identify and describe challenges to EC inclusion in their program, community, or state and to suggest solutions. Survey items were based on a similar survey conducted more than 20 years earlier (Smith & Rose, 1993; Smith, Salisbury & Rose, 1992). The authors compared the survey results with those of the previous survey (Rose & Smith, 1993; Smith & Rose, 1993; Smith et al., 1992) to understand how challenges to preschool inclusion might have changed.

The major change from 20 years ago was that the attitude and belief challenges moved from being the second most frequently cited category in 1993 to the most frequently cited challenge category in 2014 (see Table 1). Further, personnel policies were the most frequently cited category in 1993, but they moved to sixth place in the 2014 survey. These changes suggested perhaps the field has made progress in the area of personnel policies that support EC inclusion; however, attitudes and beliefs remain a major barrier to the provision of services for all children in natural and inclusive settings. We organized them into three over-arching categories: attitudes and beliefs, policies, and resources for the purposes of addressing the specific challenges. Table 1 provides more specific descriptions of the common challenges identified in these surveys.

While not mentioning them directly, many of the challenges and solutions related directly to implementing the DEC Environment recommended practices (2014). In fact, the provision of services in natural and inclusive environments is an essential component of all DEC Recommended Practices. Although it is important to identify the challenges, EC professionals and policy makers have a responsibility to overcome these challenges and work with families of children with disabilities to provide services in natural and inclusive environments. Thus, we focused the next sections of this article on solutions and strategies that ensure children with disabilities, at risk for developmental delay, and with typical development have access to educational services in high-quality natural and inclusive EC environments. Nearly all of the stated attitude and belief challenges were related to whether inclusive EC settings can be of sufficient quality to address the needs of all the children, particularly those with disabilities. Particular attention is paid to the solutions and strategies related to addressing beliefs and attitudes about EC inclusion and concerns that inclusive settings would be less high quality than separate settings, which was a persistent theme throughout all challenges (Barton & Smith, 2015a).

Solutions and Strategies

According to the DEC Recommended Practices (2014), the "environment" refers to the physical spaces themselves that include materials and toys, the social interactions that occur in those spaces, and how activities are structured and sequenced in those spaces. In high-quality and effective inclusive EC environments, it is important to consider and intentionally plan all of these aspects of the environment: the materials and toys chosen, the density of the space (e.g., how children move in the space), the peer group, and how routines and activities are scheduled. Quality inclusive EC environments facilitate the participation of children with disabilities and typically developing children with supports that lead to positive social relationships, learning, and attitudes and beliefs that support inclusion, diversity, and a sense of community for all involved (Odom et al., 2011). In the next sections, we outline strategies and solutions that comprehensively support the Environment recommended practice E1: "Practitioners

Quality inclusive EC environments facilitate the participation of children with disabilities and typically developing children with supports that lead to positive social relationships, learning, and attitudes and beliefs that support inclusion, diversity, and a sense of community for all involved.

Table 1
Common Challenges to Providing Services for All Children in Inclusive and Natural Environments

Overall Challenge	Specific Challenges	Description
Attitudes and belief challenges	Quality of comprehensive services	Districts might struggle with how to provide comprehensive services in private programs or might believe that comprehensive services cannot be provided outside of public schools.
	Someone will lose	Early childhood special educators and regular early childhood educators might believe that children with disabilities need segregated environments to meet their educational requirements.
	Turf issues and lack of respect	Personnel across community and public school programs do not respect each other's skill sets. Public school personnel have no "control" over the methods and curricula that the community-based programs use. This also includes beliefs that private and community-based programs might not have the expertise to serve children with disabilities.
	Lack of awareness and understanding	This includes a lack of awareness of current recommended practices and their use in inclusive settings and the benefits of inclusive settings for children with and without disabilities.
Perceived policy challenges	Use of nonpublic school setting	Private or nonpublic school agencies often cannot be "approved" to deliver special education and related services.
	Conflicting policies	Private and charter schools often do not accept children with disabilities, hours of the school or program day vary across settings, and private schools are not mandated to address state or common core standards.
	Personnel policies	Personnel policies are different across public and private systems, which might limit the provision of services to children with IEPs. For example, professional development systems might be separate and have different requirements.
	Fiscal and contracting	Funding streams create challenges such as contracting with church-affiliated or nonpublic programs, state legislation prohibits state general funds to be used for education below kindergarten, Head Start and state preschool programs require income or at-risk eligibility, and, in some cases, programs cannot get reimbursed from state special education funds if children are in "general education" or if the teacher is not "highly qualified." This also can include a lack of funding to pay for special education and related services personnel to provide itinerant services in the community.
	Transportation	These are often perceived policy barriers such as a lack of funding for transportation to all children, transportation can only be provided to students with IEPs, preschool age children cannot use school district transportation, busses cannot travel outside specific geographic areas, preschool children with IEPs who use the bus arrive later than other children, and parents must transport children regardless of income level.

Table 1 (continued)
Common Challenges to Providing Services for All Children in Inclusive and Natural Environments

Overall Challenge	Specific Challenges	Description
Resource challenges	Resources related to personnel	This can include the fact that personnel in community settings make low wages and that it is difficult to recruit and retain qualified teachers.
	Program quality	Districts might have a lack of high-quality early childhood programs.
	Commitment to collaboration	Public school personnel often report that community providers are not receptive to training and technical assistance from the special education community. A lack of information sharing can occur at all levels. Community programs might be full with no available slots for the school districts to buy for children with IEPs.

provide services and supports in natural and inclusive environments during daily routines and activities to promote the child's access to and participation in learning experiences."

Strategy 1: Focus on Changing Attitudes and Beliefs

As noted above, the most frequently cited challenge to preschool inclusion reported in the Barton and Smith (2015a) survey was attitudes and beliefs. This challenge has likely contributed to the lack of progress in EC inclusion because it suggests key decision makers have negative or inaccurate beliefs about EC inclusion. For instance, public school administrators are reported to lack the knowledge about the developmental importance of young children with disabilities being in settings with their typical peers. Survey respondents also reported that families of both typically developing children and children with disabilities have concerns about the quality of inclusive settings. Finally, the lack of collaboration and partnering across regular EC settings and programs and those that have traditionally served only children with disabilities is a challenge that is directly linked to attitudes and beliefs. This lack of collaboration restricts the ability to blend funding, personnel, and program placement efforts.

A first step for changing attitudes and beliefs might be to educate administrators, families, and personnel through two main activities: (1) developing and disseminating short, easy-to-read fact sheets on the research and legal base for preschool inclusion as well as professional guidance such as the DEC/NAEYC position statement; and (2) holding forums for administrators, families, and providers to discuss with decision makers their concerns and challenges and what they perceive as barriers. These forums could address such issues as blending funding streams and offer guidance about how to provide all the needed services and supports for children in inclusive settings as well as other "barrier busting" strategies. Once these are in place, state agencies might provide incentives for local programs to develop and serve as models of preschool inclusion, which could provide a place for administrators, families, and providers to visit, learn from, and see first hand the benefits of preschool inclusion.

Attitudes and beliefs also can improve through increasing and supporting collaboration within school districts as well as across district and community programs, and principals and program directors are key to making this happen. For example, Salisbury and McGregor (2002) found successful inclusive elementary programs had administrators who created supportive learning communities focused on facilitating high-quality inclusion and collaborative decision-making; the same is true for EC programs. Administrators in high-quality programs create teams of stakeholders (administrators, families, providers) who identify concerns, develop and implement solutions, and meet regularly to build trust and relationships to help address fears and concerns (Gupta & Rous, 2016; Odom et al., 2011). These stakeholder teams might:

- Create coordinated resources such as blending district EC resources (Title I, PreK, IDEA, etc.) to create inclusive classrooms within the district.
- Establish resource sharing between district and community programs (e.g., district paid specialized staff supporting community settings and community programs providing transportation).
- Provide collaborative professional development across regular early childhood education (ECE) and early childhood special education (ECSE) programs based on evidence-based practices.
- Enlist ECSE service providers to support regular ECE teachers with ideas and strategies, behavioral support services where needed, and on-site coaching.
- Generate an evaluation and communication plan to ensure that the preschool inclusion effort is successful for children, teachers, and families.

Strategy 2: Use a Blended Instructional Approach

A blended instructional approach is suggested for inclusion of young children with disabilities because it incorporates the intentional teaching of developmentally appropriate practice (DAP) for all children and embeds individualized learning opportunities across the day for children with disabilities (Grisham-Brown, Hemmeter, & Pretti-Frontczak, 2005). In this approach, teachers create meaningful and frequent opportunities for each child, use prompting and feedback to support learning, and take data to monitor the effectiveness of instruction (Barton, Pribble, & Joseph, 2015). For example, child care teachers can teach a 4-year-old working on one-to-one correspondence to count and say the number of food items (e.g., four strawberries, two crackers) during snack, lunchtime, and dramatic play. The number of learning opportunities (i.e., trials) embedded throughout the day and the schedule for embedding (e.g., massed, distributed) should be based on the child's learning history, goals, and his/her progress (Barton, Bishop, & Snyder, 2014; Wolery, 2012).

This approach, which is intentionally flexible and responsive to individual learning differences, would facilitate the provision of services and supports in natural and inclusive environments for young children with disabilities as recommended by E1. In a blended instructional approach, the learning environment is accessible and intentionally constructed to foster learning for each child and his/her goals. It allows for minimal changes to the learning environment (e.g., child care classroom) while ensuring that all children, including those with disabilities, are meaningfully engaged and receiving individualized support toward their learning goals. A blended instructional approach might address resource challenges because it does not require additional materials or costly curricula to implement.

Strategy 3: Provide Accommodations and Modifications

The third strategy is to provide effective accommodations and modifications so that all children have access to and participate in natural and inclusive environments. Further, Environment recommended practice E3 suggests that "practitioners work with the family and other adults to modify and adapt the physical, social, and temporal environments to promote each child's access to and participation in learning experiences." There are various ways that programs can allow full access to all children, including (a) changing the physical (e.g., widening walkways), social (e.g., creating partner activities), or temporal (e.g., providing a picture schedule) environments; (b) adapting materials (e.g., using high-contrast materials); (c) simplifying an activity (e.g., providing pieces to a puzzle one by one); and (d) providing specialized equipment (e.g., touchscreens, pencil grips; Sandall & Schwartz, 2008).

Using specialized equipment such as assistive technology can make an important difference in a child's access and independent participation in classroom activities and routines. Assistive technologies are flexible and can involve low-tech tools (e.g., teacher-made visuals or picture cues) or high-tech devices (e.g., computers, switches, or augmentative communication tablets; Campbell, Milbourne, Dugan, & Wilcox, 2006). Low-tech assistive technologies, such as visual schedules, slant boards, lap trays, Velcro, adapted books, pencil grips, triangular crayons, adapted scissors, and knobbed puzzles, can be easy to make, flexible to use, and easy to fix when they break! These tools can help children independently participate in classroom activities and routines alongside their peers. Some

Attitudes and beliefs also can improve through increasing and supporting collaboration within school districts as well as across district and community programs, and principals and program directors are key to making this happen.

children might benefit from more sophisticated devices such as switch-operated battery toys, touchscreens, voice output devices, and walkers. These devices might be less flexible than low technology tools, but they provide a wider range of outputs and supports.

Children also might benefit from high-technology devices such as computer augmentative and alternative communication systems (e.g., DynaVox), software programs for tablets (e.g., Proloquo2Go), seating devices, and high-powered wheelchairs (Sadao & Robinson, 2010). Tools and devices should be selected based on the child's needs and goals, developmental level, abilities, and the setting in which the child will use the device (Barton et al., 2015). The identification and use of assistive technology for individual children is supported by two Environment recommended practices: "Practitioners work with families and other adults to identify each child's needs for assistive technology to promote access to and participation in learning experiences" (E4) and "Practitioners work with families and other adults to acquire or create appropriate assistive technology to promote each child's access to and participation in learning experiences" (E5). These might challenge an EC program's resources; however, the low-technology options are usually viable and feasible for EC settings. Overall, these two recommended practices (E4 and E5) support children's access to and participation in inclusive and natural environments (E1) and provide guidance on how programs might use their resources efficiently and effectively.

Strategy 4: Ensure a Rich Social Environment

All young children learn social skills through interactions with peers and adults in their natural and inclusive environments. When a learning environment includes a high ratio of socially competent peers, young children with disabilities show greater gains in their language and social skills than children in classrooms with low ratios of socially competent peers (Guralnick, Neville, Hammond, & Connor, 2007; Justice et al., 2014; Strain & Bovey, 2011). For this reason, it is important that the ratio of young children with disabilities to typically developing children in an inclusive classroom is carefully considered when planning for young children's access and participation in natural and inclusive environments. Specific considerations include the ratio of children with and without disabilities, the severity of their disabilities, the daily schedule, and the activities that encourage or require collaboration among peers.

In addition to these considerations, it is also important to plan for intentionally teaching social skills. A primary developmental task of preschoolers is to develop friendships and become a member of a peer group. Children develop friendships and peer groups through a history of interactions with each other. In fact, children with disabilities in inclusive classrooms who have opportunities to interact with typically developing peers demonstrate higher levels of social competence and better communication skills (Guralnick et al., 2007). However, placement in an inclusive setting alone is not sufficient to promote learning and development (McConnell, 2002). Some children with disabilities will need intentional, systematic instruction to learn appropriate social skills. Specialized instruction and individualized adaptations to daily routines and activities might

Specialized instruction and individualized adaptations to daily routines and activities might be necessary to ensure all children successfully participate and engage in the physical *and* social environment.

be necessary to ensure all children successfully participate and engage in the physical *and* social environment. Systematic instruction focused on social skills might include incidental teaching of friendship skills (e.g., getting a peer's attention, asking a peer to play, entering group play), recognition of emotions, and problem solving. Commercial curricula are available to guide social skills instruction with young children (Barton, Steed, et al., 2014) and incidental teaching of social skills (Fox & Lentini, 2006). Children with disabilities and their typically developing peers should have a sufficient number of opportunities to interact with each other.

Play provides children with multiple opportunities to learn and engage with the environment, including promoting meaningful interactions across peers and contexts (Barton & Wolery, 2010; Lifter, Mason, & Barton, 2011; McConnell, 2002). For example, play provides children with disabilities multiple natural learning opportunities, meaningful social interactions with their peers,

and natural opportunities to practice and generalize other skills (Barton, 2015; Lifter et al., 2011). When children are playing near each other with the same objects or materials in the same manner, they are more likely to interact with each other (McConnell, 2002). Similarly, when children with disabilities use fewer different play responses or less creativity in their play, the opportunities for learning are limited. Children with disabilities, however, are more likely to use objects or materials inappropriately, engage in repetitive behaviors, and use fewer complex behaviors, which potentially limit the opportunities for learning and the benefits of play. Research indicates that intentional, systematic interventions are necessary to increase play skills in young children with disabilities (Lifter et al., 2011) and there are specific practices related to increased generalized pretend play skills in young children with disabilities that can be implemented within natural and inclusive environments (Barton, 2015).

Strategy 5: Practice an Evidence-Based Professional Development Approach

The fifth strategy suggestion is to use an effective professional development (PD) approach that is based on research on adult learning principles and implementation science to increase the number of professionals who are competent and confident in supporting young children with disabilities in natural and inclusive environments. The PD approach should involve workshops with lecture and discussion about inclusion, live or video demonstrations to see and practice skills, ongoing coaching in the classroom or natural setting, and performance-based feedback about the teachers' use of targeted skills (Steed & Smith, 2015). Private nondistrict programs need to reflect high quality and meet the child's needs, and they can do so with supports from the school district such as training, coaching, and technical assistance. For example, school districts can provide itinerant special education teachers or related service personnel to work with child care programs, community preschools, Head Start classrooms, or other nondistrict programs where children with IEPs attend. Too often PD approaches only use workshops where teachers or administrators are passively listening to information with no follow-up on site for them to translate the new information to their practice. Research confirms that the steps of practice, coaching, and performance-based feedback are necessary for true change and implementation of the recommended practices (Fixsen, Blase, Duda, Naoom, & Van Dyke, 2010; Snyder, Hemmeter, & McLaughlin, 2011).

Strategy 6: Support Social Emotional Skills

> It's important to examine one's program policies to see whether they are supporting or prohibiting the provision of services in natural and inclusive environments.

The sixth strategy involves a specific focus on young children's social-emotional development so that all children, including those with challenging behavior, have access to and can fully participate in natural and inclusive learning environments. Young children with challenging behavior are at increased risk for suspension and expulsion (Gilliam, 2005). To be successfully included and to promote positive social-emotional skills, it is important for an EC program to use a comprehensive, multitiered approach that includes evidence-based practices, such as those noted in Strategy 4 and programmatic structures (e.g., administrator support, leadership team, data-based decision-making), to promote sustainability of the approach.

The Pyramid Model is a conceptual framework based on evidence-based practices and developed specifically for infants and young children (Fox, Dunlap, Hemmeter, Joseph, & Strain, 2003). It involves three tiers of intervention, including (a) universal prevention through nurturing and responsive relationships, (b) secondary promotion of children's social-emotional skills through intentional teaching, and (c) individualized, function-based interventions for challenging behaviors (Hemmeter, Ostrosky, & Fox, 2006). The Pyramid Model (Fox et al., 2003) examines the levels of prevention, promotion, and intervention that must be in place to address the needs of all children. It includes the provision of high-quality natural and inclusive settings as the universal prevention strategy, intentional and systematic instruction of social-emotional competencies at the secondary level, and the provision of assessment-based interventions to children with behavior challenges at the tertiary level.

Universal preventive interventions include positive, proactive interventions that are applied to all children in natural and inclusive settings; they work to promote skills while reducing problems. Targeted interventions are used with children at risk for social-emotional delay, and individualized interventions are used for children with severe, persistent challenging behavior. Other features, such as a leadership team that uses data-based measures to track the program's adoption of Pyramid Model practices, support initial and sustained implementation in a program. Adopting the Pyramid Model framework is a long-term investment, but it is likely to result in improved access and meaningful engagement of all young children in natural and inclusive environments.

Strategy 7: Engage in Ongoing Program Evaluation

It is important that EC programs measure whether they are implementing practices and supports associated with high-quality natural and inclusive environments that are in line with Environment recommended practice E1. A dedication to ongoing monitoring of inclusion will allow the program to see what aspects of inclusion they are implementing, areas in need of improvement, and child and program outcomes. Typical measures of EC program quality are unlikely to highlight inclusion practices and provide a meaningful measure for preschool inclusion implementation. Measures specific to preschool inclusion are better options and can supplement other evaluative tools.

Some examples of classroom measures of preschool inclusion are the Inclusion Self-Checklist (Barton & Smith, 2015b), the Inclusive Classroom Profile (ICP; Soukakou, 2012), and the Quality Inclusive Practices Checklist (Wills et al., 2012). These tools provide a way to self-assess implementation of specific aspects of inclusion and plan adjustments and modifications to make the environment better support young children with disabilities and their families. In addition to measuring whether strategies are working at the classroom level, teachers should also evaluate whether individual children are sup-  ported. These measures are completed on one or more individual children who are included in a classroom, and the results are used to adjust or refine current adaptations and modifications. An example is the Quality Inclusive Experiences Measure (Wolery, Pauca, Brashers, & Grant, 2000).

Strategy 8: Examine Policies and Refine/Revise

Finally, it's important to examine one's program policies to see whether they are supporting or prohibiting the provision of services in natural and inclusive environments. Policies should reinforce the program's values and goals around inclusion and support Environment recommended practice E1. A first step to take is to look at the program's policies. Sometimes there is a perceived policy barrier that is actually an attitude or myth guiding practice and does not exist in writing. For example, a teacher may believe his/her district only allows for a 50-50 ratio of children with disabilities and with children who are typically developing in their district preschool programs because this is "how it has always been." The teacher may believe there is a written policy guiding her district's practices that conflicts with research on effective ratios for inclusive classrooms. However, there may be no such written policy in her district.

One should look at all governing policies, including national, state, and local policies. The types of policies to examine include federal IDEA policies, state and district eligibility policies, and policies that inform school assessments, professional development, tuition payments, enrollment, and budgeting. Local policies are often the easiest to change or modify (Smith, Steed, & Joseph, 2015). Once a specific policy is identified as a challenge, there are steps that a team may go through to push for policy change, including developing support and an action plan, creating materials to raise awareness of the issue, proposing the new policy or procedure, and following up with policy makers (Smith et al., 2015). While policy change may be a long process, it is critical to look at policy issues because they can be profound barriers to inclusion and when fixed can allow for more meaningful and sustained inclusion efforts into the future.

> It is critical to look at policy issues because they can be profound barriers to inclusion and when fixed can allow for more meaningful and sustained inclusion efforts into the future.

Conclusion

High-quality inclusion is more than just a long-term goal; high-quality inclusion is an issue of social justice and education equity. Children with disabilities should have equal opportunities to benefit from EC programs. Unfortunately, current data indicate that many children with disabilities are not educated alongside their peers and siblings and are thus not participating as full members of their families, classrooms, or communities. In fact, IDEA requires that each child's educational team, including the child's family, should collaboratively identify the inclusion preschool site, supports and services needed, and accommodations or modifications that are necessary to enhance the child's learning and development. Further, there is a legal, empirical, professional, and moral basis for preschool inclusion. As the U.S. Departments of Education and Health and Human Services (2015) outline in their position statement, numerous districts and states have evidence-based, clearly outlined guidelines, handbooks, or listed procedures supporting preschool inclusion. This suggests that despite the dismal increases in preschool inclusion over the past 30 years, there are exemplars of high-quality EC inclusion across the United States. Further, with the Environment recommended practices (DEC, 2014), practitioners can create and provide effective, inclusive learning environments that foster all children's learning and development. Thus, there is good reason to be optimistic and hopeful about the future and making *inclusion for all a reality*.

References

Barton, E. E. (2015). Teaching generalized pretend play and related behaviors to young children with disabilities. *Exceptional Children, 81,* 489–506. doi:10.1177/0014402914563694

Barton, E. E., Bishop, C. C., & Snyder, P. (2014). Quality instruction through complete learning trials: Blending intentional teaching with embedded instruction. In K. Pretti-Frontczak, J. Grisham-Brown, & L. Sullivan (Eds.), *Blending practices for all children* (Young Exceptional Children Monograph Series No. 16; pp. 73–96). Los Angeles, CA: Division for Early Childhood.

Barton, E. E., Pribble, L. M., & Joseph, J. D. (2015). Evidence-based practices for successful inclusion. In E. E. Barton & B. J. Smith (Eds.), *The preschool inclusion toolbox: How to build and lead a high-quality program* (pp. 113–132). Baltimore, MD: Paul H. Brookes.

Barton, E. E., & Smith, B. J. (2015a). Advancing high quality preschool inclusion: A discussion and recommendations for the field. *Topics in Early Childhood Special Education, 35,* 69–78. doi:10.1177/0271121415583048

Barton, E. E., & Smith, B. J. (2015b). *The preschool inclusion toolbox: How to build and lead a high-quality program.* Baltimore, MD: Paul H. Brookes.

Barton, E. E., Steed, E. A., Strain, P., Dunlap, G., Powell, D., & Payne, C. J. (2014). An analysis of classroom-based and parent-focused social-emotional programs for young children. *Infants and Young Children, 27,* 3–29. doi:10.1097/IYC.0000000000000001

Barton, E. E. & Wolery, M. (2010). Training teachers to promote pretend play in children with disabilities. *Exceptional Children, 77,* 85–106. doi:10.1177/001440291007700104

Camilli, G., Vargas, S., Ryan, S., & Barnett, W. S. (2010). Meta-analysis of the effects of early education interventions on cognitive and social development. *Teachers College Record, 112,* 579–620.

Campbell, P. H., Milbourne, S., Dugan, L. M., & Wilcox, M. J. (2006). A review of evidence on practices for teaching young children to use assistive technology devices. *Topics in Early Childhood Special Education, 26,* 3–13. doi:10.1177/0271121406026001010101

Division for Early Childhood. (2014). *DEC recommended practices in early intervention/early childhood special education 2014.* Retrieved from http://www.dec-sped.org/recommendedpractices

Division for Early Childhood. (2015). *DEC recommended practices glossary.* Retrieved from http://www.dec-sped.org/recommendedpractices

Division for Early Childhood & National Association for the Education of Young Children (2009, April). *Early childhood inclusion* (Joint position statement). Chapel Hill: The University of North Carolina, FPG Child Development Institute.

Espinosa, L. M. (2002). High-quality preschool: Why we need it and what it looks like. *Preschool Policy Matters, 1.* Retrieved from http://nieer.org/resources/policybriefs/1.pdf

Fixsen, D. L., Blase, K. A., Duda, M. A., Naoom, S. F., & Van Dyke, M. (2010). Sustainability of evidence-based programs in education. *Journal of Evidence-Based Practices for Schools, 11,* 30–46.

Fox, L., Dunlap, G., Hemmeter, M. L., Joseph, G., & Strain, P. (2003). The Teaching Pyramid: A model for supporting social competence and preventing challenging behavior in young children. *Young Children, 58*(4), 48–52.

Fox, L., & Lentini, R. (2006). "You got it!": Teaching social and emotional skills. *Young Children, 61*(6), 36–42.

Gilliam, W. S. (2005). *Prekindergarteners left behind: Expulsion rates in the state prekindergarten systems*. New York, NY: Foundation for Child Development.

Grisham-Brown, J., Hemmeter, M. L., & Pretti-Frontczak, K. (2005). *Blended practices for teaching young children in inclusive settings*. Baltimore, MD: Paul H. Brookes.

Gupta, S. S., & Rous, B. S. (2016). Understanding change and implementation: How leaders can support inclusion. *Young Children, 71*(2), 82–91.

Guralnick, M. J. (Ed.). (2001). *Early childhood inclusion: Focus on change*. Baltimore, MD: Paul H. Brookes.

Guralnick, M. J., Neville, B., Hammond, M. A., & Connor, R. T. (2007). The friendships of young children with developmental delays: A longitudinal analysis. *Journal of Applied Developmental Psychology, 28*, 64–79. doi:10.1016/j.appdev.2006.10.004

Hayden, P., Frederick, L., & Smith, B. J. (2003). *A road map for facilitating collaborative teams*. Longmont, CO: Sopris West.

Hemmeter, M. L., Ostrosky, M. M., & Fox, L. (2006). Social and emotional foundations for early learning: A conceptual model for intervention. *School Psychology Review, 35*, 583–601.

Individuals With Disabilities Education Act, 20 U.S.C. § 1400 (2004).

Justice, L. M., Logan, J. A. R., Lin, T.-J., & Kaderavek, J. N., (2014). Peer effects in early childhood education: Testing the assumptions of special-education inclusion. *Psychological Science, 25*, 1722–1729. doi:10.1177/0956797614538978

Lifter, K., Mason, E. J., & Barton, E. E. (2011). Children's play: Where we have been and where we could go. *Journal of Early Intervention, 33*, 281–297. doi:10.1177/1053815111429465

McConnell, S. R. (2002). Interventions to facilitate social interactions for young children with autism: Review of available research and recommendations for educational intervention and future research. *Journal of Autism and Developmental Disorders, 32*, 351–372. doi:10.1023/A:1020537805154

Musgrove, M. (2012). OSEP dear colleague letter on preschool (LRE). Retrieved from http://www2.ed.gov/policy/speced/guid/idea/memosdcltrs/preschoollre22912.pdf

Odom, S. L., Buysse, V., & Soukakou, E. (2011). Inclusion for young children with disabilities: A quarter century of research perspectives. *Journal of Early Intervention, 33*, 344–356. doi:10.1177/1053815111430094

Pianta, R. C., Barnett, W. S., Burchinal, M., & Thornburg, K. R. (2009). The effects of preschool education: What we know, how public policy is or is not aligned with the evidence base, and what we need to know. *Psychological Science in the Public Interest, 10*, 49–88. doi:10.1177/1529100610381908

Rose, D. F., & Smith, B. J. (1993). Preschool mainstreaming: Attitude barriers and strategies for addressing them. *Young Children, 48*(4), 59–62.

Sadao, K. C., & Robinson, N. B. (2010). *Assistive technology for young children: Creating inclusive learning environments*. Baltimore, MD: Paul H. Brookes.

Salisbury, C. L., & McGregor, G. (2002). The administrative climate and context of inclusive elementary schools. *Exceptional Children, 68*, 259–274. doi:10.1177/001440290206800207

Sandall, S. R., & Schwartz, I. S. (2008). *Building blocks for teaching preschoolers with special needs* (2nd ed.). Baltimore, MD: Paul H. Brookes.

Smith, B. J., & Rose, D. F. (1993). *Administrator's policy handbook for preschool mainstreaming.* Cambridge, MA: Brookline Books.

Smith, B. J., Salisbury, C. L., & Rose, D. F. (1992). Policy options for preschool mainstreaming. *CASE in Point, 7,* 17–30.

Smith, B. J., Steed, E. A., & Joseph, J. D. (2015). Creating policies and procedures that support preschool inclusion. In E. E. Barton & B. J. Smith (Eds.), *The preschool inclusion toolbox: How to build and lead a high-quality program* (pp. 63–82). Baltimore, MD: Paul H. Brookes.

Snyder, P., Hemmeter, M. L., & McLaughlin, T. (2011). Professional development in early childhood intervention: Where we stand on the silver anniversary of PL 99-457. *Journal of Early Intervention, 33,* 357–370. doi:10.1177/1053815111428336

Soukakou, E. P. (2012). Measuring quality in inclusive preschool classrooms: Development and validation of the Inclusive Classroom Profile (ICP). *Early Childhood Research Quarterly, 27,* 478–488. doi:10.1016/j.ecresq.2011.12.003

Steed, E. A., & Smith, B. J. (2015). Administrative support: Effective professional development for high-quality preschool inclusion. In E. E. Barton & B. J. Smith (Eds.), *The preschool inclusion toolbox: How to build and lead a high-quality program* (pp. 97–112). Baltimore, MD: Paul H. Brookes.

Strain, P. S. (1990). LRE for preschool children with handicaps: What we know, what we should be doing. *Journal of Early Intervention, 14,* 291–296. doi:10.1177/105381519001400401

Strain, P. S., & Bovey, E. H. (2011). Randomized, controlled trial of the LEAP model of early intervention for young children with autism spectrum disorders. *Topics in Early Childhood Special Education, 31,* 133–154. doi:10.1177/0271121411408740

Strain, P. S., & Hoyson, M. (2000). The need for longitudinal, intensive social skill intervention: LEAP follow-up outcomes for children with autism. *Topics in Early Childhood Special Education, 20,* 116–122. doi:10.1177/027112140002000207

Strain, P. S., McGee, G., & Kohler, F. W. (2001). Inclusion of children with autism in early intervention: An examination of rationale, myths, and procedures. In M. J. Guralnick (Ed.), *Early childhood inclusion: Focus on change* (pp. 337–363). Baltimore, MD: Paul H. Brookes.

U.S. Department of Health and Human Services & U.S. Department of Education. (2015, September, 14). *Policy statement on the inclusion of children with disabilities in early childhood programs.* Retrieved from: http://www2.ed.gov/policy/speced/guid/earlylearning/joint-statement-full-text.pdf

Wills, D., Darragh-Ernst, J., & Presley, D. (2012). *Quality inclusive practices checklist.* Normal, IL: Heartland Community College, Heartland Equity and Inclusion Project.

Wolery, M. (2012). Voices from the field: Reflections on instruction and naturalness in classrooms. *Young Exceptional Children, 15*(4), 41–44. doi:10.1177/1096250612466379

Wolery, M., Pauca, T., Brashers, M. S., & Grant, S. (2000). *Quality of inclusive experiences measure* [Unpublished assessment manual]. Chapel Hill, NC: Frank Porter Graham Child Development Center, Early Childhood Research Group on Inclusion.

2

The International Classification of Functioning, Disability, and Health (ICF)
Focusing on the Environment

LYNN JEFFRIES
University of Oklahoma Health Sciences Center

ALYSSA FISS
Mercer University

George is a 5-year-old child with cerebral palsy. He lives in a single-story home with his mom, dad, and older sister and attends half-day kindergarten five days a week. George loves to be around his friends and is very social. His parents would like him to engage fully in his home, school, and community.

Introduction

Practitioners, health professionals, and researchers use frameworks to provide a common language so individuals from many fields can relate to each other's findings (Stucki, Reinhardt, Grimby, & Melvin, 2007). A common framework used specifically in health professions is the International Classification of Functioning, Disability, and Health (ICF) proposed by the World Health Organization (2001). This framework focuses on enablement and highlights an individual's function, ability, and participation in all aspects of life. A key component of the ICF is the inclusion of environment. Because one of the Division for Early Childhood (DEC) Recommended Practices (2014) topic areas is Environment, linking the recommended practices and the ICF framework will provide early childhood practitioners a tool to support children with disabilities.

Ultimately, the ICF focuses on participating in life situations. For young children, this means participating in typical activities and routines within home, school, and community environments (Campbell, 2005). While recognizing that the child's health condition may be permanent, the goal for practitioners and families is to determine how to help the child fully engage in daily routines and activities. In this way, the ICF is a framework that provides a system of examining the child's functional abilities by considering a variety of factors that influence those abilities. The ICF also provides for the consideration of environmental and personal factors that help practitioners focus assessment and services to encourage child participation. This paper will introduce ICF components focusing specifically on the components of the environment. We will discuss how early childhood practitioners can consider the impact the environment has on a young child with a disability, and we will use vignettes to illustrate the application of the ICF to decision-making related to intervention.

The ICF Components

Early childhood practitioners can use the ICF framework to examine how children live with various health conditions and determine how to help them achieve full participation in life. The DEC recommended practice topic area of assessment refers to the process of gathering relevant information to develop plans for instruction (DEC, 2014). Practitioners and families can use the ICF framework as a tool for gathering information related to the children's strengths, needs, and environments. During program planning, the ICF then affords practitioners a framework to ensure everyone is considering all possible facets of the children and their lives that may be limiting their ultimate success.

The components of the ICF are *body function, structure, activities, participation*, and *environmental* and *personal* factors. Body functions are defined as the physiological functions of body systems. Anatomical parts of the body, such as organs, muscles, or bones, are identified as *body structures*. The significant loss or deviation from the typical is an *impairment of body functions and structure* (World Health Organization, 2001). Difficulties executing tasks or activities are considered *activity limitations*, and difficulties experienced while participating in life situations are *participation restrictions*. Additionally, the ICF includes consideration of children's environments, which can include the proximal (home/family) and distal (neighborhood, community, school) environments (Kolobe, Arevalo, & Catalino, 2012) as well as the personal factors that include age, gender, race, and socioeconomic status (World Health Organization, 2001). Table 1 contains definitions and examples of each ICF component that practitioners can assess and consider during program planning.

To facilitate the use of the ICF, practitioners and families should understand that the framework is a multidimensional and interactive tool that allows for the consideration of multidirectional relationships between many components of a child's functional ability (World Health Organization, 2006). Figure 1 illustrates the ICF's multidirectional relationships. However, practitioners typically focus child assessment and services on areas contained in the first part of the ICF: functioning and disability. *Functioning* is an umbrella term for body functions, activities, and participation. Similarly, *disability* is an umbrella term for impairment, activity limitation, or participation restriction (World Health Organization, 2001). Therefore, disability is the outcome of the interaction between a health condition and the context (environment) children experience when the outcome is less than fully functioning in all areas of their lives (Schneidert, Hurst,

ICF affords practitioners a framework to ensure everyone is considering all possible facets of the children and their lives that may be limiting their ultimate success.

Table 1
ICF Components, Definitions, and Examples

Component	Definition	Examples
Body function	The physiological functions of body systems	• Mental function • Sensory function • Voice and speech function • Muscle and joint function • Heart function
Body structures	The anatomical parts of the body	• Body organs • Muscles • Bones
Activities	The execution of a task or action by an individual	• Communication • Mobility • Self-care • Learning and applying knowledge
Participation	The involvement in a life situation reflecting the interaction of the person, activity, and environment	• Participating in school activities • Playing on the playground • Being part of a dance class
Environmental factors	The physical, social, and attitudinal components that can either enhance or limit participation in naturally occurring activities	• Family and societal attitudes • Supports and relationships • Physical structure of the natural environment • Services and policies • Products and technology
Personal factors	The person's internal factors that may influence their experiences	• Age • Gender • Social background • Past and current expereinces

Source: World Health Organization, 2001

Miller, & Üstün, 2003). Practitioners should also consider the contextual factor of environment when assessing the children's abilities and planning services.

Applying the ICF to Assessment

To apply the ICF to an assessment example, consider the vignette below.

During assessment, team members interacted with George and his parents at his school. The team noted that George had poor breath support for speech production. He also presented with limited joint movement because of contractures,

Figure 1
ICF's Multidirectional Relationships

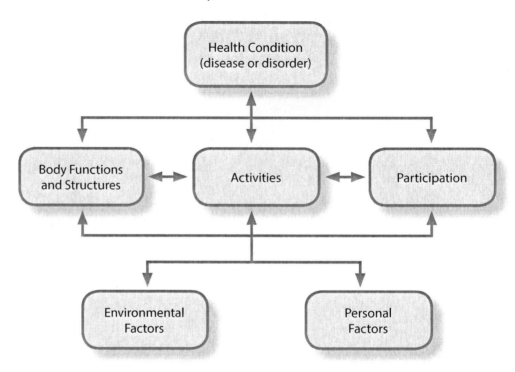

increased muscle tone in his legs, poor balance, and decreased strength. All of these were identified as body function impairments. In addition, George presented with a rotational deviation of his hips, which was an example of a body structure impairment.

George used a power wheelchair for mobility and needed help getting in and out of the chair. When placed on the floor, he could roll from one place to another, but he required support to maintain a sitting position. He used his left hand to drive the chair, play with toys, and feed himself finger foods. He was very talkative, and once accustomed to his verbal pattern, he was easy to understand. He was completing most age-appropriate educational activities when given enough time to accommodate his motor challenges. The difficulties George was experiencing in these areas would be considered activity limitations.

George liked to play games in the classroom with his peers and enjoyed singing and participating in circle time. However, he often had difficulty accessing materials during these activities. Outside on the playground, George tended to sit to the side and watch the other children. His parents noted that outside of school, George would like to attend a local karate class; however, his parents reported the teacher was unsure how to adapt the program for George. These would be considered participation restrictions.

George was extremely motivated to participate in classroom activities. He demonstrated a calm temperament and was persistent in attempting to complete tasks independently. George also presented with several health conditions, including seizures and difficulties with growth. Each of these characteristics would be considered personal factors.

Based on this assessment, the team decided additional assessment was needed to determine which components of environment could be addressed to facilitate increased activity and participation in the school and community environment.

Environmental Factor

The DEC Environment recommended practices include six practices that consider the physical (e.g., space and terrain), social (e.g., interactions with people), and temporal environments (e.g., time it takes to complete a routine) that young children encounter. The ICF environmental factor includes the physical, social, and attitudinal components that complement the DEC Environment recommended practices (World Health Organization, 2001). However, specific definitions of attitudinal and social components vary between the two models and will be discussed in this paper. It will be important for practitioners and families to clarify which terminology is being used when conversing or using literature to support program instruction.

Within each environmental factor, supports, which facilitate participation, and barriers, which hinder participation, exist. Understanding the supports and barriers may allow practitioners and families to reflect on the environments young children with disabilities encounter daily and then adjust or modify the environment to support the child's participation.

Physical Environment

The physical environment includes the space, terrain, and temperature of the natural environments where individuals live, work, and play as well as the materials and technology available (World Health Organization, 2006). The ICF physical environment is related to all of the DEC Environment recommended practices: (E1) natural and inclusive environments, (E2) universal design for creating accessible environments, (E3) modifying and adapting the physical environments, (E4) identifying assistive technology (AT) needs, (E5) acquiring and creating appropriate AT, and (E6) creating environments that provide movement and physical activity opportunities (DEC, 2014). Practitioners and families should assess not only the home environment but also the classroom, school, playground, and community buildings, programs, and play areas. When assessing these physical environments, aspects of accessibility and access to appropriate supports or modifications should be considered for each individual child because the needs of one child may vary from those of another child.

During discussions between team members and George's parents, several supports and barriers were identified related to the physical environment. Supports included access to his power wheelchair, enough room at home and in the classroom to drive his power chair, room in the school bathroom for his wheelchair, and adapted toilet seats at home and school. Mrs. Jones, the classroom teacher, identified that it would be nice if George could sit at the same level as the other children during snack time, circle time, and while playing on the floor. She also noted that George is often distracted by loud noises during playtime and when the room door

> Understanding supports and barriers may allow practitioners and families to reflect on the environments young children with disabilities encounter daily and then adjust or modify the environment to support the child's participation.

opens. He also seems cold compared with the other children in class. Mr. Anderson, his principal, stated he noticed George was sitting by himself to the side while on the playground and had difficulty maneuvering his wheelchair over the mulch. Moreover, his parents and teachers both commented that his food often ends up on the floor more than the other kids because he keeps raking it off the plate.

Based on the discussion, team members discussed strategies and solutions to address several barriers that were identified when developing George's instructional program. Ms. Minor, the physical therapist, would explore different floor sitters and table chairs for George and his teachers to try in the classroom. Mr. Pemberton, the occupational therapist, said he knew of different plates and bowls that might help during snack and mealtime, and he said he would also spend more time on the playground to assess what options could be implemented to engage George in play with peers. Mr. Anderson stated he would see if the playground surface was solid enough for George's chair to navigate. Together they brainstormed ideas regarding room arrangements to help decrease the sound and visual distraction from the classroom door and to alter George's position in the classroom away from the windows and vent to decrease the drafts in the room that may be causing him to be cold.

Social Environment

Social components of the ICF relate to the policies, rules, and laws within programs and the community but also include the relationships that enhance children's opportunities to engage and interact with others (World Health Organization, 2006). Federal and state funding policies for services and equipment and community and program policies related to access and inclusion are examples of social supports and resources (Colver et al., 2012; McManus et al., 2006).

George attended an inclusive school program (laws, rules, and policies), and his family had sufficient funding support for equipment and a van for transporting his power wheelchair. The family had a close extended family that is available to provide child care and other supports as needed. The team considered each of these an asset to George's successful participation.

Attitudinal Environment

The attitudinal component of the ICF environment is most closely related to the social component of the DEC Environment recommended practices. The attitudes of family, community members, and peers toward supporting and encouraging participation are essential for successful engagement. Researchers have identified parent's positive attitudes, perseverance, and assertiveness as facilitators of children's participation (Majnemer et al., 2008; Verschuren, Wiart, Hermans, & Ketelaar, 2012). Similarly, positive attitudes of school and community program personnel lead to improved child participation (McManus et al., 2006).

George was well liked by his peers at school, and they enjoyed assisting him in

Table 2

Examples of Supports and Barriers Related to the Physical, Social, and Attitudinal Environmental Factors

Supports	Barriers
Environment • Accessible environment: ramps, lifts, different surfaces, adapted toilets (Fauconnier et al., 2009; Verschuren et al., 2012) • Transportation: appropriate vehicles, parking, modified sidewalks (Lawlor, Mihaylov, Welsh, Jarvis, & Colver, 2006) • Modified playgrounds: ramps, adapted swings, space for movement (Yuill, Strieth, Roake, Aspden, & Todd, 2007)	**Environment** • Lack of opportunity (Verschuren et al., 2012) • Inaccessible: lack of space, elevators, ramps (Verschuren et al., 2012) • Lack of equipment (Lawlor et al., 2006) • Crowds, layout of building, distance from parking to building (Palisano, Shimmell, et al., 2009)
Social • Policies supporting inclusion (Majnemer et al., 2008) • Resources within an acceptable geographic region (Anaby et al., 2013) • Accessible funding for equipment (Colver et al., 2012) • Coordinated services: social, medical, educational (Colver et al., 2012) • Peer support (Lindsay & McPherson, 2012)	**Social** • Lack of financial resources (Verschuren et al., 2012) • Lack of community resources, services, and personnel (Law, Petrenchik, G. King, & Hurley, 2007; McManus et al., 2006) • Noninclusive policies (Fauconnier et al., 2009; G. King et al., 2006; Law et al., 2007)
Attitudinal • Awareness of benefits for participating (Verschuren et al., 2012) • Having a positive attitude: child and family (McManus et al., 2006) • Perseverance and assertiveness (Verschuren et al., 2012) • Emotional support: family, friends, practitioners (Colver et al., 2012) • Being accepted and supported by peers, friends, and parents (Verschuren et al., 2012)	**Attitudinal** • Fear of child not fitting in (Verschuren et al., 2012) • Not "open" to children with disabilities being involved (Verschuren et al., 2012) • Fear of "hurting" the child (Verschuren et al., 2012) • Child's ability being underestimated (Verschuren et al., 2012) • Not accepted by peers or other parents (Verschuren et al., 2012)

tasks throughout the day. His parents were engaged and set realistic high expectations for George's participation at home, school, and in the community. George's teachers and therapists all displayed positive perceptions of inclusion in the classroom environment. The community karate instructor was open to allowing George to participate in his classes, but he was uncertain how other parents and peers in the class might react. He was also uncertain how to modify the karate activities to accommodate George. The team noted that attitudinal components were largely an area of support for George. However, additional support and resources may have been beneficial to help facilitate George's participation in his chosen community activity. The family's home-based physical therapist agreed to attend the community karate session to assist the instructor in modifying activities and determining the best way to address the concerns of other parents.

Additional examples of supports and barriers within each environmental factor are provided in Table 2.

Research Supporting the Importance of Environments to Child Outcomes/Participation

The Home Environment

For infants, a supportive home environment that provides social and physical stimulation accounts for positive achievements in development (Hwang et al., 2014). The quality of mother-infant interactions are related to child development as well as the mother's mental health (Holditch-Davis, Miles, Burchinal, & Goldman, 2011). Positive mother-infant interactions and caregiving behaviors, which are components of the child's environment, were identified as enhancing the child's motor, cognitive, language, and adaptive skills (Holditch-Davis et al., 2011; Treyvaud et al., 2009).

The School Environment

Much of the research related to participation in the school environment has been completed with children over age 8 because of their ability to express facilitators and barriers to participation. Using the results of this research, one can gain a picture of school environments that support or hinder child participation. Examples of supports included peer assistance (Eriksson, Welander, & Granlund, 2007) and inclusive school activities (Michelsen et al., 2009). However, children identified negative attitudes of peers and adults (Díez, 2010; Morrison & Burgman, 2009); poor physical design, such as stairs and other structural barriers that limited mobility (Coster et al., 2013); and a lack of transportation for school field trips (Mancini & Coster, 2004) as negatively affecting their participation in school activities.

Use of Supports

As children with disabilities transition into the community (e.g., child care centers, schools, or community environments), practitioners should consider potential supports to facilitate child participation. Campbell and others (Campbell, 2005; Campbell, Milbourne, Dugan, & Wilcox, 2006) have developed a framework for considering and implementing supports for young children with disabilities. The supports include adaptations to the environment (e.g., rearranging space, using mobility equipment), adaptations of the activities and routines (e.g., providing more time for task completion), adaptations of materials (e.g., enlarging the puzzle knobs, using a two-handled cup), adaptations to the instruction (e.g., simplifying the task, adding picture cues), and providing adult or peer assistance.

Using this framework, Trivette, Dunst, Hamby, and O'Herin (2010) completed a research synthesis to identify the relationship among environment, activities, and material adaptations to child development in the areas of cognition, communication, motor, and social behaviors. All three adaptations were positively associated with child outcomes, and the more frequently the adaptations were used, the more effective the adaptations. These results support the consideration of adaptations to the environment, activity, and materials to facilitate participation of young children with disabilities in the home, classroom, and community.

Assistive Technology

Assistive technology (AT) includes the adaptation and devices used within the environment to enhance child participation and capacity as well as the services needed to teach the children and families to use the AT (Campbell et al., 2006). Two of the DEC Environment recommended practices are linked to AT (DEC, 2014). Recommended practice E4 relates to the identification of the children's need for AT, and E5 relates to acquiring or creating AT to promote the children's access and participation in natural learning environments. Assistive technology ranges from off-the-shelf or low-tech devices to specifically designed high-tech devices. Examples of AT use within the environment include hearing supports, such as sound-field systems; personal FM systems (Nelson, Poole, & Muñoz, 2013); speech generating devices (Watson, Ito, Smith, & Andersen, 2010); adaptive seating (Ryan et al., 2009); wheel-

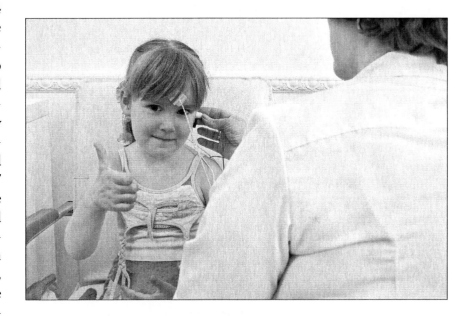

chairs (Guerette, Furumasu, & Tefft, 2013); and powered cars (Logan, Huang, Stahlin, & Galloway, 2014). For each assistive device, practitioners should consider the child's needs and the environments in which the child will use the devices.

For children with cerebral palsy, the environment where children use their devices has been found to influence their independence (Palisano, Tieman, et al., 2003). Children were less reliant on adult support when using AT for mobility in the school and at home compared with outside and in community settings. Additionally, environmental modifications (e.g., toilet armrests, elimination of thresholds, and alterations in lighting) enhanced the children's ability to participate and decreased the caregiver burden in the areas of mobility, self-care, and social function (Østensjø, Carlberg, & Vøllestad, 2005).

Dunst, Trivette, Hamby, and Simkus (2013) completed a meta-analysis of studies using different types of AT (e.g., switch interfaces, powered mobility, computers, and augmentative communication) with young children with disabilities. Results suggest AT positively enhances child outcomes including cognitive, social, communication, literacy, adaptive, and motor development as well as behavioral engagement. Additionally, all children, no matter their level of ability, successfully used AT to participate in educational activities. Early childhood practitioners may consider appropriate AT and individualized aspects of the environment to help increase children's participation in home, school, and community activities.

Conclusion

Early childhood practitioners should consider all aspects of the ICF and examine how each component affects a child. This paper introduces the ICF framework to provide practitioners and families with a common means of assessing multiple factors. Practitioners often tend to focus on the child's impairments in body structure function and activity limitations when planning educational programs. We encourage practitioners to use the ICF's multidirectional framework to thoughtfully examine all aspects of the child and environment to determine what is needed to allow the child to participate fully in home, school, and community activities. Specifically, early childhood practitioners should consider all aspects of the environment (physical, social, and attitudinal) to support the success of young children with disabilities. While the physical environment is often the simplest to assess and modify, close scrutiny is needed of the attitudinal and social components of the environment. Focusing on creating a supportive environment should assist children to more easily and successfully participate in daily life.

References

Anaby, D., Hand, C., Bradley, L., DiRezze, B., Forhan, M., DiGiacomo, A., & Law, M. (2013). The effect of the environment on participation of children and youth with disabilities: A scoping review. *Disability and Rehabilitation, 35,* 1589–1598. doi:10.3109/09638288.2012.748840

Campbell, P. H. (2005). Participation-based services: Promoting children's participation in natural settings. *Young Exceptional Children, 8*(1), 20–29. doi:10.1177/109625060400800103

Campbell, P. H., Milbourne, S. A., Dugan, L. M., & Wilcox, M. J. (2006). A review of evidence on practices for teaching young children to use assistive technology devices. *Topics in Early Childhood Special Education, 26,* 3–14. doi:10.1177/02711214060260010101

Colver, A., Thyen, U., Arnaud, C., Beckung, E., Fauconnier, J., Marcelli, M., . . . Dickinson, H. O. (2012). Association between participation in life situations of children with cerebral palsy and their physical, social, and attitudinal environment: A cross-sectional multicenter European study. *Archives of Physical Medicine and Rehabilitation, 93,* 2154–2164. doi:10.1016/j.apmr.2012.07.011

Coster, W., Law, M., Bedell, G., Liljenquist, K., Kao, Y.-C., Khetani, M., & Teplicky, R. (2013). School participation, supports and barriers of students with and without disabilities. *Child: Care, Health & Development, 39,* 535–543. doi:10.1111/cch.12046

Díez, A. M. (2010). School memories of young people with disabilities: An analysis of barriers and aids to inclusion. *Disability and Society, 25,* 163–175. doi:10.1080/09687590903534346

Division for Early Childhood. (2014). *DEC recommended practices in early-intervention/early childhood special education 2014.* Retrieved from http://www.dec-sped.org/recommendedpractices

Dunst, C. J., Trivette, C. M., Hamby, D. W., & Simkus, A. (2013). Systematic review of studies promoting the use of assistive technology devices by young children with disabilities. *Tots N Tech Research Brief, 8*(1), 1–21.

Eriksson, L., Welander, J. & Granlund, M. (2007). Participation in everyday school activities for children with and without disabilities. *Journal of Developmental and Physical Disabilities, 19,* 485–502. doi:10.1007/s10882-007-9065-5

Fauconnier, J., Dickinson, H.O., Beckung, E., Marcelli, M., McManus, V., Michelsen, S. I., . . . Colver, A. (2009). Participation in life situations of 8–12 year old children with cerebral palsy: Cross sectional European study. *British Medical Journal, 338,* b1458. doi:10.1136/bmj.b1458

Guerette, P., Furumasu, J., & Tefft, D. (2013). The positive effects of early powered mobility on children's psychosocial and play skills. *Assistive Technology, 25,* 39–48. doi:10.1080/10400435.2012.685824

Holditch-Davis, D., Miles, M. S., Burchinal, M. R., & Goldman, B. D. (2011). Maternal role attainment with medically fragile infants: Part 2. Relationship to quality of parenting. *Research in Nursing & Health, 34,* 35–48. doi:10.1002/nur.20418

Hwang, A.-W., Liao, H.-F., Chen, P.-C., Hsieh, W.-S., Simeonsson, R. J., Weng, L.-J., & Su, Y-N. (2014). Applying the ICF-CY framework to examine biological and environmental factors in early childhood development. *Journal of the Formosan Medical Association, 113,* 303–312. doi:10.1016/j.jfma.2011.10.004

King, G., Law, M., Hanna, S., King, S., Hurley, P., Rosenbaum, P., . . . Petrenchik, T. (2006). Predictors of the leisure and recreation participation of children with physical disabilities: A structural equation modeling analysis. *Children's Health Care, 35,* 209–234. doi:10.1207/s15326888chc3503_2

Kolobe, T. H. A., Arevalo, A., & Catalino, T. A. (2012). The environment of intervention. In S. K. Campbell, R. J. Palisano, & M. N. Orlin (Eds.), *Physical therapy for children* (4th ed., pp. 879–902). St. Louis, MO: Elsevier.

Law, M., Petrenchik, T., King, G., & Hurley, P. (2007). Perceived environmental barriers to recreational, community, and school participation for children and youth with physical disabilities. *Archives of Physical Medicine & Rehabilitation, 88,* 1636–1642. doi:10.1016/j.apmr.2007.07.035

Lawlor, K., Mihaylov, S., Welsh, B., Jarvis, S., & Colver, A. (2006). A qualitative study of the physical, social and attitudinal environments influencing the participation of children with cerebral palsy in northeast England. *Pediatric Rehabilitation, 9,* 219–228.

Lindsay, S., & McPherson, A. C. (2012). Strategies for improving disability awareness and social inclusion of children and young people with cerebral palsy. *Child: Care, Health & Development, 38,* 809–816. doi:10.1111/j.1365-2214.2011.01308.x

Logan, S. W., Huang, H. H., Stahlin, K., & Galloway, J. C. (2014). Modified ride-on car for mobility and socialization: Single-case study of an infant with Down syndrome. *Pediatric Physical Therapy, 26*, 418–426. doi:10.1097/PEP.0000000000000070

Majnemer, A., Shevell, M., Law, M., Birnbaum, R., Chilingaryan, G., Rosenbaum, P., & Poulin, C. (2008). Participation and enjoyment of leisure activities in school-aged children with cerebral palsy. *Developmental Medicine & Child Neurology, 50*, 751–758. doi:10.1111/j.1469-8749.2008.03068.x

Mancini, M. C., & Coster, W. J. (2004). Functional predictors of school participation by children with disabilities. *Occupational Therapy International, 11*, 12–25. doi:10.1002/oti.194

McManus, V., Michelsen, S. I., Parkinson, K., Colver, A., Beckung, E., Pez, O., & Caravale, B. (2006). Discussion groups with parents of children with cerebral palsy in Europe designed to assist development of a relevant measure of environment. *Child: Care, Health & Development, 32*, 185–192. doi:10.1111/j.1365-2214.2006.00601.x

Michelsen, S. I., Flachs, E. M., Uldall, P., Eriksen, E. L., McManus, V., Parkes, J., . . . Colver, A. (2009). Frequency of participation of 8–12-year-old children with cerebral palsy: A multi-centre cross-sectional European study. *European Journal of Paediatric Neurology, 13*, 165–177. doi:10.1016/j.ejpn.2008.03.005

Morrison, R., & Burgman, I. (2009). Friendship experiences among children with disabilities who attend mainstream Australian schools. *Canadian Journal of Occupational Therapy, 3*, 145–152. doi:10.1177/000841740907600303

Nelson, L. H., Poole, B., & Muñoz, K. (2013). Preschool teachers' perception and use of hearing assistive technology in educational settings. *Language, Speech, and Hearing Services in the Schools, 44*, 239–251. doi:10.1044/0161-1461(2013/12-0038)

Østensjø, S., Carlberg, E. B., & Vøllestad, N. K. (2005). The use and impact of assistive devices and other environmental modifications on everyday activities and care in young children with cerebral palsy. *Disability and Rehabilitation, 27*, 849–861. doi:10.1080/09638280400018619

Palisano, R. J., Shimmell, L. J., Stewart, D., Lawless, J. J., Rosenbaum, P. L., & Russell, D. J. (2009). Mobility experiences of adolescents with cerebral palsy. *Physical & Occupational Therapy in Pediatrics, 29*, 133–153. doi:10.1080/01942630902784746

Palisano, R. J., Tieman, B. L., Walter, S. D., Bartlett, D. J., Rosenbaum, P. L., Russell, D., & Hannah, S. E. (2003). Effect of environmental setting on mobility methods of children with cerebral palsy. *Developmental Medicine & Child Neurology, 45*, 113–120. doi:10.1111/j.1469-8749.2003.tb00914.x

Ryan, S. E., Campbell, K. A., Rigby, P. J., Fishbein-Germon, B., Hubley, D., & Chan, B. (2009). The impact of adaptive seating devices on the lives of young children with cerebral palsy and their families. *Archives of Physical Medicine & Rehabilitation, 90*, 27–33. doi:10.1016/j.apmr.2008.07.011

Schneidert, M., Hurst, R., Miller, J., & Üstün, B. (2003). The role of environment in the international classification of functioning, disability and health (ICF). *Disability and Rehabilitation, 25*, 588–595. doi:10.1080/0963828031000137090

Stucki, G., Reinhardt, J. D., Grimby, G., & Melvin, J. (2007). Developing "human functioning and rehabilitation research" from the comprehensive perspective. *Journal of Rehabilitation Medicine, 39,* 665–671. doi:10.2340/16501977-0136

Treyvaud, K., Anderson, V. A., Howard, K., Bear, M., Hunt, R. W., Doyle, L. W., . . . Anderson, P. J. (2009). Parenting behavior is associated with the early neurobehavioral development of very preterm children. *Pediatrics, 123,* 555–561. doi:10.1542/peds.2008-0477

Trivette, C. M., Dunst, C. J., Hamby, D. W., & O'Herin, C. E. (2010). Effect of different types of adaptations on behavior of young children with disabilities. *Tots N Tech Research Brief, 4*(1), 1–25.

Verschuren, O., Wiart, L., Hermans, D., & Ketelaar, M. (2012). Identification of facilitators and barriers to physical activity in children and adolescents with cerebral palsy. *Journal of Pediatrics, 161,* 488–494. doi:10.1016/j.jpeds.2012.02.042

Watson, A. H., Ito, M., Smith, R. O., & Andersen, L. T. (2010). Effect of assistive technology in a public school setting. *American Journal of Occupational Therapy, 64,* 18–29. doi:10.5014/ajot.64.1.18

World Health Organization. (2001). *International classification of functioning, disability and health.* Geneva, Switzerland: World Health Organization.

World Health Organization. (2006). *The international classification of functioning, disability and health: An overview.* Geneva, Switzerland: World Health Organization.

Yuill, N., Strieth, S., Roake, C., Aspden, R., & Todd, B. (2007). Brief report: Designing a playground for children with autistic spectrum disorders— effects on playful peer interactions. *Journal of Autism & Developmental Disorders, 37,* 1192–1196. doi:10.1007/s10803-006-0241-8

3

Optimizing Accessibility Through Universal Design for Learning

SERRA DE ARMENT
YAOYING XU
HEATHER COLEMAN
Virginia Commonwealth University

YOUNG CHILDREN COME IN ALL SHAPES AND SIZES WITH A WIDE variety of abilities, backgrounds, and family structures. From infancy through preschool years, diverse children have learning opportunities across home, community, and school contexts. For young children with additional learning needs because of disability, developmental delay, or risk factors that threaten development, maximizing learning experiences across these settings is essential for enhancing developmental progress. Through early childhood intervention, practitioners and families apply a collaborative approach to improving developmental outcomes for young children with disabilities. Regardless of unique constellations of characteristics, all children have the right to grow and engage in environments that are natural learning spaces for typically developing children (Bruder, 2010). This essential tenet of early childhood intervention is made salient not only through naturalistic and least restrictive environment provisions in federal law (Individuals With Disabilities Education Act [IDEA], 2004) but also through the Division for Early Childhood (DEC) Recommended Practices (2014) and the DEC/National Association for the Education of Young Children (NAEYC) joint position statement on early childhood inclusion (2009).

Universal Design for Learning (UDL) is a framework that supports inclusion through three key principles for eliminating barriers to teaching and learning for *all* learners, not just children and not just individuals with disabilities (see sidebar on next page; Center for Applied Special Technology [CAST], 2011; Lapinski, Gravel, & Rose, 2012; Meyer, Rose, & Gordon, 2014; Rose, Harbour, Johnston, Daley, & Abarbanell, 2006). Though the concept of universal design was born from the field of architecture (Hall, Meyer, & Rose, 2012), applying the principles

Figure 1

Applying UDL Principles to Support Accessible and Inclusive Learning Environments

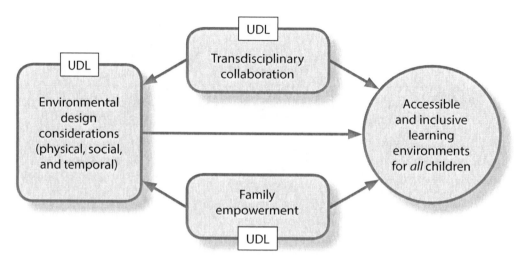

Universal Design for Learning Principles

1. Provide multiple means of representation
2. Provide multiple means of action and expression
3. Provide multiple means of engagement

of UDL in early childhood extends beyond physical access to the learning environment. Applied cohesively, UDL principles can support children's access to learning opportunities and inclusion across physical, temporal, and social environments within school, home, and community settings (DEC, 2014).

UDL requires flexibility of thought and openness to others' perspectives. Practitioners can use the UDL framework to think critically about how environmental design considerations and practitioner-family interactions can be leveraged to ensure all children are fully included and engaged (Bertling, Darrah, Lyon, & Jackson, 2010; Conn-Powers, Cross, Traub, & Hutter-Pishgahi, 2006). In this article, we explain UDL and offer suggestions for applying the principles to enhance the access and inclusion of young children and their families across learning environments. As illustrated in Figure 1, we envision the thoughtful application of UDL principles embedded in the design of varied learning environments, within transdisciplinary collaborations, and in support of family empowerment for the creation of accessible environments to include the full range of diverse young children.

Understanding UDL

UDL is a framework designed to guide the development of curricula that are flexible and supportive of all students and children (Dolan & Hall, 2001; Meyer & Rose, 1998; Pisha & Coyne, 2001; Rose, 2001), including children who have disabilities or developmental delays, children who are from culturally and/or linguistically diverse backgrounds, and children who are from low-income families. UDL helps meet the challenges of diversity by suggesting flexible instructional materials, techniques, and strategies that empower not only educators, but also families, to meet various individual needs while simultaneously addressing developmental appropriateness. UDL principles and practices help ensure that every young child has access to learning environments and typical home or educational routines and activities.

The first UDL principle, multiple means of representation, speaks to varied ways of presenting information to be learned (Israel, Ribuffo, & Smith, 2014; Rose et al., 2006). Different representations help learners understand the presented information. According to Meyer et al. (2014), "Learners' ability to perceive, interpret, and understand information is dependent upon the media and methods through which it is presented" (p. 54). One learner may learn best through hands-on manipulation of materials, and another learner may learn best when material is read aloud. Thus, learning environments become more accessible when practitioners and care providers give children options for perception and comprehension through varied and multisensory ways of presenting information (Lapinski et al., 2012).

Children's learning and access are further enhanced through the second UDL principle: multiple means of action and expression. Under this principle, learners are provided with a variety of opportunities to act on and respond to information (Rose et al., 2006). Learners recognize they can act upon materials and media in a variety of ways and are given multiple, varied opportunities to show what they know (Israel et al., 2014). Rather than employing a prescriptive approach to promoting learning and assessing children's understanding, this UDL principle supports the DEC Recommended Practices (2014) and developmentally appropriate practices (NAEYC, 2009), which emphasize the importance of frequent, meaningful, and systematic assessment within the early childhood population. Using multiple approaches to assessing what children know allows for a deeper understanding of the child as a learner and can better inform activity planning and the development of learning targets. In early childhood intervention, practitioners may seek verbal feedback to questions presented but can flexibly apply other options if verbal communication is difficult. For example, a child may require visual cues or an augmentative communication device for responding to teacher or caregiver questions.

The third principle in the UDL framework, multiple means of engagement, encourages interest in learning and motivation to learn further (CAST, 2014). Through application of this principle, educators capitalize on learners' interests and beliefs to promote engagement through a variety of means (Rose et al., 2006). Meyer et al. (2014) explain that the extrinsic environment, consisting of adults providing knowledge and activities that are relevant and valuable to learners' differing interests and goals, supports learners' motivation and engagement. Developing multiple means of engagement is not simply the process of being entertaining. It is important to understand learners' needs and what motivates them. For example, Meyer et al. suggest spontaneity and novel environments are highly engaging for some learners, while others get very frightened and anxious when their environment is different, thus becoming extremely disengaged. Advanced planning for multiple ways to engage learners in response to their interests helps ensure accessibility and inclusion.

When applied, UDL principles are inherently intertwined. As a guiding framework, UDL can steer practitioners' and families' critical thinking about young children's learning across environments so they can take advantage of all

> UDL requires flexibility of thought and openness to others' perspectives. Practitioners can use the UDL framework to think critically about how environmental design considerations and practitioner-family interactions can be leveraged to ensure all children are fully included and engaged.

potential learning and engagement opportunities (Bruder, 2010; McWilliam & Casey, 2008). The resources section at the end of this article presents additional UDL resources for informing practices with young children and families. Next, we consider how UDL principles relate to elements of physical, temporal, and social learning environments.

Environmental Design Considerations

Young children have the potential to learn across any setting, whether that environment is a home, playground, child care center, classroom, or other naturalistic setting in their lives. However, these settings may not be fully accessible to children with varying abilities, cultural and/or linguistic diversities, or high-need backgrounds. Likewise, the families of diverse young children may find these settings inaccessible as well. To improve inclusion and accessibility across environments such as these, early childhood intervention professionals, in partnership with families, must consider who young children are as learners and thoughtfully design environments and supports within environments to promote positive developmental outcomes.

As recognized by the DEC Recommended Practices (2014), learning environments in early childhood consist not solely of physical spaces and materials but also social and temporal environments. This means that UDL principles can guide intentional planning for peer, sibling, and family interactions (social environment), scheduling and timing of routines and activities (temporal environment), and placement of furniture, materials, and equipment (physical environment) within a home, school, or community setting. Creating inclusive environments that embrace multiple paths for achieving learning outcomes involves flexibility and thoughtful planning for incorporating variety and choice in anticipation of potential barriers to learning.

In preschool and child care settings, practitioners, in collaboration with other professionals and families, consider whether the early childhood environment provides "all children with multiple and varied ways to learn . . . to express and show what they learn . . . [and] to become engaged, motivated, excited and challenged" (Cunconan-Lahr & Stifel, 2013, p. 1). Though practitioners may not have direct control over settings within the home and community, multiple and varied ways of learning, expression of learning, and engagement can similarly be considered in collaboration with families and other professionals within these nonschool environments. To illustrate this, we offer three vignettes about how the UDL principles might be used in child care, home, and children's museum settings. While these vignettes are only a snippet of how those who work with young children might consider the UDL principles, they highlight the relevance of the principles for supporting inclusive practices across environments.

School setting: *At Rainbow Child Development Center, Coronda is thinking ahead to next month when a new group of diverse 3-year-olds will transition to her classroom from the toddler room down the hall. Coronda wants to ensure her classroom is a comfortable and engaging learning space for each child. After meeting with their families and current teacher, Coronda feels she has an initial*

> Though practitioners may not have direct control over settings within the home and community, multiple and varied ways of learning, expression of learning, and engagement can similarly be considered in collaboration with families and other professionals within these nonschool environments.

understanding of their backgrounds, interests, and needs. She uses this information to make thoughtful changes to her classroom. First, she expands her classroom library to include books that depict children in wheelchairs and books representing children from different cultures. She even finds a few books in Spanish, and a parent gives her a book in Swahili. Then, Coronda restructures classroom shelves and adds new bins with visual labels to ensure all toys and materials can be safely and securely stored when not in use. Coronda knows she'll want to make more improvements to her classroom and instructional approach once she gets to know each child, but she feels good about these initial steps toward improving her classroom's accessibility.

Home setting: *As equal members of their daughter's transdisciplinary team, Jordan and Carlos have regularly communicated with service providers about supporting 2-year-old Makayla's developmental progress. Born prematurely, Makayla exhibits significant language delays; however, she is very social and loves playing with her big sister Olivia. To support Makayla's developing oral language, Jordan and Carlos strive to make their home a language-rich environment while ensuring that both daughters are fully included in routines and play activities. Together, they sing songs and read stories; Olivia particularly likes teaching her little sister silly rhymes and chants. Makayla's parents also are in the habit of narrating daily activities and modeling language during play. Like their service coordinator, Danise, taught them, Jordan and*

Carlos watch for Makayla's nonverbal communication attempts and use those as opportunities to interact meaningfully around her interests.

Community setting: *As the director of education at the local children's museum, Shun's biggest priority is improving the museum's accessibility for diverse children and families. Recently, Shun brought together a group of local stakeholders, including child care providers, preschool teachers, families, and university faculty in early childhood special education, to serve as an advisory committee for museum programming. As a result of their collaboration and shared perspectives, Shun has added new seating options across museum spaces, widened pathways between exhibits, and incorporated new multisensory materials across existing thematic learning experiences. Next month he excitedly anticipates the museum's first of many specialized sensory-based events solely for young children with autism and their families. Surveys of museum visitors and regular advisory committee meetings will continue to support Shun's efforts for improving the museum experience for all children.*

Table 1
Application of UDL Principles Across Developmental Domains Within Physical, Temporal, and Social Environments

	Physical Environment	**Temporal Environment**	**Social Environment**
Representation	• Include a variety of materials (e.g., blocks, cars, books, photos) to represent learning themes through hands-on learning • Expose children to a variety of sights, sounds, textures, and motor-centered experiences • Rotate toys and materials • Consider low-tech and high-tech options across materials	• Establish daily routines • Represent the schedule in concrete ways (e.g., pictures, objects, timers) • Use incidental teaching opportunities during routines and in response to children's interests • Signal transitions through nonverbal and verbal means (e.g., flash lights, play a song) • Balance adult-initiated and -directed activities with child-initiated and -directed activities	• Use scripted stories, books, role playing, and naturalistic interactions as opportunities for learning about social skills • Incorporate texts, visuals, and cultural artifacts that represent all children and families • Visit a variety of social environments (e.g., library story time, public playgrounds, children's museums) • Offer directions and communication to children in multiple ways (e.g., pictures, signs, words, gestures)
Action & Expression	• Provide writing materials of varying types (e.g., jumbo pencils and crayons, crayon rocks, markers, Slick Sticks, pencil grips) • Offer opportunities for expression through singing and dancing • Supply materials and time for children to show what they know • Let children choose their supplies for creating • Establish wide pathways for movement • Consider levels of sensory input (e.g., lighting, noise, visual stimulation)	• Incorporate various ways for children to show what they know across the day (e.g., sing Old MacDonald, name animals in a picture book, point to a dog on the street, pretend to be a cow) • Encourage persistence across activities by supporting children through completion of a task • Provide opportunities for children's independence	• Provide opportunities for children to communicate with each other through various means (e.g., spoken language [English or other], pictures, signs) • Build frequent opportunities for peer socialization into routines (e.g., passing out snacks, taking turns on swing) • Prompt communication and questions through eye-level placement of children's artwork, photos, etc. • Provide opportunities for children to express emotions in various ways

No matter the setting, it is important to note that variety, choice, and engagement are not synonymous with high technology and high expense. Though technology such as computers and iPads can enhance access (Stockall, Dennis, & Miller, 2012), especially when thoughtfully facilitated and mediated by an adult (Brown, Shifrin, & Hill, 2015), it is not a requirement of UDL (Hall et al., 2012). As illustrated in Table 1 and outlined next, flexible and collaborative thinking following UDL principles allows for low-tech and low (or no) expense variations and choice across physical, temporal, and social environments as well.

Table 1 (continued)
Application of UDL Principles Across Developmental Domains Within Physical, Temporal, and Social Environments

	Physical Environment	Temporal Environment	Social Environment
Engagement	• Offer multiple seating options (e.g., floor, carpet, chair) • Offer specialized seating such as cube chairs, bean bags, balance disks, and seating wedges • Ensure child-size seating options and appropriate table heights • Use furniture placement to define areas for play, meals, and group activities • Consider activity levels and group quiet activities such as reading away from noisy areas such as blocks and music • Label storage for toys and materials using words, pictures, and textures	• Keep structured activities brief and flexible; consider extending if children are engaged and participating • Be sensitive to times of day and sequences that work best for certain activities and routines • Vary pacing of activities • Provide opportunities for quiet/rest time • Use incidental teaching strategies to respond to children's initiations	• Use children's interests, strengths, and preferences to partner or group children • Provide enough materials that children can engage in parallel play while also encouraging social interaction and sharing

Suggestions adapted, in part, from Conn-Powers et al. (2006); Cunconan-Lahr and Stifel (2013); Dinnebeil et al. (2013); Dixon (2008); and McWilliam and Casey (2008).

Physical Environment

Conn-Powers et al. (2006) recommend that the physical environment allow all children the opportunity to participate fully in all activities through consideration of (a) how the environment can be arranged, (b) what seating accommodations are needed, and (c) what kind of materials are needed for all children. Environmental arrangement, whether at home or in a more structured setting such as a child care center or school, refers to how furniture and materials are placed within a space to allow for access. Breaking up wide-open spaces and structuring specific areas for particular activities supports children's engagement for learning (McWilliam & Casey, 2008). Bookshelves, seating, and rugs can be used to create spots for quietly looking at books or building a tower out of blocks. Maintaining wide aisles allows for easy navigation throughout the space for children in wheelchairs or those who use other equipment for mobility (Cunconan-Lahr & Stifel, 2013). Young children like to explore, and learning spaces should allow them to independently access materials (Dinnebeil, Boat, & Bae, 2013). Therefore, toys, books, and other supplies can be placed in clearly labeled bins on low shelves for easy and well-defined access.

Seating for young children can take many forms. In general, seating should be child-sized with complementary table height. However, some children may need specific supports to sit independently and access the learning environment, such as a cube chair with a tray attached. Other seating could include a child-sized rocking chair for movement and sensory input or a chair with an antislip mat in the seat to help prevent falls. Offering multiple seating options allows all children to engage in seated learning activities (Conn-Powers et al., 2006; Cunconan-Lahr & Stifel, 2013). Furthermore, varied seating can signal certain types of activities such as calm and cozy time on a beanbag in a reading area.

UDL principles suggest that materials within an early childhood environment should reflect children's interests, cultural backgrounds, and strengths

while also providing for appropriate challenges and goal-directed behavior (Conn-Powers et al., 2006; Cunconan-Lahr & Stifel, 2013; McWilliam & Casey, 2008). Material selection should be made through consideration of how characteristics of objects affect levels of interest and how the developmental level of the child affects the level of interest and action patterns. For every child, there is an optimal level of novelty, responsivity, and complexity, as well as an appropriate level of difficulty. To engage all learners, materials should be varied and multisensory, and children should have options for how to interact with them. For example, one child may prefer listening to a story about the changing colors of leaves, while another prefers to collect and sort leaves by color, and another chooses to press leaves into several colors of dough. In addition to these low-tech materials, other high-tech options could include listening to a leaf song on a tablet, matching leaf clip art using an interactive whiteboard, or video recording children's narrative stories or descriptions about leaves for later viewing.

Children should be allowed choice across materials according to their preferences. However, adults need to offer guidance by limiting the number of available choices and rotating materials to promote engagement and prevent children from being overwhelmed (McWilliam & Casey, 2008; Stockall et al., 2012). The first column of Table 1 provides some additional suggestions for applying UDL principles to the design of physical environments across developmental domains.

Temporal Environment

The temporal environment consists of schedules and routines as well as pacing and sequence of activities that serve to engage young children in learning experiences. In action, the UDL principles help practitioners and families structure time spent within learning spaces and across activities to support children's access and inclusion. Schedules set the sequence of activities and establish routines across the day. To increase children's access, schedules need to be child-friendly and understandable through multiple formats. Schedules should be posted at children's eye level and represented in multiple and meaningful ways such as in simple words, pictures, photographs, or objects as well as spoken words in English or children's home languages (McWilliam & Casey, 2008). At home, caregivers can alert children of routines within the daily schedule as well. For example, a parent can display a bottle or cup in anticipation of mealtime or consistently use low lighting as part of the bedtime routine. These strategies can be used alongside language-rich transitions within daily routines, such as singing a song or speaking a simple sentence, that also signal it is time for a particular activity.

The design of temporal learning environments requires balance across routines, planned activities, and child-initiated activities. Pacing of activities within routines and schedules should reflect young children's limited attention spans but also allow for extended time in response to in-depth engagement. Capitalizing on opportunities for incidental (i.e., unplanned) teaching within the temporal environment, caregivers can respond to the unique needs of diverse children by identifying and responding to their self-initiated attempts to communicate and engage with materials across any context (Curiel & Sainato, 2016; see also Fenske, Krantz, & McClannahan, 2001 for more information on incidental teaching). This flexibility across pacing and planned and unplanned activities gives children time to produce a response as needed, greater opportunity for interest- and strengths-based learning, and breaks from challenging or unmotivating activities when engagement wanes (Cunconan-Lahr & Stifel, 2013).

The sequence of activities within the temporal environment also requires consideration for maximally engaging young learners. By alternating active and more sedentary activities, adults can address children's varying needs for movement and rest (Copple & Bredekamp, 2009). Activities also can be sequenced with attention to varying whether they are adult- or child-directed. Over-reliance on one type of activity or set durations for activities can limit children's opportunities to meaningfully access learning environments. The second column of Table 1 provides suggestions for other temporal environment variations across each UDL principle.

Social Environment

A critical aspect of inclusive learning environments is children's and families' sense of belonging within the social environment. This comprises "equitable access to and full membership in the social-emotional life of the group" (Conn-Powers et al., 2006, p. 5) made possible by repeated and thoughtfully planned opportunities to promote children's social-emotional development (Strain, 2014). Though children are naturally social, some may have difficulty engaging in social relationships because of communication delays or cultural and linguistic diversity. Using a variety of materials (books, dolls, and cultural artifacts) as well as options for social engagement (songs, sharing, signed or picture-based communication) can enable all children to understand expectations for social skill development and offer multiple opportunities for children to practice social skills.

The design of temporal learning environments requires balance across routines, planned activities, and child-initiated activities. Pacing of activities within routines and schedules should reflect young children's limited attention spans but also allow for extended time in response to in-depth engagement.

Adults across home, school, and community settings can capitalize on children's interests and preferences to promote language and peer interaction. For example, by strategically limiting the number of toys available at a time, a teacher can promote peer-to-peer communication around turn-taking and sharing (McWilliam & Casey, 2008). At home, families can encourage sibling communication through cooperative games or shared story time. Children also need various opportunities to understand and express their emotions (Copple & Bredekamp, 2009; Cunconan-Lahr & Stifel, 2013). Scripted stories, such as Social Stories (Gray & Garand, 1993), may help some young learners process their responses to frustrating or fearful situations. This approach entails the use of a brief and simple story that explains the expectations for a given situation, as well as why, and that is tailored for the perspective of the particular child (Gray & Garand, 1993). Other children might benefit from peer modeling and pretend social play as means for improving their understanding of feelings and emotions in a given circumstance. The third column of Table 1 presents other ideas in this area.

The ideas presented in Table 1 are a place to start when considering UDL principles for environmental design in early childhood. These suggestions can, and should, be expanded upon and adapted to fit particular settings (school, home, and community) and meet the needs of unique children and families. In our experience, colleagues and families are essential sources of information and ideas for UDL-based variations to support inclusion and access. Specifically, as we discuss next, transdisciplinary collaboration and family empowerment, when supported by application of UDL principles, further allow for children's access to naturalistic and inclusive environments.

> Application of the UDL framework to transdisciplinary collaboration highlights the reciprocal teaching and learning that takes place among diverse members of the team and reveals the inseparable links among topic areas of the DEC Recommended Practices.

Transdisciplinary Collaboration

Early childhood intervention inherently involves a team of adults who work together to improve developmental outcomes for young children with or at-risk for developmental delays or disabilities. Inclusion and access to diverse learning environments are enhanced through collaborative teamwork across service providers and families (Catalino & Meyer, 2015; Hunt, Soto, Maier, Liboiron, & Bae, 2004; Kilgo, 2006; National Professional Development Center on Inclusion, 2009; Wesley & Buysse, 2001). Application of a transdisciplinary team approach recognizes the integrated nature of services and supports for promoting development of the whole child within inclusive environments. Further, this model signifies that all members of the team, including service providers and especially families, have equal involvement and equally important roles to play within the team structure (Kilgo, 2006). However, all members must recognize the limits of their knowledge, skills, and expertise and collaborate with others to ensure access and positive outcomes. Working together to share knowledge and responsibilities, transdisciplinary teams must engage in "intensive, ongoing interaction" (King et al., 2009, p. 213) that is strengthened by openness to other perspectives and ultimately a shared vision of goals and outcomes for the child and family (Kilgo, 2006). When considering early learning environments, teams must have a shared vision of inclusion and access.

Application of the UDL framework to transdisciplinary collaboration

Table 2
Multiple Means of Representation, Action/Expression, and Engagement Across Transdisciplinary Practice

Communication	• Provide flexible options for communication among team members, including time of day and mode (e.g., informal and formal face-to-face meetings, Skype or other video-based Internet communication, e-mail, phone conversations) • Use multiple approaches for actively welcoming and engaging all members of the team • Consider individual team members' preferences in light of culture and background
Teaching and Learning	• Share discipline-specific knowledge through verbal exchange, sharing of literature, observation, or modeling of approaches • Invite questions, perspectives, and communication of understanding from other team members • Offer options for how team members can implement discipline-specific strategies

Service Delivery	Use discipline-specific expertise and collective brain power to expand
	  • the range of materials and experiences for children across environments
	  • understanding of what challenges and motivates children across environments

highlights the reciprocal teaching and learning that takes place among diverse members of the team and reveals the inseparable links among topic areas of the DEC Recommended Practices (2014). In this case, Environment recommended practices intersect with Teaming and Collaboration recommended practices. As learners working alongside one another, each team member must gain discipline- or family-specific knowledge from the teaching of other members of the team. Within this adult structure, UDL principles help maximize the impact of the team for supporting inclusion and access by providing a common framework to guide and sustain the team's continuous communication and information sharing (Aldridge, 2006). Simultaneously, a cohesive team approach to implementation of UDL principles in direct or indirect service to young children with or at-risk for disabilities (through strategies illustrated in this article) will further maximize access.

In practice, application of UDL principles to transdisciplinary team processes and services will naturally take many forms. All team members should be well versed in UDL principles and know where to access information about UDL, such as through resources identified at the end of this article. Beginning with a shared understanding of UDL allows for integration of the principles into three key aspects of transdisciplinary practice: team communication, teaching and learning among the team, and team collaboration for service delivery (Aldridge, 2006). Specific ideas for application across these three areas are outlined in Table 2.

Family Empowerment

Families play a critical role in promoting accessibility to learning environments across home, community, and school settings. As an integral part of the child's learning, families are involved as decision makers to reflect the diverse needs or the uniqueness of each family. To do this, application of UDL principles helps ensure families also have access and are involved in the full range of children's early learning experiences (Conn-Powers et al., 2006). Again, we see tight linkages among topic areas encompassed within the DEC Recommended Practices (2014) with Family recommended practices overlapping not only with the Environment recommended practices associated with UDL but also with Teaming and Collaboration practices.

Family empowerment is to enhance the family's capacity by encouraging service delivery in naturalistic, least restrictive settings where child needs and family preferences are the priority (Howard, Williams, Miller, & Aiken, 2014). Family capacity building involves providing support to families, helping families access resources, and building on the strengths of families (Friend, Summers, & Turnbull, 2009; Trivette, Dunst, & Hamby, 2010). Central to family empowerment is an assumption of the family's equal and reciprocal participation in accessing resources and in the process of decision-making. Families can be empowered in many ways based on the individual family needs and priorities. For example, some parents may need to learn about their infant's physical characteristics and behavioral states. Others may need help in developing specific strategies such as how to recognize and respond to their child's cues. Still others may need emotional support and resources to enable them to feel more confident and comfortable in caring for their child's needs.

> Instead of feeling insufficient or deficient when expressing their needs and concerns, empowered families are provided *choices* that help them identify their intra- and interfamily resources for optimal accessibility to multiple learning opportunities within and outside the family environment.

Instead of feeling insufficient or deficient when expressing their needs and concerns, empowered families are provided *choices* that help them identify their intra- and interfamily resources for optimal accessibility to multiple learning opportunities within and outside the family environment. Intrafamily resources refer to resources that are available within the core family system, such as babysitting from an older sibling, parents' continuing education related to a child's special needs, or a vacation tradition for the whole family. Interfamily resources are supports from outside the core family, such as in-home respite from an extended family member, after-school child care from a church, or a parent-child reading group hosted by a community library.

As members of the team, family members have an opportunity to share their concerns and express their feelings toward the issue of the individual, often unique needs of the child with disabilities or delays. Reflecting the UDL principles, parents and other caregivers should be encouraged to express their concerns through flexible approaches that are meaningful to the child and the family. For example, parents can tell their story to the team, invite a friend to share the experience, or show family photos and describe vacation experiences. All these naturalistic settings help the team identify learning opportunities that are unique for the child.

According to Bailey et al. (2006), the family empowerment approach includes five primary outcomes: (1) families can articulate their child's abilities and special needs, (2) families are clear about their rights and can advocate for their child by using their rights, (3) families acquire and implement strategies to facilitate their child's development, (4) families have support systems and use them, and (5) families access desired services and programs in their communities.

Table 3

Empowering Families to Optimize Learning Opportunities Within the UDL Framework

UDL Principles	What Professionals Do	What Families Accomplish
Representation	Professionals help families identify resources in multiple formats to meet the various needs of families. • Intrapersonal support for parental development and training (e.g., parent continuing education on child development and learning) • Interpersonal support directly related to the target child's needs (e.g., sibling support for child care, extended family support for transportation, emotional support for child transition) • External family support (e.g., community activities, local or state professional organizations, nonprofit agencies)	Families are empowered to identify their needs and prioritize goals/objectives. • Parents are able to identify their target child's individual strengths and unique needs with confidence. • Families are able to identify each family member's contribution and function as a unit to develop prioritized goals and objectives. • Families are well informed of services that are available and most relevant to the target child's goals and objectives.
Action & Expression	Professionals help families access resources with multiple materials, processes, and strategies. • Information about child's characteristics is shared in a way that is clearly understood by families from culturally and/or linguistically diverse backgrounds. • The process of accessing resources is clearly and meaningfully described with multiple ways to meet family needs (e.g., electronic communication, hard copy newsletters, home visits from professionals). • Examples for multiple learning opportunities are explored with families.	Families are empowered to use multiple sources of information and create learning opportunities benefiting the target child and the whole family. • Families are able to develop strategies for implementing the prioritized goals and objectives related to the child's needs within home routines. • Families are comfortable to make choices based on existing resources as well as information provided from the professionals. • Families make decision about what services are needed and how they are delivered.
Engagement	Professionals provide multiple ways to reflect and assess the effects of using the resources for implementing the prioritized goals and objectives. • Let families tell their stories. • Multiple means of formative assessments are provided to families throughout the process. • Professionals share their reflections and development as diverse learners.	Families are empowered to identify their strengths in the process of using resources to achieve the prioritized goals and objectives. • Every family member is given an opportunity to share his or her voice. • Families are part of the decision-making in how to demonstrate their progress. • Family members reflect on what has been successful and what they would like to do differently in the future.

Through the UDL principles, professionals can engage families in taking advantage of multiple naturalistic learning environments that are most relevant to the family and most meaningful to the child. Empowering families means "helping families help themselves" in the process of identifying needs, accessing resources, and prioritizing goals and objectives. Table 3 provides some practical tips on what professionals can do to empower families to achieve their prioritized goals and objectives for the target child and the whole family within the UDL framework.

Empowering families of young children with disabilities or delays begins with informing them about the possible differences in physical, behavioral, social, and cultural characteristics between their child and children who are typically developing. It also involves helping parents assume their parental role in multiple settings such as the neonatal intensive care unit (NICU), child care centers, and home setting as well as developing appropriate interactions with their infants and young children. Using families' everyday activities and places is a noninvasive approach to family capacity building to increase the likelihood of improving caregiver competence and confidence (Swanson, Raab, & Dunst, 2011). In addition, effective early intervention with young children with disabilities involves providing parents with concrete, objective information about the likely course of development. This is often the first step for developing emotionally focused coping strategies (Johnson, Fieler, Jones, Wlasowicz, & Mitchell, 1997). Objective information means that the information is developmentally appropriate and individually specific. It should be information that parents can easily understand and therefore should be presented in multiple ways. Clear understanding of children's development decreases the discrepancy between what is expected and what actually occurs, and thus it increases predictability. Further, it also provides parents with practical and meaningful strategies that can be achieved through routines and daily activities.

Conclusion

The UDL framework requires consideration at the outset of design and planning for inclusive and accessible learning environments, rather than solely in response to barriers that emerge in practice. Like the DEC Recommended Practices (2014) and NAEYC's developmentally appropriate practice recommendations (2009), application of the UDL principles are often enmeshed, and one variation or approach can address two or all of the principles. In this article we have highlighted how the principles of UDL can, and should, be strategically applied to maximize the inclusion of all children across environments and through transdisciplinary collaboration and family empowerment. Embracing the principles as an integral part of reflective professional practice not only addresses multiple topic areas of the DEC Recommended Practices, it also reinforces the inclusion imperative.

Yet, we recognize this is a tall, though critically important, order. As Catalino and Meyer (2015) note, applying Environment recommended practices, such as the practice of focus here, is not likely to be instinctive but rather requires conscious planning and thought. It is our hope that through the illustrative examples presented here, readers can readily identify elements of UDL principles in action

The principles of UDL can, and should, be strategically applied to maximize the inclusion of all children across environments and through transdisciplinary collaboration and family empowerment.

within their work with colleagues and diverse young children and their families. Focusing on existing strengths can be a useful catalyst for change. Some questions to consider are:

- How have I designed the physical environment, schedules and/or routines, and opportunities for social engagement to improve child and family outcomes?
- Where and how do I apply flexible approaches to sharing information and teaching and learning alongside families and other professionals?
- What strategies do I use to empower families as active agents who support their children's learning across environments?

Using answers to these questions as a starting point, conscious effort must be directed toward bringing UDL principles to the forefront of practice to support children's access to and participation in early learning environments.

References

Aldridge, J. (2006). Making transdisciplinary teaming work: Pulling it all together. In J. L. Kilgo (Ed.), *Transdisciplinary teaming in early intervention/early childhood special education: Navigating together with families and children* (pp. 69–76). Olney, MD: Association for Childhood Education International.

Bailey, D. B., Jr., Bruder, M. B., Hebbeler, K., Carta, J., Defosset, M., Greenwood, C., . . . Barton, L. (2006). Recommended outcomes for families of young children with disabilities. *Journal of Early Intervention, 28*, 227–251. doi:10.1177/105381510602800401

Bertling, J., Darrah, M., Lyon, D., & Jackson, S. (n.d.). *Early childhood building blocks: Universal design for learning in early childhood inclusive classrooms.* Columbus, OH: Resources for Early Childhood

Brown, A., Shifrin, D. L., & Hill, D. L. (2015). Beyond "turn it off": How to advise families on media use. *AAP News, 36.* Retrieved from http://www.aap publications.org/content/36/10/54

Bruder, M. B. (2010). Early childhood intervention: A promise to children and families for their future. *Exceptional Children, 76*, 339–355. doi:10.1177/001440291007600306

Catalino, T., & Meyer, L. E. (2015). Improving access and participation. In *DEC recommended practices: Enhancing services for young children with disabilities and their families* (DEC Recommended Practices Monograph Series No. 1, pp. 53–63). Los Angeles, CA: Division for Early Childhood.

Center for Applied Special Technology. (2011). *Universal design for learning guidelines version 2.0.* Wakefield, MA: Author.

Center for Applied Special Technology. (2014). *What is UDL?* Retrieved from http://www.udlcenter.org/aboutudl/whatisudl

Conn-Powers, M., Cross, A. F., Traub, E. K., & Hutter-Pishgahi, L. (2006, September). The universal design of early education: Moving forward for all children. *Beyond the Journal: Young Children on the Web.*

Copple, C., & Bredekamp, S. (2009). *Developmentally appropriate practice in early childhood programs serving children from birth through age 8* (3rd ed.). Washington, D.C.: National Association for the Education of Young Children.

Cunconan-Lahr, R. L., & Stifel, S. (2013). *Universal design for learning (UDL) checklist for early childhood environments.* Bethlehem, PA: Building Inclusive Child Care Project.

Curiel, E. S. L., & Sainato, D. M. (2016). Teaching your tot to talk: Using milieu teaching strategies. *Young Exceptional Children, 19*(1), 39–47. doi:10.1177/1096250615576805

Dinnebeil, L. A., Boat, M., & Bae, Y. (2013). Integrating principles of universal design into the early childhood curriculum. *Dimensions of Early Childhood, 41*(1), 3–13.

Division for Early Childhood. (2014). *DEC recommended practices in early intervention/early childhood special education 2014.* Retrieved from http://www.dec-sped.org/recommendedpractices

Division for Early Childhood & National Association for the Education of Young Children. (2009, April). *Early childhood inclusion* (Joint position statement). Chapel Hill: The University of North Carolina, FPG Child Development Institute.

Dixon, S. D. (2008). Language is everywhere! Universally designed strategies to nurture oral and written language. *Young Exceptional Children, 11*(4), 2–12. doi:10.1177/1096250608320283

Dolan, R., P., & Hall, T. E. (2001). Universal design for learning: Implications for large-scale assessment. *Perspectives: The International Dyslexia Association, 27*(4), 22–25.

Fenske E. C., Krantz P. J., & McClannahan L. E. (2001). Incidental teaching: A not-discrete-trial teaching procedure. In C. Maurice, G. Green, & R. M. Foxx (Eds.), *Making a difference: Behavioral intervention for autism* (pp. 75–82). Austin, TX: PRO-ED.

Friend, A. C., Summers, J. A., & Turnbull, A. P. (2009). Impacts of family support in early childhood intervention research. *Education and Training in Developmental Disabilities, 44*, 453–470.

Gray, C. A., & Garand, J. D. (1993). Social stories: Improving responses of students with autism with accurate social information. *Focus on Autistic Behavior, 8*(1), 1–10. doi:10.1177/108835769300800101

Hall, T. E., Meyer, A., & Rose, D. H. (Eds.). (2012). *Universal design for learning in the classroom: Practical applications.* New York, NY: Guilford.

Howard, V. F., Williams, B. F., Miller, D., & Aiken, E. (2014). *Very young children with special needs: A foundation for educators, families, and service providers* (5th ed.). Upper Saddle River, NJ: Pearson.

Hunt, P., Soto, G., Maier, J., Liboiron, N., & Bae, S. (2004). Collaborative teaming to support preschoolers with severe disabilities who are placed in general education early childhood programs. *Topics in Early Childhood Special Education, 24*, 123–142. doi:10.1177/02711214040240030101

Individuals With Disabilities Education Act, 20 U.S.C. § 1400 (2004).

Israel, M., Ribuffo, C., & Smith, S. (2014). *Universal design for learning: Recommendations for teacher preparation and professional development* (Document No. IC-7). Gainesville, FL: The CEEDAR Center.

Johnson, J. E., Fieler, V. K., Jones, L. S., Wlasowicz, G. S., & Mitchell, M. L. (1997). *Self-regulation theory: Applying theory to your practice.* Pittsburgh, PA: Oncology Nursing Press.

Kilgo, J. L. (2006). Overview of transdisciplinary teaming in early intervention/early childhood special education. In J. L. Kilgo (Ed.), *Transdisciplinary teaming in early intervention/early childhood special education: Navigating together with families and children* (pp. 9–15). Olney, MD: Association for Childhood Education International.

King, G., Strachan, D., Tucker, M., Duwyn, B., Desserud, S., & Shillington, M. (2009). The application of a transdisciplinary model for early intervention services. *Infants & Young Children, 22,* 211–223. doi:10.1097/IYC.0b013e3181abe1c3

Lapinski, S., Gravel, J. W., & Rose, D. H. (2012). Tools for practice: The universal design for learning guidelines. In T. E. Hall, A. Meyer, & D. H. Rose (Eds.), *Universal design for learning in the classroom: Practical applications* (pp. 9–24). New York, NY: Guilford.

McWilliam, R. A., & Casey, A. M. (2008). *Engagement of every child in the preschool classroom.* Baltimore, MD: Paul H. Brookes.

Meyer, A., & Rose, D. H. (1998). *Learning to read in the computer age.* Cambridge, MA: Brookline Books.

Meyer, A., Rose, D., & Gordon, D. (2014). *Universal design for learning: Theory and practice.* Wakefield, MA: Center for Applied Special Technology.

National Association for the Education of Young Children. (2009). *Developmentally appropriate practice in early childhood programs serving children from birth through age 8* (Position statement). Washington, DC: Author.

National Professional Development Center on Inclusion. (2009). *Research synthesis points on early childhood inclusion.* Chapel Hill: The University of North Carolina, FPG Child Development Institute, Author.

Pisha, B., & Coyne, P. (2001). Smart from the start: The promise of universal design for learning. *Remedial and Special Education, 22,* 197–203. doi:10.1177/074193250102200402

Rose, D. (2001). Universal design for learning. *Journal of Special Education Technology, 16*(4), 66–67. doi:10.1177/016264340101600411

Rose, D. H., Harbour, W. S., Johnston, C. S., Daley, S. G., & Abarbanell, L. (2006). Universal design for learning in postsecondary education: Reflections on principles and their application. *Journal of Postsecondary Education and Disability, 19,* 139–151.

Stockall, N. S., Dennis, L., & Miller, M. (2012). Right from the start: Universal design for preschool. *Teaching Exceptional Children, 45*(1), 10–17. doi:10.1177/004005991204500103

Strain, P. S. (2014). *Inclusion for preschool children with disabilities: What we know and what we should be doing* (Handout). Retrieved from http://www.eclre.org/media/88372/strain_what_we_know_.pdf

Swanson, J., Raab, M., & Dunst, C. J. (2011). Strengthening family capacity to provide young children everyday natural learning opportunities. *Journal of Early Childhood Research, 9,* 66–80. doi:10.1177/1476718X10368588

Trivette, C. M., Dunst, C. J., & Hamby, D. W. (2010). Influences of family-systems intervention practices on parent-child interactions and child development. *Topics in Early Childhood Special Education, 30,* 3–19. doi:10.1177/0271121410364250

Wesley, P. W., & Buysse, V. (2001). Communities of practice: Expanding professional roles to promote reflection and shared inquiry. *Topics in Early Childhood Special Education, 21,* 114–123. doi:10.1177/027112140102100205

UDL Resources

The following are a select group of resources to learn more about Universal Design for Learning. All but those with specific web addresses can easily be found with a popular search engine.

General Information

National Center on Universal Design for Learning (NCUDL)
    NCUDL videos
    UDL Guidelines 2.0

Center for Applied Special Technology (CAST)
    UDL at a glance YouTube video
    UDL Exchange

IRIS Module: Universal Design for Learning

Questions to Consider in UDL Observations of Early Childhood Environments

Universal Design for Learning (UDL) in Action: The Smart Inclusion Toolkit

Other Resources to Support UDL Principles Across Developmental Domains

Literacy
    UDL Book Builder
    Tar Heel Reader

Social-Emotional
    Carol Gray Social Stories
    Touch Autism: Wait Timer

Fine Motor
    Fine Motor Activities
    http://www.finemotoractivities.net

    Handwriting Without Tears

    Make your own line writing paper
    http://www.do2learn.com/
    activities/writingtools/index.htm

4

Role of Universal Design for Learning and Differentiation in Inclusive Preschools

Eva Horn
University of Kansas

Jean Kang
University of North Carolina at Greensboro

Audra Classen
University of Southern Mississippi

Gretchen Butera
Indiana University

Susan Palmer
University of Kansas

Joan Lieber
University of Maryland

Amber Friesen
San Francisco State University

Alina Mihai
Indiana University Kokomo

The phone call came: "Ms. Vega, we would like to hire you as the lead teacher in our state-funded inclusive prekindergarten program." Teresa Vega was elated and eager to get started as she thought about the types of activities she would plan for her young students. Soon enough she'd be helping them learn about the world around them and get ready for formal schooling. The children enrolled in her classroom would be a diverse group with a wide range of abilities, experiences, and backgrounds. Teresa remembered that to enroll in the program in her state, a child must be 4 years old no later than August 30. It was quite possible, and even likely, that she would have children who had their 4th birthday during the summer as well as children who had turned 4 the previous fall. These classmates, almost a year apart in age, would certainly present different levels of development, growth, and social-emotional maturity. In addition, children qualify to attend the program based on a variety of circumstances, including family poverty, English as a second language status, and coming from a single-parent family. Finally, the school district was committed to serving their 3- to 5-year-old children with special needs in inclusive settings, which included the prekindergarten classes. Thus, Teresa would no doubt have children in her classroom with a range of learning abilities and needs. The school district was well aware that Teresa would need to get started early to plan curriculum for her classroom. During the phone call, she was told, "Ms. Betzler is the early childhood special educator who will be working with you to address the needs of children with disabilities in the classroom. She worked in the classroom last year and is anxious to meet with you to help with the planning." Teresa was eager to begin planning the curriculum and setting up a learning environment that would support all of the children in her class in accessing, participating, and making meaningful progress in the curriculum.

Research has consistently demonstrated that attending high-quality preschool programs is related to better outcomes for many children (Barnett, 2008). By planning for developmentally appropriate learning environments, teachers can

support the learning of all young children as they progress toward meeting learning standards. However, as our opening vignette illustrates, early education programs today are enrolling children from increasingly diverse families. Children and families from diverse backgrounds—ethnic, linguistic, and economic—and children with differing abilities are found in early education programs throughout the country, reflecting the increasing diversity of the nation (BUILD Initiative, 2008). While diversity brings richness to the work, ensuring that all children's needs are effectively met requires thoughtful, intentional planning by educators. How can early education programs ensure appropriate access, participation, and opportunities for learning for all young children?

As articulated in the Division for Early Childhood (DEC) Recommended Practices (2014) as a part of the Environment topic area, programs such as Teresa's have taken the first step by committing to provide "services and supports in natural and inclusive environments during daily routines and activities to promote the child's access to and participation in learning experiences" (p. 8). The first step in this process is for teachers such as Teresa to implement specific strategies that support all children's access to, participation in, and learning within the general curriculum. Two key strategies that are associated with well-designed learning environments and general curriculum access and participation for all children are universal design for learning, or UDL (Conn-Powers, Cross, Traub, & Hutter-Pishgahi, 2006) and differentiation (Tomlinson, 2003). These two terms are also central to DEC's Environment recommended practices (2014). Specifically, recommended practice E2 includes a recommendation to "consider Universal Design for Learning principles" (p. 8). E3, while not directly using the term, does address key elements of differentiation in recommending that educators "modify and adapt the physical, social, and temporal environment" (p. 8). That is, as we will articulate further below, differentiation when accounting for supporting access and participation in the general curriculum focuses on making modifications and adaptations to aspects of the general curriculum to support children's active engagement with the material and learning activities.

Universal Design for Learning and Differentiation

UDL has at its roots the concept of universal design often used in architecture. The basic premise is that all products, buildings, and spaces should be useable by all people to the greatest extent possible without need for adaptation (Mace, Hardie, & Place, 1996). With universal design, the developer meets diverse needs at the design stage rather than building a structure or product before considering modifications. UDL extends the concept of universal design to the learning environment and specifically to the curriculum. Using UDL, teachers focus on designing learning environments from the start for the widest range of learners rather than making individual accommodations and modifications that focus on making the learning environment work for an individual child (Conn-Powers et al., 2006; Dinnebeil, Boat, & Bae, 2013; DEC, 2007).

Differentiation, on the other hand, moves to the next step. That is, in differentiation the teacher's focus is on making the learning environment work for individual children. Differentiation provides a cluster of strategies that the teacher uses to vary and adapt materials and activities to support individual children's active participation and learning of the general curriculum content (Hall, 2002; Tomlinson, 2003). In practice, the teacher implementing differentiation strategies resists the "one size fits all" approach and relies instead on designing modifications and adaptations based on children's assessment data and careful observation of the children's engagement in their environments.

Certainly, UDL and differentiation have commonalities and overlap in some respects. Both UDL and differentiation, at their core, address the fact that all children are unique and learn and grow in different ways and at their own pace. Both require the teacher to resist the "one size fits all" approach to designing curriculum and arranging and managing the learning environment for young children. While UDL and differentiation are related concepts, each represents a different step in teachers' planning and implementation processes. In UDL, the focus is on the starting point or the "design stage" as the teacher thinks about how the children will move through the curriculum. The teacher then uses differentiation strategies in an ongoing manner to plan for and make adjustments for individual children to address their participation and engagement in the learning environment.

As depicted in Figure 1, UDL and differentiation—and ultimately individualized instruction—are each steps in the process of designing inclusive, accessible, and supportive learning environments for all children. In fact, the planning and

Using UDL, teachers focus on designing learning environments from the start for the widest range of learners rather than making individual accommodations and modifications that focus on making the learning environment work for an individual child.

Figure 1
Three-Step Planning Process

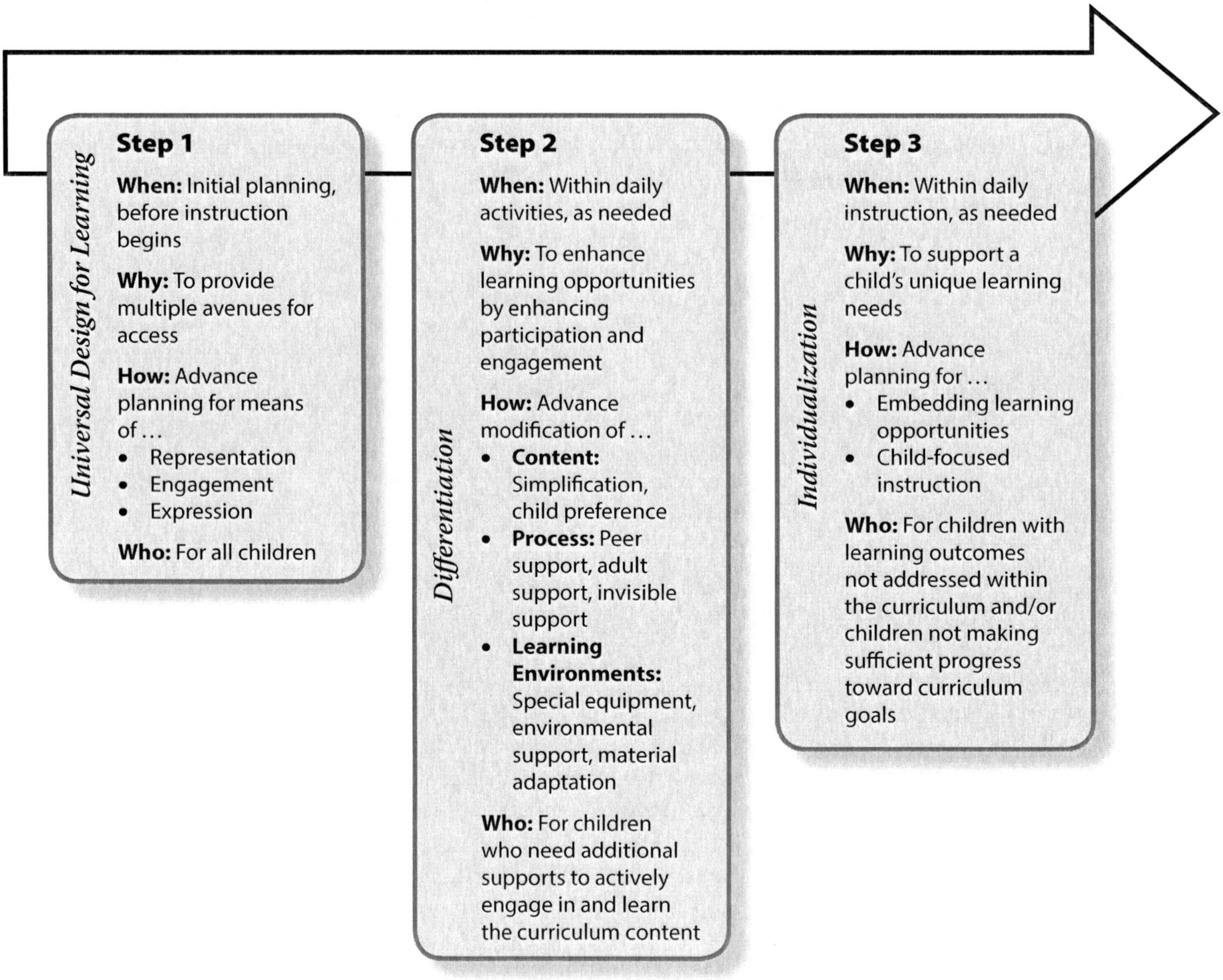

Universal Design for Learning

Step 1

When: Initial planning, before instruction begins

Why: To provide multiple avenues for access

How: Advance planning for means of …
- Representation
- Engagement
- Expression

Who: For all children

Differentiation

Step 2

When: Within daily activities, as needed

Why: To enhance learning opportunities by enhancing participation and engagement

How: Advance modification of …
- **Content:** Simplification, child preference
- **Process:** Peer support, adult support, invisible support
- **Learning Environments:** Special equipment, environmental support, material adaptation

Who: For children who need additional supports to actively engage in and learn the curriculum content

Individualization

Step 3

When: Within daily instruction, as needed

Why: To support a child's unique learning needs

How: Advance planning for …
- Embedding learning opportunities
- Child-focused instruction

Who: For children with learning outcomes not addressed within the curriculum and/or children not making sufficient progress toward curriculum goals

implementation process can be viewed as a series of increasingly individualized steps. As the first step, UDL addresses all children's needs for varied strategies for accessing the learning environment. The second step, differentiation, addresses specific children's needs for increased opportunities to engage in and learn the curriculum content. The third step, individualization, moves beyond a focus on the learning environment to the instructional process. Thus, while depicted in the figure, we do not discuss specific strategies for Step 3.

As she begins planning for her new position, Teresa has the opportunity to ensure that her learning environments are universally designed from the start to support access and participation for the widest range of learners. Later, through careful observation and monitoring, she will begin to understand individual children's participation and engagement with the curriculum content and other aspects of the learning environment, and she will create intentional plans for providing modifications and adaptations (differentiation). Throughout the process, Teresa strives to make the environment accessible for all children to participate in learning experiences by providing naturally and inclusively delivered services and supports in the same settings that other preschool children experience (DEC, 2015). In the remainder of this paper, we take a closer look at how Teresa can accomplish these first two steps: UDL and differentiation. Note that we will not address the third step of individualization. A more complete description of all three steps of the curriculum planning process is available in Horn, Palmer, Butera, and Lieber (2016).

UDL in Early Education

By using UDL to guide planning from the beginning, the teacher ensures that all children are provided with a variety of ways to access and process new information and demonstrate what they are learning. That is, a curriculum that incorporates UDL from the beginning rather than as an after-the-fact adaptation provides all children with a variety of formats for using resources and materials; engaging with learning content; demonstrating what they know; and expressing their ideas, feelings, and preferences (Karger & Hitchcock, 2003). By initially planning for the broadest range of young learners, the teacher spends less time modifying or adapting later. UDL encompasses three primary principles: (a) means of representation to give learners a variety of ways to access information and content, (b) means of engagement to gain and maintain learners' interest, and (c) means of expression to provide learners with a variety of ways for demonstrating what they know (Center for Applied Special Technology [CAST], n.d.).

Using the guiding questions checklist (Horn et al., 2016) shown in Table 1, Teresa can conduct a self-check on her adherence to the three UDL principles as she plans curriculum activities. The following sections provide a closer look at each of the key principles and aligns with the guiding questions checklist.

Means of Representation

Means of representation has been referred to as the "what" of the learning process (DEC, 2007; Rose & Meyer, 2006). Young children differ in how they receive and understand information that is presented to them. Some may grasp information more readily by seeing it, hearing it, touching it—or a combination of all three. For example, research has established young children are initially more able to learn concepts that are presented using concrete objects and through multiple examples (Clements, 1999). Means of representation can be thought of as both a focus on the means used to support how the children receive information and how information is communicated to the children. While these two foci are not discrete and many teaching strategies address both, the important message is that teachers must reflect carefully on each to ensure that they are fully addressing the means of representation principle as they plan. The guiding questions provided in Table 1 for means of representation are organized to address these two areas and they are further detailed below.

> By using UDL to guide planning from the beginning, the teacher ensures that all children are provided with a variety of ways to access and process new information and demonstrate what they are learning.

Table 1
Guiding Questions for Universal Design for Learning

Means of Representation

Consider	Ask These Questions	Yes/No — How?
Formats for communication	1. Have I considered all appropriate options for presenting materials and content in different formats, including visual, auditory, and/or tactile forms? 2. Have I provided for the simultaneous presentation in more than one format?	
Complexity of communication	1. Have I identified the key concept and made plans for providing scaffolding to address multiple levels of complexity? 2. Have I reviewed my instructions, questions, and expectations and planned for providing simultaneous options for children's understanding?	

Means of Engagement

Consider	Ask These Questions	Yes/No — How?
Recruiting children's engagement	1. Have I identified multiple types of activities and materials that children in my class are currently drawn to and systematically incorporated several into my activity plan? *Note: Consider the influence of gender, temperament, life experiences, and family culture as you generate ideas.* 2. Have I identified opportunities for child choice and systematically incorporated several options into my activity plan? 3. Have I identified and planned for multiple opportunities for incorporating novelty and connecting to "known" or prior experiences so there is a good balance of both?	
Sustaining children's attention	1. Have I considered the difficulty/complexity level of the activity/concept/materials and planned for flexibility in providing for a range of challenging, yet not frustrating, complexity levels throughout the activity? 2. Have I planned for multiple types and opportunities for feedback, encouragement, and scaffolding for children throughout the activity? 3. Across the children's day and/or work on particular concepts, have I ensured that activity plans represent multiple learning contexts, including large group, small group and independent time?	

Table 1 (continued)
Guiding Questions for Universal Design for Learning

	Means of Expression		
Consider	**Ask These Questions**		**Yes/No — How?**
Acceptable formats for making responses	Have I identified multiple acceptable formats for children to appropriately respond, including: • Verbal • Physical (e.g., pointing, nodding or shaking head, gestures, acting out the response) • Nonverbal symbolic (e.g., pictures, drawings, symbols, writing) produced by adult • Nonverbal symbolic (e.g., pictures, drawings, symbols, writing) produced by child		
Acceptable levels of complexity of responding	1. Have I identified multiple acceptable levels of complexity for children to appropriately respond, including: • Nonverbal • Single responses • Multiple component responses 2. Have I identified multiple acceptable levels of scaffolding or independence in children's responses, including: • Following adult prompt or partial cue • Following adult or peer model • As a part of choral responding • Independent responding • Independent, self-initiated behavior or communication		

Adapted with permission from Horn, E., Palmer, S. B., Butera, G. D., & Lieber, J. A. (2016). Six steps to inclusive preschool curriculum: A UDL-based framework for children's school success. Baltimore, MD: Paul H. Brookes.

Means for receiving information. In recognizing that young children have a range of learning styles, the teacher should support all learning modalities (i.e., auditory, visual, and tactile) by providing information using multiple and, as appropriate, simultaneous presentation through auditory (e.g., verbally stating the information), visual (e.g., providing a picture of the information), and tactile (e.g., using concrete objects to illustrate the information) means. For example, during a storybook reading activity, Teresa could provide multiple copies of the book and/or a large book format so that the children can follow along visually as she reads aloud (auditory). In addition, she could bring in concrete objects related to key concepts in the story (tactile).

Means of communication. In addressing multiple forms of communication, the teacher considers both the format of the communication and the complexity level. Strategies for varying the format include the use of pictures and signs or gestures paired with verbal communication. Strategies for addressing multiple levels of complexity include stating the word and then stopping to define it, repeating and restating key concepts, and breaking the communication into discrete components or steps (e.g., "First, choose your paper color. Second, choose . . ."). A strategy that Teresa could implement would be to routinely model the steps and verbally describe them as she provides the children instructions for an activity.

An additional aspect that can be addressed through multiple means of communication is supporting the use of multiple languages, especially important for dual language learners. Research confirms the importance of supporting children's continued learning in their primary language while at the same time fostering their ability to learn to speak English or any "new" language (Hammer, Lawrence, & Miccio, 2008). Furthermore, the learning of a second language is enhanced when learning occurs in context. Adding the use of Spanish, American Sign Language (ASL), or any other language used by the children in the classroom addresses specific child needs and also serves as a UDL strategy for all the children. For example, Teresa could include storybooks in multiple languages, invite family members or other community volunteers to read books in different languages or with sign language interpretation, and sing songs in multiple languages and with signing.

Means of Engagement

Means of engagement is sometimes referred to as the "why" of the learning process (DEC, 2007; Rose & Meyer, 2006). Teachers should think about "why" the young children in class might want to participate in planned activities or interact with the materials and people in the classroom environment. As a group, young children are interested in spontaneity and novelty, but they also need to be grounded by predictable routines. Young learners differ greatly in what captures their attention and motivates them to engage in activities that lead them to learn. How can we tap into the children's interest, offer appropriate challenges, and help them to become motivated, engaged, and excited about learning? The UDL principle of means of engagement provides a guide for the teacher. Engagement in this case includes both a focus on recruiting children's interest and sustaining their attention and persistence to a task. Again, the guiding questions checklist (see Table 1) provides Teresa with a way to systematically address these two areas of means of engagement.

Recruiting child attention. An effective strategy for recruiting children's attention is to brainstorm about the types of activities and materials that children of this age group tend to gravitate toward. In doing so, it is important to remember to address a number of factors that often influence child interests, including gender, temperament, life experiences, and family culture as well as the current popular themes, characters, and toys (e.g., princesses, dinosaurs, superheroes). Materials and activities should reflect responsiveness to these differences while communicating that the classroom is a place to explore freely. Another well-documented, successful strategy for recruiting children's engagement is providing them with choices as they participate in learning activities (Brewer, 2004; Dunlap et al., 1994). For example, even something as simple as allowing the children to choose where they will sit as a small group (e.g., "We could sit by the window at the small table or we could sit in the book corner in the beanbags") can entice the children to join the storybook reading group.

The teacher can also use the strategy of providing a balance between the novel and the familiar and making meaningful connections to children's prior experiences and current environments. For example, during a science activity as a part of a fall season theme, Teresa plans to have the children weigh and measure apples. She can have a variety of apples available. As they prepare to weigh and measure the apples, she can lead a discussion about apples, including who likes to eat apples, the ways they like to eat apples (e.g., whole, peeled, sliced), and where their family buys apples. To add some novelty, she can include a hedge apple from her yard to spark a great discussion on weight and size as well as other concepts (e.g., same/different, food/nonfood).

Sustaining children's attention. Sustaining children's attention requires that the teacher closely monitor children's level of engagement and routinely implement strategies that are known to be effective in preventing wandering attention and supporting children's persistence. The research and theory that provide the evidence base for developmentally appropriate practice principles provide excellent guidance about how to effectively support children's attention and persistence (National Association for the Education of Young Children [NAEYC], 2009). Specifically, an important factor in sustaining children's attention and persistence is ensuring that the difficultly/complexity level of the task is such that children are not bored and remain challenged yet not frustrated. Furthermore, children should have a high proportion of experiences in which they are successful and thus encouraged to continue. The teacher can also support children's persistence with experiences that are just beyond their mastery by providing appropriate levels of feedback, encouragement, and scaffolding.

The organization of the activities also plays an important role in supporting children's sustained engagement. That is, Teresa will want to use a variety of learning contexts, including large group, small group, independent time, and even one-on-one time. As she does so, she will need to ensure that the learning contexts selected reflect an appropriate match with the learning content. Small group instruction, for example, has been shown to be highly effective for introducing new skills and concepts (Castle, Deniz, & Tortora, 2005; Early et al., 2005; Vaughn, & Linan-Thompson, 2003). Paying close attention to the length of activities and alternating between active participation and more quiet observation are also important features of recruiting and maintaining young children's active engagement.

> Paying close attention to the length of activities and alternating between active participation and more quiet observation are also important features of recruiting and maintaining young children's active engagement.

Means of Expression

Means of expression is sometimes referred to as the "how" of the learning process (DEC, 2007; Rose & Meyer, 2006). Young learners differ in the ways in which they can best demonstrate how and what they have learned. Some young children may provide long verbal responses while others provide brief responses or partial responses. Yet other children are more comfortable drawing or writing about what they know, while another group of children may prefer using gestures, finger plays, or singing. In fact, most children use all of these approaches to express their growing knowledge about their world. Of concern to Teresa and other

teachers is how to provide children with alternatives for demonstrating what they know. How can support be provided to help them organize what they know and then show what they have learned? Strategies that can be used by the early education teacher to address multiple means of expression can be divided into the three components. First, teachers should consider how they might provide multiple acceptable options for physical responses to questions, including verbal responses, gestures, pointing, drawing, and writing. Second, teachers must consider how they will communicate feedback to the children based on the length and complexity of the response. For example, if Teresa asks a question of the children in a small group storybook reading, one child may provide a one-word response, whereas another child may answer the question in a multiple-word sentence, and yet another child may add new information connecting the question asked to her/his experience. Third, during the planning process teachers should consider how to provide scaffolding to support a range of responses. They must consider the variety of child responses and think about how to support a range of independence in responding. This may include choral responding, responding in imitation following a peer's response, and responding after an adult model. The guiding questions checklist (see Table 1) for means of expression again can be used by teachers to check whether they have considered all aspects of the UDL principle of means of expression.

Differentiation in Early Education

In moving from UDL to differentiation, the teacher's focus shifts. That is, for UDL the teacher's focus is on "designing barrier-free, instructionally rich learning environments and lessons that provide access to all students" (Nelson, 2014, p. 2). In every classroom, however, there are children with and without disabilities who will need additional modifications and adaptations to the learning environment beyond those provided through UDL in order to enhance their active participation with and learning of the planned curricular content. Thus the task for Step 2 (see Figure 1) shifts from addressing children's curricular learning to a more focused look at specific children's access, participation, and learning opportunities within the curriculum by developing plans for providing *differentiation* to address identified support needs. Specifically, differentiation provides for modifications and adaptations for all children's learning of a common concept, but each child is doing so within his/her comfort level and at a pace that meets his/her needs (Horn et al., 2016).

Differentiation *is not individualization* in which the focus moves from participation in the general curriculum to addressing the unique learning needs of a given child (Horn & Banerjee, 2009). Differentiation supports increased participation within the learning environment classroom that creates more opportunities for the child to learn. Differentiation should occur when children are interested in the ongoing curriculum activities but are not able to fully participate. A child may watch the other children and may try to participate, but not succeed, or may not stay with the activity long enough to make progress on the content. Sometimes a child performs a skill but does so in a way that needs improvement/refinement. Sometimes a child has acquired the basic skills to participate in the curriculum activities but has stalled in making further progress. This child might do some, but not all, of the skills expected.

Central to differentiation is the process of modifying and adjusting the learning environment to meet the needs of each child based on an understanding of his/her current abilities, engagement, and interests (Tomlinson, 2000). Following careful observation and monitoring of children's performance and engagement in the learning environment, the teacher is prepared to make modifications. The modification can take the form of adjustments in the content (i.e., information the children need to learn), the process (i.e., types and format of the activities in which the children are engaged), the product (i.e., children's "work" in which they apply and extend the content in order to make sense of it and master it), and/or the learning environment (i.e., types and levels of learning support provided to the child).

Differentiation and/or curriculum modification have been organized in a number of ways to guide implementation by early education teachers. One such organization focuses on three key elements of "what" needs to be modified or differentiated and includes: (a) the *learning environment* or the types and levels of support provided to the child, (b) the *content* or the information the child needs to learn, and (c) the *process* or the types and format of the activities in which the child is engaged (Tomlinson, 2001). Another organizational approach focuses on how to accomplish curricular modifications and adaptations. This approach includes eight types of strategies: environmental support, material adaptations, special equipment, use of children's preferences, simplification of the activity, adult support, peer support, and invisible support (Sandall & Schwartz, 2008). In yet another organizational approach, Horn and her colleagues (2016) have combined these two organizational strategies into a single approach. That is, as shown in Table 2, the eight types of curricular modifications have been organized to align with the three key elements of what needs to be modified or

Differentiation supports increased participation within the learning environment classroom that creates more opportunities for the child to learn. Differentiation should occur when children are interested in the ongoing curriculum activities but are not able to fully participate.

Table 2
Components of Differentiation

Learning Environment

Modification	Definition	Strategies
Environmental support	Special or adaptive devices to promote maximum independence in participation	• Change physical environment (e.g., place footprints on floor to make pathways) • Change the social environment (e.g., support children in group activity by sitting them next to a peer who doesn't distract them) • Change temporal environment (e.g., provide activity/space the child can move to as needed during group activity)
Material adaptation	Special or adaptive devices to promote maximum independence in participation	• Have materials in optimal position (e.g., height) • Stabilize materials • Modify the material to make larger • Modify to create higher contrast (e.g., remove background visual or highlight important content) • Modify material to lessen physical demands (e.g., glue small piece of Styrofoam to book pages to separate them and make them easier to turn)
Special equipment	Special or adaptive devices to promote maximum independence in participation	• Use of special equipment to increase access (e.g., use loop scissors) • Use of special equipment to increase participation (e.g., when children are sitting on floor, use a bean bag or other supports for child who cannot easily sit independently)

Content

Modification	Definition	Strategies
Child preferences	Identify and integrate child preferences and choice to enhance child participation	• Incorporate multiple choices for the child as he/she participates in the activity (e.g., choice of materials, choice of peers or adult, choice of location) • Allow child to retain item that provides comfort (e.g., hold a preferred object) as long as it's unobtrusive
Simplification	Simplify complicated task by breaking it into smaller parts or reducing number of steps	• Break task into clearly delineated steps (e.g., provide cue cards to assist with retelling the story) • Reduce number of steps by partially completing task and support child in finishing with success (e.g., child writes name on their project by only writing first letter, with others written by teacher)

Table 2 (continued)
Components of Differentiation

Process		
Modification	**Definition**	**Strategies**
Adult support	Provide direct individualized support	• Adult provides support through additional cues for appropriate behavior, including verbal cue, model, physical prompt, and physical guidance • Adult provides support through praise and scaffolding to work on expanding the child's response
Peer support	Arrange for a peer to provide support	• Pair children so one child can model for the other on how to complete the task • Designate a peer to help accomplish a specific task for a child (e.g., peer designated as helper for pushing wheelchair)
Invisible support	Intentionally rearrange aspects of environment in an unobtrusive manner to provide support	• Plan sequence of turns for a child to simplify task (e.g., third or fourth child to report on weekend activity so they can use previous responses as example) • Plan for enhanced access or proximity to adult or peer for support • Plan for enhanced access to materials

Adapted with permission from Horn, E., Palmer, S. B., Butera, G. D., & Lieber, J. A. (2016). Six steps to inclusive preschool curriculum: A UDL-based framework for children's school success. Baltimore, MD: Paul H. Brookes.

adapted. Sandall and Schwartz (2008) provide a comprehensive listing of each of the eight curricular modifications with multiple examples for each that teachers can adopt.

It is important to use a curriculum modification only when necessary to help the child participate, rather than as a standard practice, because in many cases the universally designed curriculum will be sufficient for children to actively participate and learn. Modifications should be provided in the least intrusive and obvious manner possible. Finally, remember to always evaluate the impact of the differentiation strategy on the child's active participation in the environment. Because the ultimate goal is promoting learning, not just engagement, the teacher should also monitor the child's performance to assess whether the child is becoming more competent and engaged in the activity and learning the curricular content.

In Summary

Teachers like Teresa will continue to find that the children they serve represent a range of learning assets and needs. Striving to reach all learners must be front and center in their planning. A framework that includes UDL as the first step in planning and differentiation as the second step in implementation can assist Teresa and other teachers with taking on the challenge. UDL and differentiation, used well, can help us achieve one goal of supporting all children, that is, active participation and engagement with the learning environment. By considering the range of learners at these stages, teachers will meet the needs of a greater number of learners with less need for instructional individualization. The need for individualization will continue but will be easier to accomplish if built upon a foundation of UDL and differentiation. When teachers use UDL in their planning process followed by differentiation to adjust the learning environment, teachers are addressing key aspects of DEC Recommended Practices (2014) to provide an accessible and supportive environment for all children.

References

Barnett, W. S. (2008, September). *Preschool education and its lasting effects: Research and policy implications.* Boulder, CO: Education and the Public Interest Center & Education Policy Research Unit. Retrieved from http://nieer.org/resources/research/PreschoolLastingEffects.pdf

Brewer, J. A. (2004). *Introduction to early childhood education: Preschool through primary grades* (5th ed.). Boston, MA: Pearson.

BUILD Initiative. (2008, January). *Building early childhood systems in a multi-ethnic society: An overview of BUILD's briefs on diversity and equity.* Boston, MA: Author.

Castle, S., Deniz, C. B., & Tortora, M. (2005). Flexible grouping and student learning in a high-needs school. *Education and Urban Society, 37,* 139–150. doi:10.1177/0013124504270787

Center for Applied Special Technology. (n.d.). *About universal design for learning.* Retrieved from www.cast.org/our-work/about-udl.html

Clements, D. H. (1999). "Concrete" manipulatives, concrete ideas. *Contemporary Issues in Early Childhood, 1,* 45–60. doi:10.2304/ciec.2000.1.1.7

Conn-Powers, M., Cross, A. F., Traub, E. K., & Hutter-Pishgahi, L. (2006, September). The universal design of early education: Moving forward for all children. *Beyond the Journal: Young Children,* 1–9. Retrieved from http://journal.naeyc.org/btj/200609/ConnPowersBTJ.pdf

Dinnebeil, L. A., Boat, M., & Bae, Y. (2013). Integrating principles of universal design into the early childhood curriculum. *Dimensions of Early Childhood, 41*(1), 3–13.

Division for Early Childhood. (2007, March). *Promoting positive outcomes for children with disabilities: Recommendations for curriculum, assessment, and program evaluation.* Missoula, MT: Author.

Division for Early Childhood. (2014). DEC recommended practices in early intervention/early childhood special education 2014. Los Angeles, CA: Author. Retrieved from http://www.dec-sped.org/recommendedpractices

Division for Early Childhood. (2015). *DEC recommended practices: Enhancing services for young children with disabilities and their families* (DEC Recommended Practices Monograph Series No. 1). Los Angeles, CA: Author.

Dunlap, G., dePerczel, M., Clarke, S., Wilson, D., Wright, S., White, R., & Gomez, A. (1994). Choice making to promote adaptive behavior for students with emotional and behavioral challenges. *Journal of Applied Behavior Analysis, 27,* 505–518. doi:10.1901/jaba.1994.27-505

Early, D., Barbarin, O., Bryant, D., Burchinal, M., Chang, F., Clifford, R., . . . Barnett, W. S. (2005, May). *Pre-kindergarten in eleven states: NCEDL's multi-state study of pre-kindergarten and study of state-wide early education programs (SWEEP).* Chapel Hill, NC: Frank Porter Graham Child Development Institute. Retrieved from http://www.fpg.unc.edu/node/4654

Hall, T. (2002, June). *Differentiated instruction.* Retrieved from http://teachingcommons.cdl.edu/education/_media/documents/NCACDifferentiatedInstructionPaper.doc

Hammer, C. S., Lawrence, F. R., & Miccio, A. W. (2008). Exposure to English before and after entry into Head Start: Bilingual children's receptive language growth in Spanish and English. *International Journal of Bilingual Education and Bilingualism, 11,* 30–56. doi:10.2167/beb376.0

Horn, E., & Banerjee, R. (2009). Understanding curriculum modifications and embedded learning opportunities in the context of supporting all children's success. *Language, Speech, and Hearing Services in Schools, 40,* 406–415. doi:10.1044/0161-1461(2009/08-0026)

Horn, E., Palmer, S. B., Butera, G. D., & Lieber, J. A. (2016). *Six steps to inclusive preschool curriculum: A UDL-based framework for children's school success.* Baltimore: MD. Paul H. Brookes.

Karger, J., & Hitchcock, C. (2003). *Access to the general curriculum for students with disabilities: A brief legal interpretation.* Wakefield, MA: National Center on Accessing the General Curriculum. Retrieved from http://opi.mt.gov/pdf/Assessment/MCPresents/IEPs/curriculum_access_legal.pdf

Mace, R. L., Hardie, G. J., & Place, J. P. (1996). *Accessible environments: Toward universal design.* Raleigh: The Center for Universal Design, North Carolina State University.

National Association for the Education of Young Children. (2009). *Developmental appropriate practice in early childhood programs serving children from birth through 8* (Position statement). Washington, DC: Author. Retrieved from http://www.naeyc.org/files/naeyc/file/positions/PSDAP.pdf

Nelson, L. L. (2014). *Design and deliver: Planning and teaching using universal design for learning.* Baltimore, MD: Paul H. Brookes.

Rose, D. H., & Meyer, A. (Eds.). (2006). *A practical reader in universal design for learning.* Cambridge, MA: Harvard Education Press.

Sandall, S. R., & Schwartz, I. L. (2008). *Building blocks for teaching preschoolers with special needs* (2nd ed.). Baltimore, MD: Paul H. Brookes.

Tomlinson, C. A. (2000). *Differentiation of instruction in the elementary grades.* Eric Digest, (ED443572). Champaign, IL: ERIC Clearinghouse on Elementary and Early Childhood Education.

Tomlinson, C. A. (2001). *How to differentiate instruction in mixed-ability classrooms* (2nd ed.). Upper Saddle River, NJ: Prentice Hall.

Tomlinson, C. A. (2003). *Fulfilling the promise of the differentiated classroom: Strategies and tools for responsive teaching.* Alexandria, VA: Association for Supervision and Curriculum Development.

Vaughn, S., & Linan-Thompson, S. (2003). Group size and time allotted to intervention: Effects for students with reading difficulties. In B. R. Foorman (Ed.), *Preventing and remediating reading difficulties: Bringing science to scale* (pp. 299–324). Baltimore, MD: York Press.

5

Practitioners as Architects
Constructing High-Quality Environments for Physical Activity in Inclusive Early Childhood Settings

LORELEI E. PISHA
The George Washington University

KARIN H. SPENCER
Shepherd University

TODAY'S TECHNOLOGY-FOCUSED LIFESTYLE IS LESS PHYSICALLY active than that of previous generations. Adults and children alike are spending more and more time in front of screens for work, learning, and leisure activities, as well as opting to travel by motorized vehicles rather than by foot (American Heart Association, 2015). This decline in physical activity is associated with increased rates of obesity, including childhood obesity. Obesity during the early years is especially problematic because research indicates obesity continues from childhood through adolescence and into adulthood (Fuentes, Notkola, Shemeikka, Tuomilehto, & Nissinen, 2003; Johannsson, Arngrimsson, Thorsdottir, & Sveinsson, 2006; Nader et al., 2006; Olvera, Sharma, Suminski, Rodríguez, & Power, 2007).

Several national organizations have issued recommendations regarding physical activity for young children with suggestions ranging from 60 to 120 minutes per day (Centers for Disease Control and Prevention, n.d.; National Institute for Health and Clinical Excellence, 2009; National Association for Sport and Physical Education [NASPE], 2009a). The NASPE guidelines recommend that young children ages 3–5 participate in 120 minutes of physical activity throughout the day and across settings to promote healthy development. The recommendations specify that 60 of these minutes should be spent in adult-facilitated, structured physical activities. Unfortunately, young children are not meeting the NASPE guidelines for physical activity and are, instead, spending a vast majority of the day in sedentary activities (Brown, Pfeiffer, et al., 2009; Pate, McIver, Dowda, Brown, & Addy, 2008). This includes more than 32 hours per week in front of a screen (e.g., television, computer, tablet, phone, video game console; McDonough, 2009).

Children with and at risk for developmental disabilities tend to engage in even less physical activity and are at increased risk of obesity compared with their peers without disabilities or such risk factors (Cervantes & Porretta, 2010; De, Small, & Baur, 2008; Fox, Witten, & Lullo, 2014; Rimmer & Rowland, 2008; Zwier et al., 2010). Approximately 29% of children with disabilities and 30% of children with autism are obese (Bandini, Curtin, Hamad, Tybor, & Must, 2005; Curtin, Anderson, Must, & Bandini, 2010). Additionally, children with disabilities who are African American or Hispanic are significantly more likely to be obese than their Caucasian peers (Rimmer, Yamaki, Davis, Wang, & Vogel, 2011).

Catalino and Meyer (2015) recognize a pressing need for research-based interventions supporting physical activity in young children with physical disabil-

ities and special health care needs. Pisha (2012) found that inclusive early childhood practitioners may also struggle to promote physical activity in young children with autism who may have atypical social-communication skills, interests, and sensory profiles that interfere with participation in raucous physical activity with peers. Moreover, practitioners need to understand that vulnerable children who have experienced trauma within primary attachment relationships may display behaviors that impact their participation in physical activity. For example, children who have experienced homelessness and/or maternal depression may present with low energy levels, possibly appearing with symptoms of chronic fatigue syndrome (Mader, 2012; Swick, 2008). On the other end of the continuum, children who have experienced domestic violence may appear hypervigilant and highly reactive, which may lead to safety concerns during unstructured interactions with peers (Bassuk, Konnath, & Volk, 2006).

However, the Committee on Obesity Prevention Policies for Young Children explains that a physically active lifestyle during the early childhood years may decrease the risk for obesity throughout the lifespan (Institute of Medicine, 2011). During these early years, participation in a variety of developmentally appropriate physical activities provides opportunities for acquiring important fundamental movement skills (e.g., skipping, balancing, or catching) along with promoting an enjoyment of movement and cardiovascular health (Trost, Sirard, Dowda, Pfeiffer, & Pate, 2003). Adults, including early childhood practitioners, are the architects of these early experiences with physical activity. Specifically, early childhood practitioners may nurture a lifelong love for movement by intentionally designing engaging inclusive environments that offer sufficient access to and encourage participation in high-quality physically active play experiences.

The Division for Early Childhood (DEC) Recommended Practices (2014) directs attention to the importance of physical activity for promoting overall health and development for young children with and at risk for disabilities. Environment recommended practice E6 explains that practitioners should "create environments that provide opportunities for movement and regular physical activity to maintain or improve fitness, wellness, and development across developmental domains" (p. 8). E2 also highlights the critical role that Universal Design for Learning (UDL) principles should play in the design and delivery of inclusive learning environments that promote physical activity. We will now integrate UDL principles with recommended practices for promoting physical activity in early childhood settings to support practitioners in their work to provide all young children with access to and participation in high-quality inclusive movement experiences.

Access and Participation: UDL Principles for Physically Active Play

Although child-related factors (e.g., physical disability) certainly influence participation in physical activity, as much as 50% of the variation in young children's physical activity during preschool hours may be attributed to characteristics of the early childhood program the child attends (Bower et al., 2008). Quality is one such characteristic. The DEC/National Association for the Education of Young Children (NAEYC) joint position statement on early childhood inclusion (2009) sets forth three defining features of high-quality inclusion: access, participation, and supports. All children must have access to the physical, social, temporal, and instructional environments within the inclusive early childhood setting that offers opportunities for physically active play. However, access alone is not sufficient. Practitioners must use instructional strategies (e.g., preference assessment, adaptations, modifications, naturalistic teaching) with intentionality to design movement opportunities that promote the active participation of all children. System-level supports (e.g., professional development, provision of space/time for physically active play) are required to ensure that practitioners have the knowledge, skills, and resources to implement quality practices related to physically active play. These defining features may be applied to the design and delivery of high-quality inclusive physical activity in early childhood settings. This article focuses on practitioner-level practices for providing all children access to and participation in high-quality early childhood physical activity experiences.

DEC (2007) recommends that early childhood practitioners employ UDL principles in the design and delivery of the curriculum to intentionally provide young diverse learners with access to and participation in inclusive learning opportunities. UDL is characterized by three guiding principles: multiple means of representation, multiple means of engagement, and multiple means of action and expression (Center for Applied Special Technology [CAST], 2011). When early childhood practitioners use UDL principles to plan for physically active play, they create environments that allow all children to access and participate from the start without making significant after-the-fact adaptations or modifications to the environment on a child-by-child basis. Like architects who design

Early childhood practitioners may nurture a lifelong love for movement by intentionally designing engaging inclusive environments that offer sufficient access to and encourage participation in high-quality physically active play experiences.

Table 1
UDL Principles With Examples for Physically Active Play

UDL Principle	Definition	Physical Activity Examples
Engagement	The "Why" of Learning (CAST, 2011) Children are motivated to learn	Children have opportunities for active participation when teachers plan at least five minutes of movement activity at each large group gathering. Children have choices about how to move during transitions. Teachers promote effort and persistence by positively noting children's effort or activity level: "Wow, Johnny you are working really hard!"
Representation	The "What" of Learning (CAST, 2011) Children learn in many different ways	Children can practice the same skill in different ways at more than one movement station (i.e., throwing small soft balls at a large target drawn on the mat and throwing frog-shaped bean bags onto a lily pad [hula hoop]) to help bridge concept and skill development across activities. The stations are also offered on multiple days so children can have repeated opportunities to practice.
Action & Expression	The "How" of Learning (CAST, 2011) Children show what they have learned in many different ways	Activities provide alternatives for physical action. A track around the perimeter of the gymnasium allows children to move feely at their own pace while other children participate in movement stations. Children can choose to ride scooters on their tummies or on their bottoms. They can be self-propelled or get pushed or pulled by a peer. Children are able to demonstrate their emerging throwing skills with a variety of materials (i.e., scarves, o-balls, nerf balls, bean bags) in response to their development.

buildings and products for users with a range of characteristics, interests, and abilities (CAST, 2011), practitioners must leverage the concepts of UDL to design environments that provide movement opportunities for a diverse group of young learners. Practical application of the UDL principles of engagement, representation, and action and expression are discussed throughout the article. Table 1 provides a brief overview of each principle in relation to physical activity in early childhood settings.

Practitioners as Architects: High-Quality Inclusive Environments for Physical Activity

This section describes recommended practices the practitioner may use when designing physical, social, temporal, and instructional environments to promote access to and participation in physically active play. These practices are aligned with national guidelines and recommended practices for physical activity in early childhood settings. UDL principles are purposively integrated with these recommended practices to promote intentional planning and instruction for inclusive early childhood settings through (1) setting the stage through preparation and planning, (2) designing the environment to provide opportunities for physical activity, (3) facilitating child-led physically active play, and (4) leading structured physical activity. Interspersed within are brief rubrics or rating scales adapted from a physical activity consultant tool (Head Start Body Start National Center for Physical Development and Outdoor Play [HSBS], 2010) that teams can use to self-monitor their progress toward implementing high-quality practices. Recommended practices for promoting physically active play with UDL-informed planning will be demonstrated through the use of vignettes about Mrs. Porterfield's inclusive early childhood classroom. The vignette below introduces Mrs. Porterfield, her teaching team, and the children in her classroom.

Mrs. Porterfield is the lead teacher for an inclusive community early childhood classroom where sixteen 4-year-olds are enrolled in a full-day program. Ms. Engleside is the itinerant early childhood special education (ECSE) teacher who visits the classroom once each week to provide supports for two children who have identified developmental delays. At a team meeting in December, Mrs. Porterfield expresses concern with indoor recess. Winter has already set in, and the children are spending recess time in the gym engaging in free play with equipment such as balls, tunnels, and trikes.

Michael's sensory sensitivity and delays in social communication are restricting his play choices and activity, especially during indoor recess. He bangs on the door to leave and cannot be encouraged to stay in the gym with the other children, no matter what the teachers offer him as a choice. Mrs. Jones, her teaching assistant, has to take him in the hallway to ride a trike while she watches over all the other children. She's also worried about Alessandra, who has spina bifida and uses a walker for mobility at school. Mrs. Porterfield doesn't know how to keep her safe in the gym with balls, trikes, and children running everywhere. Alessandra's energy levels seem low these days, and she tends to stay close to teachers, preferring the company of adults over peers. The team wonders whether her resistance to exploring the indoor play environment is related to her experiences at home where she is coping with insecure housing, maternal depression, and a recent placement in foster care. Alessandra's physical therapist asked Mrs. Porterfield last week to encourage Alessandra to explore her environment more, but she questions how she can motivate Alessandra to do this while also ensuring that she stays safe during physically active play.

> " A cornerstone of high-quality early childhood practice is thoughtful preparation and planning for instruction; practitioners must set the stage for success.

Setting the Stage

A cornerstone of high-quality early childhood practice is thoughtful preparation and planning for instruction; practitioners must set the stage for success. Practitioners plan to ensure that children have opportunities across the day and routines to meet or exceed recommendations for physical activity. They consider physical activity as integral to learning across the curriculum and use UDL principles to "create flexible designs from the start that have customizable options" allowing all learners to progress and be successful (CAST, 2011).

Alignment with guidelines and recommendations. Practitioners should also intentionally plan learning experiences that align with recommendations from national organizations specializing in physical activity during the early childhood years. Several sources converge to provide recommendations for early childhood physical activity. These include *Appropriate Practices in Movement Programs for Young Children Ages 3–5* (NASPE, 2009b), *Active Start: A Statement of Physical Activity Guidelines for Children from Birth to Age 5* (NASPE, 2009a), and *Promoting Physical Activity in Preschool Settings: Teacher Behavior Rating Scale* (HSBS, 2010). The latter is a set of recommended practices based on a literature review and the professional knowledge and experience of national experts in the field of early childhood physical activity.

National guidelines for recommended practice provide guidance for both quantity and quality of physically active play. In addition to ensuring recommended quantities of structured and unstructured play, effective teaching teams intentionally implement recommended practices to ensure that physical activity is an integral part of daily plans and collaborate with families to promote opportunities across settings. Instruction should maximize opportunities for physical activity for all children while also promoting increased physical exertion along with the development of motor competence and movement literacy (HSBS, 2010). The current work in this article builds upon the recommended practices of NASPE and HSBS by aligning these practices with UDL principles for inclusive early childhood settings.

UDL-informed planning. UDL-informed planning for physical activity includes foci related to amount, variety/frequency, and individualization. It guides practitioners to create learning opportunities through both unstructured, child-directed choice and structured, adult-led activities that promote developmentally appropriate movement opportunities during the preschool day. The practitioner draws upon knowledge of child development to plan varied and frequent opportunities for physically active play. For example, adults plan for multiple bouts of varied physical activities spread throughout the daily schedule with an emphasis on moderate-to-vigorous physical activity to reflect children's nature as intermittent movers. To this end, movement is integrated throughout the daily routine, taking advantage of transitions as an opportunity to be physically active.

A UDL-informed approach to planning also focuses on individualization that aims to increase engagement by recruiting children's interest through active participation (CAST, 2011). Adults plan with attention to children's individual differences, including strengths, needs, and interests as well as language, culture, gender, race, and parental attitudes that may impact physical activity. In doing so, they further increase engagement by varying activities so they can be personalized and contextualized to learners' lives (CAST, 2011). Such responsive curriculum planning promotes cultural relevance. Observations inform planning and adults intentionally build upon skills, interests, and prior experiences by linking these to new concepts and movement patterns. Adults facilitate skill development and increase comprehension by activating prior knowledge and skill development and bridging concepts and movement patterns. They highlight critical features such as verbally noting or physically modeling movement awareness concepts, as Mrs. Porterfield does in the following vignette.

> Instruction should maximize opportunities for physical activity for all children while also promoting increased physical exertion along with the development of motor competence and movement literacy.

Mrs. Porterfield includes at least five minutes of movement activity at each large group gathering and keeps the children moving during transitions. Today while reading Eric Carle's From Head To Toe, *she led the children as they moved their bodies like a variety of animals, swinging their arms like gorillas, bending their necks like giraffes, and kicking their legs like donkeys. Then Mrs. Porterfield and the children sang and moved to "Head, Shoulders, Knees and Toes," singing it fast and slow, standing up high, and sitting down low. Children moved in a variety of nonlocomotor patterns and learned movement vocabulary such as bending, swinging, and kicking low and high.*

Sufficient opportunities for physical activity throughout the day are especially important for Alessandra. She benefits from the energy boost of physical activity. Her experiences with homelessness and maternal depression may impact her overall low energy level, and, as a result, she benefits from regular opportunities for movement throughout the day (Mader, 2012). This can be contrasted with some of her peers who come from chaotic homes. They may exhibit high energy levels, and some may even be hypervigilant, causing them to have a harder time settling in and engaging in activities (Gewirtz & Edleson, 2007; Mader, 2012). When Michael is not overwhelmed by the loudness of the gym environment, he often engages in sensory-seeking activities such as pounding on objects or running into walls or peers. Physical activities that provide proprioceptive input—big body play, heavy weight push and pull activities—can be calming and organizing for Michael and some of his "high energy" friends.

Mrs. Porterfield and Ms. Engleside brainstorm with the physical education teacher about the use of the gymnasium space and available equipment. They borrow cones and polyspots to create separate sections in the gymnasium, just like center time in the classroom. They set up some areas with more structured activity (i.e., bean bag toss) away from others with more freedom (i.e., ribbon dancing). This supports Michael and Alessandra as they participate in the areas that feel less chaotic and safer. Alessandra recently enjoyed interacting with her peers at the scarf dancing station where Mrs. Porterfield has included one polyspot for each dancer and an MP3 player loaded with De Colores and Other Latin American Folk Songs.

Michael likes to use the sensory station, often playing with the shape-shifting body socks. Classmates like to use the "track" around the perimeter when it is designated for "belly or bottom" scooters. Some especially like to get moving around the whole group while keeping an eye on all the action. Mrs. Porterfield and Ms. Engleside are sure to give Michael visual and verbal warnings when it is almost time to stop an activity because they know that sensory seekers often have a hard

Table 2
Self-Monitoring Tool: Setting the Stage

	Highly Effective	Intentional	Room to Grow
Amount	Plans include both structured and unstructured physical activity at or above the minimum recommended standards.	Both structured and unstructured physical activity are planned at the minimum standards but may be subject to other priorities that arise during the day.	Unstructured physical activity takes precedence over structured activity because of limited planning. Moderate-to-vigorous physical activity may be restricted because of safety or management concerns.
Variety and Frequency	Plans include multiple opportunities for physical activity with varying types of activities and levels of exertion throughout the day. Children are able to choose their level of exertion.	Physical activities are planned as several periods of moderate-to-vigorous activity that occur throughout the day. Children can often choose a variety of activities or level of exertion.	Physical activity is limited to specified recess time. A single time is scheduled for structured activity.
Individualization	Culturally responsive instruction consistently and intentionally reflects the strengths, needs, and interests of children.	Instruction intentionally incorporates some of the following: children's strengths, needs, interests, and culture.	Instruction is not planned to include physical activity or it includes theme-based activities rather than those responsive to children's strengths, needs, interests, and culture.

Adapted from HSBS, 2010

time transitioning and need extra support. Throughout play the teaching team is sure to positively note children's effort and comment on their activity level to facilitate an enjoyment of activity as well as increase children's ability to self-monitor. For example, Mrs. Jones says, "Alessandra, you sure look like you are having fun and really moving to the music. I bet your heart is beating faster."

Table 2 provides a rubric in which our recommended practices aligned with national guidelines are informed by UDL principles. Practitioners may use the table's rubric to assess progress toward effective planning and preparation of environments that promote physical activity.

Designing the Environment

"Environment as the third teacher" is a popular notion in early childhood education and is particularly relevant when working to ensure a wide range of opportunities for physical activity. Well-designed environments include foci on variety, participation, safety, and challenge. Adults can infuse the UDL principle of action and expression by providing a wide array of options for physical action and, in doing so, naturally increase engagement as well. Adults should thoughtfully and intentionally select and arrange toys, materials, and equipment to stimulate active play (HSBS, 2010). High-quality environments incorporate a wide variety of affordances (Sanders, 2002) with toys, equipment, materials, and space that are intentionally selected and presented to suggest many different ways to move. For example, balls of different sizes and materials might encourage various nonlocomotor skills such as throwing and catching, rolling, or kicking, while a tunnel might encourage locomotion when children crawl down low to the ground. Musical instruments or music played on a boom box might encourage children to move rhythmically and possibly start and stop on a signal.

A variety of open-ended materials might be included to spur creativity, such as a variety of loose parts (i.e., tree cookies, PVC pipes, tires, plastic containers, pallets, milk crates). Another important feature of a well-planned environment is the infusion of the principle of engagement by promoting maximum participation and safety. Adults promote active participation by avoiding activities where children participate one at a time and need to wait long periods for a turn. Adults also provide materials and space that present varying levels of challenges and complexity with the opportunity for children to self-select their degree of challenge and receive fading assistance while engaging in challenging activities. Mrs. Porterfield applies these practices as she redesigns the gymnasium environment.

Mrs. Porterfield's new gymnasium arrangement is better designed to balance safety, risk, and engagement. She uses visual markers (i.e., cones and poly spots) to create separate areas for activities with different movement opportunities. Children are able to self-select their activity, and the activities themselves encourage different levels of challenge. The team's approach provides learners with as much discretion and autonomy as possible, exemplifying the UDL principle of engagement. For example, the teaching team establishes a "track" around the perimeter of half the gym so children can move freely at their own pace while other children participate in other movement stations without the fear of getting bumped.

Mrs. Porterfield varies the equipment for the track. On this day it is scooters, and children can self-select their challenge by riding them on their tummies or their bottoms and self-propelling or getting pushed/pulled by a peer. The children have multiple options for physical action during this activity, demonstrating the UDL principle of action and expression. Mrs. Porterfield effectively redesigns the environment so all children can simultaneously be active and have multiple opportunities to practice emerging and newly achieved skills. This team knows that all learners, and especially young ones, need multiple occasions for practice, demonstrating how they infuse the UDL principle of representation in their planning.

Table 3
Self-Monitoring Tool: Designing Opportunities in the Environment

	Highly Effective	Intentional	Room to Grow
Variety	Toys, equipment, materials, and space are consistently selected and presented to suggest many different ways to move.	Toys, equipment, materials, and space are often selected and presented to suggest different ways to move.	Toys, equipment, materials, and space are limited in number and variety.
Participation	Time to move is maximized by the environment. Children can be active simultaneously rather than wait for turns.	Children have frequent opportunities to be active simultaneously. Occasionally, children may have to share and wait for turns.	Space and materials limit children's ability to be physically active simultaneously. Children often have to share materials and wait for turns.
Safety	Materials and space are arranged so that all children can be safely active simultaneously and can safely experience a sense of risk and challenge.	Materials and space are arranged to minimize safety precautions while allowing children to be active simultaneously and safely experience a sense of risk and challenge.	Materials and space are arranged to maximize safety, but doing so removes all sense of risk and challenge. Or, materials and space are not arranged with safety in mind and children are frequently hurt by other bodies or materials.
Challenge	Materials and space consistently present varying levels of challenge and complexity. Children are allowed to select or are supported as needed to self-select their challenge.	Some materials and space present varying levels of challenge and complexity. Children are both assigned to activities and allowed to select activities.	Materials and space suggest one purpose with little accommodation of ability of skill. Children are regularly assigned to activities.

Adapted from HSBS, 2010

Table 3 provides a rubric in which our recommended practices are aligned with national guidelines and informed by UDL principles to create opportunities in the inclusive early childhood environment for physically active play. Practitioners may use this rubric to assess progress toward designing effective opportunities in the environment.

Facilitating Physically Active Play

With intentionally designed environments in place, adults must next put on another hat: play facilitator. In this role, the adult must first remain outside the play to carefully observe how children play with materials or peers, their growth in different developmental domains, whether toys and materials are interesting and challenging, and the effect of props or how rearrangement of materials affects play. The adult uses this knowledge to determine which role(s) to assume to facilitate children's engagement in the play cycle (Blum & Spencer, 2010), including (1) narrator, (2) responder, (3) extender, (4) supporter, (5) collaborator, (6) integrator, and (7) includer. Each role is described next in terms of its use to support physically active play and its relation to UDL.

A narrator introduces and reinforces children's movement vocabulary through narrating play in real time, labeled "sportscasting" by Madga Gerber (Greenwald & Weaver, 2013). The narrator "sportscasts" in real time using specific movement vocabulary including action (skipping, twisting, bending), effort (slow, medium, fast), space (up, down, high, low) and relational awareness (around, over, under). Narrating children's physically active play helps to simultaneously increase children's movement literacy and cognitive development. Overlaying language for position and direction words as children move their bodies though space is essential for developing these concepts. Practitioners who "sportscast" using specific movement vocabulary are infusing the UDL principle of representation. By highlighting key terms and concepts, they support young learners' comprehension.

A responder acknowledges children's abilities or knowledge in a way that supports their self-efficacy. In doing so, this practitioner employs the UDL principle of engagement to sustain persistence, often emphasizing process, effort, or improvement rather than accuracy. Practitioners in this role provide feedback to children engaged in physically active play by commenting on the child's activity and use of toys and materials or by asking thoughtful questions while being respectful of the roles the children are pretending to be and/or the activity with which the children are engaged. Adults pose authentic questions to uncover new information rather than quizlike interrogations focused on assessment.

The extender adds a prop, asks a question, or makes a comment to scaffold more complex or elaborate play and/or facilitates connections to previous learning. Building upon his or her role as a narrator and responder, the adult draws upon his or her skill as a keen observer of children to scaffold their development. The adult serves as a more knowledgeable other, facilitating the child's creativity and experimentation while supporting the original child-initiated play. The adult's authentic interactions reflect the UDL principle of representation by including queries that serve to promote comprehension by activating children's prior knowledge and supporting the child in bridging new learning to previous learned concepts.

The supporter specifically acknowledges children's persistence and achievement, especially when engaged in a problem-solving task or practicing a challenging skill. The supporter engages children in exploring their thinking; they seek to understand the child's perception of how they engaged in an activity and what they learned from it. Skillful supporters employ the UDL principle of action and expression as they engage children in think-alouds about processes.

A collaborator joins in, participating in child-initiated play in a way that models joy in movement and is respectful of the child's chosen direction for play; the adult plays by the children's rules. The adult incorporates the UDL principle of action and expression by promoting a variety of movement opportunities and promoting executive function skills as the children share plans and organize their play.

> Narrating children's physically active play helps to simultaneously increase children's movement literacy and cognitive development. Overlaying language for position and direction words as children move their bodies though space is essential for developing these concepts.

Table 4
Self-Monitoring Tool: Facilitating Physically Active Play

	Highly Effective	Intentional	Room to Grow
Narrator	Adults narrate children's real-time activity using specific movement vocabulary. They describe exactly what is happening in play without interfering, questioning, or extending.	Adults narrate children's real-time activity using some specific movement vocabulary. They may also use praise-based vocabulary or narrate children's activity after the fact.	Adults may acknowledge after the fact that children were engaged in movement activity.
Responder	Adults acknowledge children's abilities or knowledge providing feedback on specific qualities of a child's abilities or skills that are changing or improving.	Adults acknowledge that a child's abilities or skills are changing or improving, though at times this includes generic encouragement.	Adults use primarily corrective feedback.
Extender	Adults extend children's play facilitating the child's creativity and experimentation while supporting the original child-initiated play.	Adults suggest specific changes related to the original child-initiated play. Adult involvement may at times change the nature of the activity.	Adults direct the play scenario making changes to original child-initiated play so that it is no longer the child's activity.
Supporter	Adults monitor and assist children in negotiation, cooperation, and other social interactions without taking over the play. They engage children's metacognition by consistently acknowledging children's persistence and achievement, especially when engaged in problem-solving tasks or when practicing a challenging skill.	Adults debrief children's engagement in play after the fact, scaffolding the child's learning about the steps necessary to be successful with motor skills and peer interactions.	Adults acknowledge the child's engagement in an activity, but only on-task behavior is praised.

An integrator reinforces and extends emerging skills in child-initiated play. She recognizes emerging skills across developmental domains within child-initiated play and takes advantage of teachable moments without disrupting play. She may insert vocabulary and concepts from other learning domains into physical activities in natural and contextual ways. The integrator infuses the UDL principle of representation as she highlights important information.

An includer supports social interactions among children. She supports cooperation, collaboration, and negotiation among children in ways that are consistent with different stages and types of play. This support is consistent with the UDL principle of engagement. The following vignette demonstrates how Mrs. Porterfield and Ms. Engleside use a variety of roles to facilitate physically active play for diverse learners.

Mrs. Porterfield takes the children outside for play every day. Today she starts the

Table 4 (continued)
Self-Monitoring Tool: Facilitating Physically Active Play

	Highly Effective	Intentional	Room to Grow
Collaborator	Adults consistently participate in child-initiated play as a collaborator. The adult regularly plays by the children's rules.	Adults generally play by children's rules but may subtly impose more mature structure on the play. S/he may alternate between participant and authority.	Adults take over play, participating as an authority figure.
Integrator	Adults ensure that various learning domains are integrated into the play experience while not interfering in the child-initiated play. Adults recognize emerging skills within child-initiated play and take advantage of teachable moments without disrupting play. They may insert vocabulary and concepts from other learning domains into physical activities in ways that are natural and contextual.	Adult inserts vocabulary and concepts from other learning domains into physical activities but may at times interrupt play to do so.	Adult interrupts physical play to quiz children on vocabulary and concepts from other learning domains.
Includer	Adult immediately acknowledges specific, positive social interactions among children.	Adult acknowledges specific, positive social interactions among children after play.	Adult defines positive social interactions in the midst of resolving a current conflict.

Adapted from HSBS, 2010

outdoor play period by standing near the playground structure. She "sportscasts" the children's actions, taking care to incorporate vocabulary that describes position and effort. You can hear her say, "Oooh, look Johnny climbed way up high on the ladder, now he is going to swoosh down the slide fast. Michael is waiting behind Joey for a turn to crawl through the tunnel." Yesterday, Ms. Engelside observed carefully as Seth pulled some branches over toward the grassy areas under the big tree. A skilled responder, she thoughtfully queried Seth and Julie: "You are working so hard pulling those branches. I am wondering what your plan might be?" Because their goal was to "build something," today the teachers added new materials to the play area (large foam blocks and pool noodles) to provide opportunities to extend their play. They also brought out a wagon for pulling heavy items.

Seth and Julie have revisited their construction play, and Alessandra has joined them. The trio invites Ms. Engleside to help. She joins as a collaborator: "What is your plan? How can I help?" Alessandra explains that they are making the three pigs' houses. The children have already made a cross curricular connection during their outdoor play! Ms. Engleside continues as an integrator, scaffolding their story retelling supporting oral language, comprehension, and sequencing skills. When Michael comes over to the play, standing on the perimeter, watching and then taking a pool noodle from a "house," the children screech. Ms. Engleside helps to include Michael in the play: "Oh, I think Michael might want to join your work. Let's see. Michael, your friends are building the three little pigs' houses. Say, 'I want to play, too.'"

Examine the rubric in Table 4 in which our recommended practices are aligned with national guidelines and informed by UDL principles. Practitioners may use the rubric in Table 4 to assess progress with facilitation of play during child-selected physical activity.

Leading Structured Physical Activity

While early childhood environments emphasize the open-ended nature of unstructured play opportunities, structured play is also valuable, especially when teaching fundamental movement skills, encouraging increased vigorous activity, or embedding learning opportunities for skills in other domains. The adult's role includes generating and leading structured activities, each with a specific emphasis, while keeping the activity playlike from the children's perspective (HSBS, 2010). The adults use both direct and indirect teaching methods to ensure that children are both exposed to important information about movement and encouraged to explore and discover a range of movement possibilities (NASPE, 2009b).

A variety of strategies facilitate participation at all ability levels to develop children's skills and motor literacy. When beginning an activity, the adult shares the activity's focus. He or she provides a sense of what the activity is about in age-appropriate language and concepts. The adult demonstrates the UDL principle of engagement by providing clear, purposeful outcomes that serve to sustain effort and persistence. Children are encouraged to persist, to work and play, progressing in targeted skills. When children become off-task, adults gently and respectfully return children to the activity using multimodal reinforcement (modeling, oral reminders, etc; HSBS, 2010). Adults may model or demonstrate specific actions in ways that present movement challenges. Consistent use of prompts and reminders support engagement while visual and verbal models support comprehension via the UDL principle of representation.

While modeling, adults use movement vocabulary to direct attention to relevant aspects of the demonstration. They use language specific to movement literacy, cueing and reinforcing with language specific to movement rather than behavior (HSBS, 2010). This practice of highlighting critical features is one example of representation that supports comprehension. Adults engage children in interesting learning activities and provide opportunities for repetition and variation. Adults provide "a variety of novel learning experiences that emphasize similar motor skills across different environment contexts, allowing children to develop movement patterns gradually. They plan for and provide opportunities within instructional sessions for extending and refining these skills" (NASPE, 2009b, p. 12). The following vignette describes some of our recommended practices rooted in UDL.

> While early childhood environments emphasize the open-ended nature of unstructured play opportunities, structured play is also valuable, especially when teaching fundamental movement skills, encouraging increased vigorous activity, or embedding learning opportunities for skills in other domains.

Table 5
Self-Monitoring Tool: Leading Structured Physically Active Play

	Highly Effective	Intentional	Room to Grow
Purpose	Adult consistently uses developmentally appropriate concepts and language to describe the purpose of activities and uses visual and verbal strategies to maintain children's attention to activities and corresponding foci.	Adult usually provides a sense of what activities are about in common language and concepts and may use some strategies to support children's ability to maintain attention to the activity.	Adult provides the name of the activities or perhaps the rules but does not establish a focus connected to motor learning.
Modeling	Adult consistently models specific movements and/or motor activities using movement vocabulary. He or she highlights aspects of the demonstration to support children's learning.	While modeling skills, the adult names the skills and usually uses movement vocabulary.	Adult provides a demonstration without verbal cues.
Adaptations	Adult consistently makes adaptations to motor activities to support each child's individual skills development. He or she uses own knowledge, resources, and teamwork to adapt activities and provide varying levels of challenge and complexity. He or she encourages and scaffolds children's ability to make self-referenced adaptations or choose challenges.	Adult usually makes familiar adaptations to motor activities to support children's skill development. They usually provide at least one level of challenge.	Adults rarely adapt activities. Instead they provide the same activity for all children.
Feedback	The adult provides individualized feedback and support. Positive noting emphasizes effort and comments specific to skill development tells children what "to do" rather than what "not to do."	The adult usually provides feedback, but it may be generalized based on the observed trends of the group. He or she positively notes effort.	The adult provides limited feedback for either effort or skill development. If comments are provided, they are corrective in nature rather than focused on providing a model of "what to do."

Adapted from HSBS, 2010

Mrs. Porterfield regularly includes a movement center in her early education classroom. Children may work at the center during choice time. This week, Mrs. Porterfield has a "catching" station where children are able to work on their ability to catch a ball. She challenges them with variety such as catching various sized and shaped objects, catching from a throw or a bounce, and increasing the distance from the "thrower" while keeping in mind that children must experience success. She tries to create motor-learning opportunities where children will experience a "state of flow," being successful about 80% of the time (Sanders, 2002).

Mrs. Porterfield adjusts the level of complexity of the catching task based on individual differences in children's current abilities. For example, Michael's eye-hand coordination is not well developed. Therefore Mrs. Porterfield gives him scarves to throw up in the air and then catch. This encourages Michael to track the scarf visually as it moves slowly through the air. Ms. Engleside supports Mrs. Porterfield with embedding learning opportunities so Michael can practice functional communication skills when he wants to play at this center, such as requesting, making choices, and using turn-taking language with supports.

While scarf dancing, Alessandra independently demonstrates the ability to throw and catch a scarf multiple times. Mrs. Porterfield is building upon her skills by playing catch with Alessandra using a soft sponge ball. First she demonstrates catching at an efficient level (hands catch away from the body, thumbs are up with palms facing each other and arms are extended or slightly flexed; Choosy Kids, 2005). Then Mrs. Porterfield provides verbal and visual cues to Alessandra as she practices catching. Mrs. Porterfield provides a lot of positive feedback specific to developing motor skills and effort. Once Alessandra meets success with the teacher, another child is invited to join in a game of catch, promoting fun opportunities for peer interaction and play with materials that are safe for Alessandra's physical concerns.

In Table 5, our recommended practices are aligned with national guidelines and informed by UDL principles. Practitioners may use the following rubric to self-assess progress with leading structured physically active play.

Conclusion

The Environment recommended practices highlight the relationship between the environment and young children's access to and participation in developmentally appropriate physical activity. As architects of young children's experiences and environments, practitioners may implement specific recommended practices that target physical activity, including (1) setting the stage through preparation and planning, (2) planning opportunities and designing environments for physically active play, (3) facilitating physical activity during child-selected activities, and (4) leading children in physically active play. Moreover, practitioners may use UDL principles to further effective planning of physical, social, temporal, and instructional environments to increase all young children's engagement in physical activity, enjoyment of robust movement, and development of fundamental movement skills. While the practices discussed in this article are considered "recommended" or "best" practices for promoting physical activity in young children, they are not yet vetted by high-quality research for promoting physical activity specifically for diverse, inclusive early childhood settings. Presently, the field lacks sufficient research evidence to guide practitioners with this "neglected aspect of play" (Pelligrini & Smith, 1998). With disability as a risk factor for obesity, it is imperative that the early childhood community mobilize to develop the research base to support practices for promoting a lifelong love of movement as a protective factor against obesity across the lifespan.

References

American Heart Association. (2015). *The price of inactivity*. Retrieved from http://www.heart.org/

Bandini, L. G., Curtin, C., Hamad, C., Tybor, D. J., & Must, A. (2005). Prevalence of overweight in children with developmental disorders in the continuous national health and nutrition examination survey (NHANES) 1999–2002. *Journal of Pediatrics, 146*, 738–743. doi:10.1016/j.jpeds.2005.01.049

Bassuk, E. L., Konnath, K., & Volk, K. T. (2006, February). *Understanding traumatic stress in children*. Newton Centre, MA: The National Center on Family Homelessness.

Blum, H., & Spencer, K. (2010). *The necessity of play: Preparing for the 21st century*. Paper presented at the National Head Start Association Annual Conference, Dallas, TX.

Bower, J. K., Hales, D. P., Tate, D. F., Rubin, D. A., Benjamin, S. E., & Ward, D. S. (2008). The childcare environment and children's physical activity. *American Journal of Preventive Medicine, 34*, 23–29. doi:10.1016/j.amepre.2007.09.022

Brown, W. H., Pfeiffer, K. A., McIver, K. L., Dowda, M., Addy, C. L., & Pate, R. R. (2009). Social and environmental factors associated with preschoolers' nonsedentary physical activity. *Child Development, 80*, 45–58. doi:10.1111/j.1467-8624.2008.01245.x

Catalino, T., & Meyer, L. E. (2015). Improving access and participation. In *DEC recommended practices: Enhancing services for young children with disabilities and their families* (DEC Recommended Practices Monograph Series No. 1, pp. 53–63). Los Angeles, CA: Division for Early Childhood.

Center for Applied Special Technology. (2011). *Universal design for learning guidelines version 2.0*. Wakefield, MA: Author.

Centers for Disease Control and Prevention. (n.d.). *Youth physical activity: Guidelines toolkit*. Retrieved from www.cdc.gov/healthyschools/physicalactivity/toolkit/userguide_pa.pdf

Cervantes, C. M., & Porretta, D. L. (2010). Physical activity measurement among individuals with disabilities: A literature review. *Adapted Physical Activity Quarterly, 27*, 173–190.

Choosy Kids. (2005). Choosy assessment of motor patterns. In *I am moving, i am learning: A proactive approach for addressing childhood obesity in Head Start children*. Washington, DC: Office of Head Start.

Curtin, C., Anderson, S. E., Must, A., & Bandini, L. (2010). The prevalence of obesity in children with autism: A secondary data analysis using nationally representative data from the National Survey of Children's Health. *BMC Pediatrics, 10*(11). doi:10.1186/1471-2431-10-11

De, S., Small, J., & Baur L. A. (2008). Overweight and obesity among children with developmental disabilities. *Journal of Intellectual & Developmental Disabilities, 33*, 43–47. doi:10.1080/13668250701875137

Division for Early Childhood. (2007, March). *Promoting positive outcomes for children with disabilities: Recommendations for curriculum, assessment, and program evaluation* (Position statement). Missoula, MT: Author.

Division for Early Childhood. (2014). *DEC recommended practices in early intervention/early childhood special education 2014*. Retrieved from http://www.dec-sped.org/recommendedpractices

Division for Early Childhood/National Association for the Education of Young Children. (2009, April). *Early childhood inclusion* (Joint position statement). Chapel Hill: The University of North Carolina, FPG Child Development Institute.

Fox, M. H., Witten, M. H., & Lullo, C. (2014). Reducing obesity among people with disabilities. *Journal of Disability Policy Studies, 25,* 175–185. doi:10.1177/1044207313494236

Fuentes, R. M. Notkola, I. L., Shemeikka, S., Tuomilehto, J., & Nissinen, A. (2003). Tracking of body mass index during childhood: A 15-year prospective population-based family study in eastern Finland. *International Journal of Obesity, 27,* 716–721.

Gewirtz, A. & Edleson, J. (2007). Young children's exposure to intimate partner violence: Towards a developmental and risk and resilience framework for research and intervention. *Journal of Family Violence, 22,* 151–163. doi:10.1007/s10896-007-9065-3

Greenwald, D. & Weaver, J. (Eds.). (2013). *RIE manual* (Expanded ed.). Los Angeles, CA: Resources for Infant Educators.

Head Start Body Start National Center for Physical Development and Outdoor Play. (2010). *Promoting physical activity in preschool settings: Teacher behavior rating scale*. Reston, VA: Author.

Institute of Medicine. (2011, June). *Early childhood obesity prevention policies: Goals, recommendations, and potential actions*. Washington, DC: The National Academies Press.

Johannsson, E., Arngrimsson, S. A., Thorsdottir, I., & Sveinsson, T. (2006). Tracking of overweight from early childhood to adolescence in cohorts born 1988 and 1994: Overweight in a high birth weight population. *International Journal of Obesity, 30,* 1265–1271. doi:10.1038/sj.ijo.0803253

Mader, P. (2012). *Adverse childhood experiences (ACE) and the neurobiology of trauma*. Paper presented at the 18th National Conference on Child Abuse and Neglect, Washington, DC.

McDonough, P. (2009, October 26). TV viewing among kids at an eight-year high. *Nielsen Newswire.*

Nader, P. R., O'Brien, M., Houts, R., Bradley, R., Belsky, J., Crosnoe, R., . . . Susman, E. J. (2006). Identifying risk for obesity in early childhood. *Pediatrics, 118,* E594–E601. doi:10.1542/peds.2005-2801

National Association for Sport and Physical Education. (2009a). *Active start: A statement of physical activity guidelines for children from birth to age 5*. Reston, VA: American Alliance for Health, Physical Education, Recreation and Dance.

National Association for Sport and Physical Education. (2009b). *Appropriate practices in movement programs for children ages 3–5* (3rd ed.). Reston, VA: American Alliance for Health, Physical Education, Recreation and Dance.

National Institute for Health and Clinical Excellence. (2009, January). *Promoting physical activity, active play and sport for pre-school and school-age children and young people in family, pre-school, school, and community settings.* London, England: National Institute for Health and Clinical Excellence.

Olvera, N., Sharma, S., Suminski, R., Rodríguez, A., & Power, T. (2007). BMI tracking in Mexican American children in relation to maternal BNI. *Ethnicity & Disease, 17*, 707–713.

Pate, R. R., McIver, K., Dowda, M., Brown, W. H., & Addy, C. (2008). Directly observed physical activity levels in preschool children. *Journal of School Health, 78*, 438–444. doi:10.1111/j.1746-1561.2008.00327.x

Pelligrini, A. D., & Smith, P. K. (1998). Physical activity play: The nature and function of a neglected aspect of playing. *Child Development, 69*, 577–598. doi:10.1111/j.1467-8624.1998.tb06226.x

Pisha, L. E. (2012). *Teachers' beliefs related to activity play in the preschool setting: A phenomenological investigation* (Doctoral dissertation). Retrieved from ProQuest. (Accession No. 3524210)

Rimmer, J. H., & Rowland, J. L. (2008). Health promotion for people with disabilities: Implications for empowering the person and promoting disability-friendly environments. *American Journal of Lifestyle Medicine, 2*, 409–420. doi:10.1177/1559827608317397

Rimmer, J. H., Yamaki, K., Davis, B. M., Wang, E., & Vogel, L. C. (2011). Obesity and overweight prevalence among adolescents with disabilities. *Preventing Chronic Disease, 8*, A41.

Sanders, S. W. (2002). *Active for life: Developmentally appropriate movement programs for young children.* Washington, D.C. National Association for the Education of Young Children.

Swick, K. J. (2008). The dynamics of violence and homelessness among young families. *Early Childhood Education Journal, 36*, 81–85. doi:10.1007/s10643-007-0220-5

Trost, S. G., Sirard, J. R., Dowda, M., Pfeiffer, K. A., & Pate, R. R. (2003). Physical activity in overweight and nonoverweight preschool children. *International Journal of Obesity, 27*, 834–839.

Zwier, J. N., van Schie, P. E., Becher, J. G., Smits, D.-W., Gorter, J. W., & Dallmeijer, A. J. (2010). Physical activity in young children with cerebral palsy. *Disability and Rehabilitation, 18*, 1501–1508. doi:10.3109/09638288.2010.497017

6

Creating Inclusive Playground Environments Following the Principles of Universal Design

Collaborative Strategies to Promote Family Participation in the Design and Development Process

TINA L. STANTON-CHAPMAN
University of Cincinnati

ERIC L. SCHMIDT
Playground Equipment Services

Megan and Jonathan took their children, Nathan, a 2-year-old with autism spectrum disorder, and Maddie, a 7-year-old who is developing typically, to their community playground. "Maddie is having so much fun going up and down the slide," said Jonathan. "Where is Nathan?" asked Megan. "I don't know, but let me look." Jonathan then searched for his son. "He is over here by the fence picking grass." Megan answered, "He never seems to play on the playground equipment or with his sister. I wish he would do more than wander around."

An important component of early childhood inclusion is the recognition that every child and his or her family has the opportunity, regardless of ability, to fully participate in a broad range of activities and opportunities in the local community, including playground settings (Division for Early Childhood [DEC] & National Association of the Education of Young Children [NAEYC], 2009). This requires playground developers, designers, and manufacturers to understand and be responsive to the differences in children's abilities, skills, and behaviors and also be cognizant of the varying needs of families, especially those who have a child with a disability *and* a child who is typically developing. Although there has been an increased interest and investment in building accessible playgrounds for children with disabilities, the vignette shows that many families have unmet needs.

The construction and architectural design of the overall playground environment (i.e., play equipment, ground surfacing) is often criticized for its accessibility and play value for *all* children with disabilities despite such guidelines as the Americans with Disabilities Act (ADA) Accessibility Guidelines for Play Areas (2000) and the ADA Standards for Accessible Design (2010) advocating for full inclusion. Accessibility guidelines, in general, provide the minimum accessibility requirements for a public playground, but these guidelines do not ensure that *all* children benefit from the playground environment. When playground developers target the minimum standards, play value is ignored and children with disabilities miss out on the potential social, emotional, and communication benefits that playground play has to offer.

Playgrounds should be more versatile and usable to all populations of children. Rather than focusing on meeting minimum requirements to achieve usability, playground developers, builders, and manufacturers should apply the Principles of Universal Design (UD), where every child, regardless of ability or disability, is welcomed and benefits physically, developmentally, and socially from the playground environment (Center for Universal Design, 1997). UD has seven founding principles: equitable use, flexibility in use, simple and intuitive use, perceptible information, tolerance from error, low effort, and size and space for approach and use. These principles are consistent with the DEC Recommended Practices (2014) and the DEC/NAEYC (2009) position statement on inclusion. Specifically, they address DEC Environment practice E2, which is that professionals should consider UD to create accessible environments.

Results From Prior Studies Regarding the Play Value and Usability of Current Playgrounds

Inclusion is a federal policy that promotes the integration of children with disabilities into the mainstream educational and community settings (Baker, Wang, & Walberg, 1994; Nisbet, 1994). Physical proximity with peers who are typically developing on accessible playground equipment is thought to be critical in assisting children with disabilities to develop social and communicative skills, but physical proximity of children with disabilities on accessible playgrounds *alone* is not sufficient for successful socialization. Furthermore, an accessible playground may meet the legal ADA mandates for playground accessibility but still exclude access to some or all playground equipment for some children with disabilities.

Prior observational studies examining the play behaviors of children with disabilities suggest that children with disabilities, particularly those with physical disabilities, may not be able to participate on an accessible playground to the same extent as their peers who are typically developing (Parkes, McCullough, & Madden, 2010). Children with autism spectrum disorder (ASD) may also find playground time to be a challenging and overwhelming experience because of its large, undefined space; its lack of predictable and structured play routines; and varied play styles exhibited by peers (Flynn & Kieff, 2002; Nabors, Willoughby, Leff, & McMenamin, 2001). They are also less engaged in moderate-to-vigorous physical activity than peers who are typically developing and less likely to socially interact with peers (Pan, 2008). Research investigating stress levels of children with ASD during playground play may provide a clue as to why children with ASD find typical playgrounds aversive. Edmiston, Merkle, and Corbett (2015) found that cortisol levels in children with ASD increased once they entered a

> When playground developers target the minimum standards, play value is ignored and children with disabilities miss out on the potential social, emotional, and communication benefits that playground play has to offer.

playground facility and levels became extremely high when the children were asked to interact with a peer.

Parent report studies using survey and/or interview data also indicate a lack of equity between children with disabilities and their peers who are typically developing on accessible playgrounds. Darcy and Dowse (2013) questioned caregivers of children diagnosed with an intellectual disability about the constraints they faced in locating appropriate playgrounds and sporting activities for their children. Caregivers indicated there was a lack of appropriate playgrounds in their geographic location and little information available to them that indicates where they can take their children to play. In a survey asking caregivers about their families' playground needs, caregivers of children with disabilities consistently mentioned how their child plays alone on a typical playground and often does not use the equipment provided (Stanton-Chapman & Schmidt, in press-a). Furthermore, caregivers mentioned the need for a playground that met their child's sensory needs and suggested such a structure be built near typical playground equipment so they could bring *all* of their children to one setting. Finally, Estell et al. (2009) reported that families were apprehensive in taking their child with a disability to a typical playground because of the possibility of their child being teased or bullied.

Several studies also have sampled special educators about their opinions on the play value of their school playgrounds or their beliefs on the supports students with disabilities require on the playground. Stanton-Chapman and Schmidt (in press-b) interviewed special education teachers regarding the experiences their students had on the school playground. They overwhelmingly discussed how the school playground was boring for most children and lacked play equipment that met the needs of all children and kept them engaged. In a literature review exploring school recess time and play behaviors of students with ASD, Lang et al. (2011) concluded that students with ASD may need additional social and communicative supports on the playground to benefit fully from what an accessible playground has to offer. O'Hara and Hall (2014) concurred with the findings of Lang et al. by demonstrating that structured work systems could be used by special education teachers to keep students with ASD engaged with playground equipment during recess on school playgrounds.

Finally, recent observational studies exploring the play value of playground equipment provide interesting feedback to special education professionals and families who have children with disabilities. In a study examining the types of playground equipment most frequently used by children on school playgrounds, Anthamatten et al. (2014) indicated that playground structures and swing sets were more popular than hard-play surfaces without equipment. Other studies (Czalczynska-Podolska, 2014; Norðdahl & Einarsdóttir, 2015) found that children prefer to play in sand areas where they can use water, sand, sticks, and sand toys to explore during play. In an investigation studying the type of play equipment children with disabilities prefer to play with on the community playground, Stanton-Chapman and Schmidt (2016) found that children with disabilities preferred to play with musical equipment, go down slides, and hide in tunnels, and they rarely used or ignored activity panels (tic-tac-toe, spinning wheels). This is an interesting finding because activity panels are typically marketed as a sensorimotor activity for children with disabilities and are ADA compatible.

Collaborative Strategy Cycle to Promote Family Participation in the Design and Development of Inclusive UD Playgrounds

Designing developmentally appropriate, inclusive, and UD environments for play is an ongoing process. Successful playgrounds are not simply ordered from a manufacturer's catalog, built from a playground installer, and left. Inclusive UD playgrounds require careful thought, planning, continued maintenance, and frequent updates to make sure they continue to meet the needs of the community. Current practice suggests that families and professionals should build relationships and work together to achieve mutually agreed upon outcomes and goals that address families' priorities and concerns and their children's strengths and needs (DEC/NAEYC, 2009). Specifically, DEC Family practice F4 states that professionals and the family should "work together to create outcomes or goals [and] implement practices that address the family's priorities and concerns and the child's strengths and needs." Unfortunately, professional–family collaboration does not necessarily occur when accessible playgrounds are designed and built as evidenced in the vignette. The family described in the vignette experienced an accessible playground that failed to meet Nathan's needs because he did not engage with the playground equipment or his sister.

The purpose of this article is to describe the Collaborative Strategies Cycle communities can use to support the development of inclusive UD playgrounds in their neighborhoods (see Figure 1). Local community governments, playground developers, and construction workers typically use a traditional playground cycle when they build a playground—from beginning to end (Heseltine & Holborn, 1987). Local community governments, however, often proceed through the traditional playground cycle when developing neighborhood playgrounds—without the input of local residents (Stanton-Chapman & Schmidt, 2016). Local community governments have a responsibility to make sure that their playgrounds are settings in which *all* children and their families feel accepted. For this goal to be accomplished, active participation of families in the playground development cycle is an essential component of high-quality, inclusive early childhood environments. Active family participation in the development and building of new playgrounds addresses DEC Teaming and Collaboration practice TC2: "Practitioners and families work together as a team to systematically and regularly exchange expertise, knowledge, and information to build team capacity and jointly solve problems, plan, and implement interventions." To ensure that

> Successful playgrounds are not simply ordered from a manufacturer's catalog, built from a playground installer, and left. Inclusive UD playgrounds require careful thought, planning, continued maintenance, and frequent updates to make sure they continue to meet the needs of the community.

Figure 1

The Collaborative Strategies Cycle for Building Inclusive Playgrounds That Follow the Principles of Universal Design

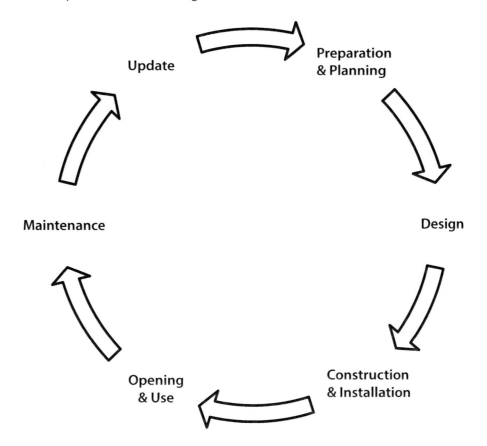

teaming and collaboration take place between families and professionals in the playground development process, we integrated many of the collaboration strategies discussed in King-Sears, Janney, and Snell (2015) with the playground development cycle discussed by Heseltine and Holborn (1987) to develop our Collaborative Strategies Cycle.

The following steps in the cycle are described in depth using Nathan's family for further clarification so that local communities can encourage active participation by families in each step of the cycle as well as use family input in supporting the social play of *all* children on community playgrounds. Tips for applying the strategies are in Table 1. These tips are suggested tasks and activities that communities can use when applying each step within the Collaborative Strategies Cycle.

Stage 1: Preparation

The overall success of an inclusive UD playground depends on how well it meets the needs of the families and their children in the community where it is built. Many families who have children with disabilities are unhappy with the accessible playgrounds in their neighborhoods because they do not meet the needs

Table 1
Tips for Applying the Steps and Strategies in the Collaborative Strategies Cycle

Principle	Definition
Preparation and planning	• Recruit families for the focus groups by posting flyers in buildings visited by families (e.g., library, post office, grocery stores, pediatrician offices, churches), sending flyers home with children in schools, and requesting their assistance in community newspapers • Serve refreshments during the focus group meetings and offer free child care to encourage maximum attendance • Form the steering committee by asking individuals who will best serve the needs of the community and keep the interests and needs of families at the forefront
Design	• Observe children of all ages and abilities playing on current community playgrounds (e.g., parks, schools) • Consult the professional literature to learn the interests and play preferences of children with and without disabilities (e.g., equipment, surfacing, settings for play) • All steering committee members should consider how their beliefs, values, and experiences influence their decisions and reflect on whether their idea or vote is a personal choice or is based on what the community truly needs • Consult the services of several playground equipment manufacturers after all data has been collected to ensure that the best decisions are made for the community
Construction and installation	• Schedule several site visits by committee members at the beginning of construction and installation and place these dates on the calendar. They can be rescheduled, if needed, but this ensures site visits will not be forgotten as things become hectic • Recruit families for the site visits and the volunteer workforce by posting flyers in buildings visited by families (e.g., library, post office, grocery stores, pediatrician offices, churches), sending flyers home with children in schools, and requesting their assistance in community newspapers
Opening and use	• For ribbon-cutting ceremonies, invite local disability organizations to the event to make them aware of the inclusive UD playground. These organizations may be potential funders for maintenance and future repairs. • Develop a parent social committee whose purpose is to plan events and activities at the inclusive UD playground. Members can be recruited by asking families who frequently visit the inclusive UD playground or through flyers posted throughout the community.

of their children with disabilities (as evidenced by Nathan) and sometimes their children without disabilities (Stanton-Chapman & Schmidt, in press-a). Once a community has decided to build an inclusive UD playground, it is important to develop focus groups and engage local families in a conversation about the type of playground that is needed. Focus groups are a form of research in which a group of people are asked about their opinions, beliefs, and attitudes toward a concept (Gibbs, 2012). Questions are posed to the group and the participants are free to talk interactively. For the focus groups, it is important to recruit families who have children with disabilities as well as families who have children who are typically developing. These focus groups can provide input on the needs of the families and their children in their community, the community's willingness to assist in the long-term maintenance of the playground, and their overall happiness with the final product. Furthermore, this practice addresses DEC Family

Table 1 (continued)
Tips for Applying the Steps and Strategies in the Collaborative Strategies Cycle

Principle	Definition
Maintenance	• The steering committee should meet with local officials to make certain a maintenance budget for repairs to the inclusive UD playground is in its yearly operational budget. The steering committee should also investigate potential foundation or grant funding for maintenance. • Recruit families for litter collections and the parent-playground satisfaction committee by posting flyers in buildings visited by families (e.g., library, post office, grocery stores, pediatrician offices, churches), sending flyers home with children in schools and requesting their assistance in community newspapers • Recruit high school students for litter collections as part of a service project for a social club or community service hours
Update	• Recruit families for the playground satisfaction surveys by posting flyers in buildings visited by families (e.g., library, post office, grocery stores, pediatrician offices, churches), sending flyers home with children in schools, and requesting their assistance in community newspapers • Develop paper and pencil and online surveys using questions that focus on family demographics (e.g., ages of children in the household, the types of disabilities the children in their home have, if any), children's interests, preferences, and abilities; family interest in visiting the inclusive UD playground; and things the family likes and doesn't like at the inclusive UD playground • Conduct informal observations of children of all ages and abilities during play on the inclusive UD playground. Keep track of where children play and don't play. Observations should take place on multiple days and times (weekends, weekdays, mornings, evenings, afternoons) to obtain a representative sample

practice F3: "Practitioners are responsive to the family's concerns, priorities, and changing life circumstances."

Several focus group families, if not all of the families identified in the early stages of preparation, should be formally asked to participate in a steering group. A steering group's purpose is to manage the general course of operations for the inclusive UD playground. At a minimum, at least one family who has a child with a disability and one family who has a child who is typically developing should be invited members of the steering committee.

Given their recent experience with Nathan and Maddie at their community playground, Megan and Jonathan joined their community's steering committee to develop a new community playground in their neighborhood for children with and without disabilities. Megan and Jonathan represent families who have children with autism. Other members of the steering committee should include playground designers, playground manufacturers, a council member from the representative community who has knowledge of local laws and policies, a parks and recreation representative who will be involved in the maintenance of the playground, and special educators and related service personnel (e.g., occupational therapists, physical therapists) who may offer professional expertise regarding children with disabilities. Together, the steering group team can be more responsive to families' concerns, priorities, and changing life circumstances and come up with an agreed-upon philosophy of how all children in the community can be included within the playground setting (DEC/NAEYC, 2009).

Stage 2: Design

Once a steering group is formed, the next step is designing the inclusive UD playground. A series of meetings to discuss what will benefit the community's children the most are needed to ensure that the needs of *all* families in the community are considered. It is important that the committee starts with the following questions rather than beginning their conversation with what type of playground equipment is needed or browsing through manufacturer catalogs. Quite often, sales representatives from playground manufacturer companies

show communities the type of equipment that is available for purchase and typically "push" communities to purchase the more expensive items regardless whether the items are appropriate for the community or beneficial to its children (Stanton-Chapman & Schmidt, 2016). This process can lead to playgrounds that may not be appropriate for the children in the given community and many unhappy families.

Questions to answer during steering group meetings include: (a) What does an inclusive UD playground look like? (b) How should children be engaged on an inclusive UD playground? (c) What do you want children to be doing on an inclusive UD playground? (d) How can adults support children during play on an inclusive UD playground? and (e) How should families feel when they are visiting an inclusive UD playground? The answers to these questions will provide insight to what color schemes, sounds, textures, surfacing, and equipment the children may like and will meet DEC Environment practice E6: "Practitioners create environments that provide opportunities for movement and regular physical activity to maintain or improve fitness, wellness, and development across domains." Additionally, the answers also will help the steering committee address accessible parking, fencing, and nearby hazards and move on to the construction and installation of the inclusive UD playground.

Megan and Jonathan, as members of their community's steering committee, state that their community's current playground does not offer equipment that Nathan enjoys and, thus, his physical needs are not met. They recommend that the steering committee consider more sensory equipment and activities (e.g., musical equipment, tactile experiences, olfactory experiences) to meet their son's sensory needs.

Stage 3: Construction and Installation

Typically in the construction and installation phase, the playground installer assumes responsibility for the building of the playground. However, it is still critical that the steering committee, especially the family members on the committee, be involved. One strategy to consider is to arrange several site visits with the local community during the construction and installation stage. Frequent on-site visits to the construction site by community members may help create a sense of ownership of the new playground to the community. In addition, inviting families who have children with disabilities to the construction site may develop positive rapport between the families and construction staff, further enhancing recommended practices of building trust and respectful partnerships with the family (DEC, 2009).

Revisiting the vignette, we learn that Megan and Jonathan frequently visit the new playground site and discuss progress with the construction workers. They hope to prepare Nathan for the "grand opening" by taking many pictures of the playground's progress over time.

It may also be possible to enlist the local community in the construction and installation of the inclusive UD playground through volunteer involvement. Provided that all safety concerns are addressed prior to volunteer assistance, it may be possible to reduce labor costs by enlisting family members who are able to donate time to the cause. By using a local volunteer workforce, it is hoped that community members feel a sense of ownership toward the finished product as well as feel empowered that they contributed to their local community, resulting in a beautifully constructed expression of shared pride.

Step 4: Opening and Use

Once construction and installation of the inclusive UD playground is complete, the next step in the Collaborative Strategies Cycle is opening and use. Opening and use of the inclusive UD playground should begin with a ribbon-cutting ceremony. Ribbon-cutting ceremonies bring enthusiasm and pride to the local community. They also provide an opportunity to thank the steering committee, the volunteer workforce, funding sources, and local government officials for their time and effort.

The ribbon-cutting ceremony should be a community fun day where children of all abilities take an active role in play. If planned appropriately (e.g., inviting television and newspaper reporters, providing refreshments), the ribbon-cutting ceremony also can raise the profile of the inclusive UD playground and bring visitors from nearby neighborhoods who may be willing to contribute financially and physically to the overall maintenance of the playground. One strategy to increase the chance of news coverage would be to approach a newspaper or television station well before the ribbon-cutting ceremony and suggest a family they could interview about their involvement in the process and how much they are looking forward to enjoying the new playground.

Inviting families who have children with disabilities to the construction site may develop positive rapport between the families and construction staff, further enhancing recommended practices of building trust and respectful partnerships with the family.

Megan and Jonathan bring their children, Nathan and Maddie, to the ribbon-cutting ceremony for their new community playground so they can celebrate the first day they are able to play together as a family. After the ribbon is cut, Megan and Jonathan are excited to see Nathan and Maddie play together for the first time on a playground with musical instruments.

Publicity of the inclusive UD playground is critical to its sustainability. Publicity may be occasional or ongoing, depending on the local community's preferences. The steering committee or a parent committee formed for this purpose may take the lead in planning events and activities at the inclusive UD playground. Family picnics, peer-buddy play groups between children with and without disabilities, and school field trips are just a few examples of the activities or events that can be planned by the steering or parent committee. These activities can help families who have children with disabilities feel comfortable with the environment and more willing to take their children to the playground on a frequent basis. Additionally, memories of positive, quality family experiences may be developed, alleviating previous caregiver concerns of negative situations experienced by their children with disabilities on playgrounds (Stanton-Chapman & Schmidt, in press-a).

Step 5: Maintenance

Ongoing maintenance of the inclusive UD playground is crucial to its success. In the early stages of planning and development, the steering committee should make financial plans for maintenance because successful playgrounds tend to have excessive wear and tear. Equipment and surfacing may need to be replaced, and funds need to be readily available to replace these items.

Family members can contribute to this step of the Collaborative Strategies Cycle in several ways. First, frequent and organized litter cleanup events can be planned to keep the inclusive UD playground free of trash. Second, the inclusive UD playground should have signs that indicate the appropriate age range for the playground and contact information for playground patrons to call if there is broken equipment, vandalism, or a possible safety concern. Families should contact the individuals responsible for repairs to maintain a safe environment for their children. Communities should do their best to respond to these concerns in a timely manner. Prompt repair of problematic items is crucial for the community's morale and pride. Twenty-four to 48 hours is the expected time to have minor repairs fixed (e.g., repairs not requiring equipment to be ordered and installed).

Finally, another parent committee can be established to evaluate the current equipment and surfacing to determine whether it continues to meet the community's needs. Community residents may come and go, and it is crucial to make a list of needed changes so the community continues to be satisfied with the inclusive UD playground. Additionally, it is possible that children will move into the community and have disabilities that vary from the disabilities previously considered during the preparation and planning step of the playground. Their needs must be addressed, and this process meets DEC Environment practice E3:

Community residents may come and go, and it is crucial to make a list of needed changes so the community continues to be satisfied with the inclusive UD playground.

"Practitioners work with the family and other adults to modify and adapt the physical, social, and temporal environments to promote each child's access to and participation in learning experiences." Any needed changes to the inclusive UD playground will assist the steering committee during the final step of the Collaborative Strategies Cycle.

Megan and Jonathan serve on their community's safety committee. Their role is to visit the playground weekly and report any issues that need to be addressed, such as broken equipment, graffiti, and/or public nuisances.

Step 6: Update

As new residents move into the community and current residents move and/ or age, use of the inclusive UD playground will change, requiring the steer-

ing committee to evaluate the overall satisfaction of the playground to see whether it is still meeting the families' needs. Playground satisfaction surveys should be completed every one to three years using paper and pencil and/or on-line surveys. Observations of children of all ages and abilities on the playground also should be conducted frequently to determine which equipment is preferred or not preferred. The information from the surveys and observations will provide the steering committee with data on what is working and what is not working in terms of the playground equipment, surfacing, and environment. Any needed changes, whether major or minor, can be made during this step. It is critical that the community's park and recreation agency have a budget for improvements. This budget can come from the local community, state funding, or foundations and grants. This will allow the inclusive UD playground to have continued success rather than fail from neglect or nonuse for not meeting the needs of the community.

In Megan and Jonathan's community, the steering committee reports that the rubber surfacing needs to be replaced and that the playground would benefit from a community garden with raised planting beds so grandparents with physical disabilities could grow vegetables with their grandchildren. The local parks and recreation agency agrees to these improvements and pays for the project.

Conclusion

Participation in inclusive UD playgrounds can provide many opportunities for children with disabilities to play and socially interact with peers with a wide range of abilities and skills. However, some children, such as Nathan, may have little interest in their accessible community playground because it does not meet their specific needs. Accessible playgrounds alone are not sufficient to promote positive playground experiences in children with varying abilities, skills, and behaviors. However, communities can support the social play of *all* children in their communities by encouraging family participation in every step of the Collaborative Strategies Cycle when developing inclusive UD playgrounds in their neighborhoods. Ultimately, communities have a responsibility to make sure that their playgrounds are settings in which all children and their families feel accepted. To accomplish this goal, active participation of families in the development of inclusive UD playgrounds is an essential component of high-quality, inclusive early childhood environments.

References

ADA Accessibility Guidelines for Play Areas, 36 C.F.R. § 1191. (2000, October 18). Retrieved from http://www.access-board.gov/guidelines-and-standards/buildings-and-sites/about-the-ada-standards/background/ada-accessibility-guidelines-for-play-areas

ADA Standards for Accessible Design. (2010, September 15). Retrieved from http://www.ada.gov/2010ADAstandards_index.htm

Anthamatten, P., Brink, L., Kingston, B., Kutchman, E., Lampe, S., & Nigg, C. (2014). An assessment of schoolyard features and behavior patterns in children's utilization and physical activity. *Journal of Physical Activity and Health, 11,* 564–573. doi:10.1123/jpah.2012-0064

Baker, E. T., Wang, M. C., & Walberg, H. J. (1994). Synthesis of research: The effects of inclusion on learning. *Educational Leadership, 52*(4), 33–35.

Center for Universal Design. (1997). *The principles of universal design* (Version 2.0). Raleigh: North Carolina State University.

Czalczynska-Podolska, M. (2014). The impact of playground spatial features on children's play and activity forms: An evolution of contemporary playgrounds' play and social value. *Journal of Environmental Psychology, 38,* 132–142. doi:10.1016/j.jenvp.2014.01.006

Darcy, S., & Dowse, L. (2013). In search of a level playing field: The constraints and benefits of sport participation for people with intellectual disability. *Disability & Society, 28,* 393–407. doi:10.1080/09687599.2012.714258

Division for Early Childhood. (2014). DEC recommended practices in early intervention/early childhood special education 2014. Retrieved from http://www.dec-sped.org/recommendedpractices

Division for Early Childhood & National Association for the Education of Young Children (2009, April). *Early childhood inclusion* (Joint position statement). Chapel Hill: The University of North Carolina, FPG Child Development Institute.

Edmiston, E. K., Merkle, K., & Corbett, B. A. (2015). Neural and cortisol responses during play with human and computer partners in children with autism. *Social Cognitive and Affective Neuroscience, 10,* 1074–1083. doi:10.1093/scan/nsu159

Estell, D. B., Farmer, T. W., Irvin, M. J., Crowther, A., Akos, P., & Boudah, D. J. (2009). Students with exceptionalities and the peer group context of bullying and victimization in late elementary school. *Journal of Child and Family Studies, 18,* 136–150. doi:10.1007/s10826-008-9214-1

Flynn, L. L., & Kieff, J. (2002). Including "everyone" in outdoor play. *Young Children, 57*(3), 20–26.

Gibbs, A. (2012). Focus groups and group interviews. In J. Arthur, M. Waring, R. Coe, & L. V. Hedges (Eds.), *Research methods and methodologies in education* (pp. 186–192). Thousand Oaks, CA: Sage.

Heseltine, P., & Holborn, J. (1987). *Playgrounds: The planning, design, and construction of play environments.* New York, NY: Nichols.

King-Sears, M. E., Janney, R., & Snell, M.E. (2015). *Collaborative teaming* (3rd ed.). Baltimore, MD: Paul H. Brookes.

Lang, R., Kuriakose, S., Lyons, G., Mulloy, A., Boutot, A., Britt, C., . . . Lancioni, G. (2011). Use of school recess time in the education and treatment of children with autism spectrum disorders: A systematic review. *Research in Autism Spectrum Disorders, 5,* 1296–1305. doi:10.1016/j.rasd.2011.02.012

Nabors, L., Willoughby, J., Leff, S., & McMenamin, S. (2001). Promoting inclusion for young children with special needs on playgrounds. *Journal of Developmental and Physical Disabilities, 13,* 179–190. doi:10.1023/A:1016665409366

Nisbet, J. (1994). Education reform: Summary and recommendations. In *The national reform agenda and people with mental retardation: Putting people first* (pp. 151–165). Washington, DC: U.S. Department of Health and Human Services.

Norðdahl, K., & Einarsdóttir, J. (2015). Children's views and preferences regarding their outdoor environment. *Journal of Adventure Education and Outdoor Learning, 15,* 152–167. doi:10.1080/14729679.2014.896746

O'Hara, M., & Hall, L. J. (2014). Increasing engagement of students with autism at recess through structured work systems. *Education and Training in Autism and Developmental Disabilities, 49,* 568–575.

Pan, C.-Y. (2008). Objectively measured physical activity between children with autism spectrum disorders and children without disabilities during inclusive recess settings in Taiwan. *Journal of Autism and Developmental Disorders, 38,* 1292–1301. doi:10.1007/s10803-007-0518-6

Parkes, J., McCullough, N., & Madden, A. (2010). To what extent do children with cerebral palsy participate in everyday life situations? *Health and Social Care in the Community, 18,* 304–315. doi:10.1111/j.1365-2524.2009.00908.x

Stanton-Chapman, T. L., & Schmidt, E. L. (2016). *Children's preferences regarding accessible playground equipment: An observational study of children with disabilities participating in outdoor play.* Manuscript submitted for publication.

Stanton-Chapman, T. L., & Schmidt, E. L. (in press-a). An examination of family needs for a family inclusive recreational facility for children with and without disabilities. *Intellectual and Developmental Disabilities.*

Stanton-Chapman, T. L., & Schmidt, E. L. (in press-b). Special education professionals' attitudes towards accessible playgrounds. *Research and Practice for Persons with Severe Disabilities.*

7

Home-Based Care
An Opportunity for Promoting High-Quality Inclusive Environments for Young Children With Disabilities

Rena Hallam
Alison Hooper
University of Delaware

THE DEFINITION OF EARLY CHILDHOOD INCLUSION UNDERSCORES the significance of access, participation, and supports for young children with disabilities across different types of settings (DEC/NAEYC, 2009). The crux of the Environment recommended practices of the revised DEC Recommended Practices (2014) is a focus on building the capacity of a wide array of settings and programs to ensure that the inclusion of young children with disabilities occurs in ways that promote full participation of all children and attend to the complexity of the social, temporal, and physical aspects of a wide variety of early childhood environments. The Environment recommended practices delineate the significant features of these diverse environments that must be present to provide high-quality inclusive opportunities for young children. In this paper, we discuss the potential of home-based child care environments to provide meaningful and high-quality educational experiences for young children with disabilities. In doing so, we describe features of the home-based child care context that can be enhanced to enact the DEC Environment recommended practices in home-based settings as well as the policy and infrastructure supports needed to effectively support home-based providers in their efforts to provide quality, inclusive care.

Home-based child care includes any nonparental child care that takes place in a residential setting. This includes licensed family child care providers as well as informal care, often referred to as family, friend, and neighbor care or kith and kin care. These child care settings are an often-overlooked context of care from the perspective of researchers and policymakers; however, national data suggest that families commonly turn to home-based settings to meet their child care demands (National Survey of Early Care and Education [NSECE] Project Team, 2015b). An intentional focus on the application of the DEC Environment recommended practices in home-based settings creates an opportunity for significantly building the supply of high-quality child care for working parents of young children with disabilities.

Young Children With Disabilities in Home-Based Child Care

Recent data from the National Survey of Early Care and Education (NSECE) suggests that approximately 7 million children birth to age 5 spend time in one or more forms of home-based nonparental child care, and these children are cared for by approximately 3.7 million home-based providers (NSECE Project Team, 2015b). The NSECE provides the first nationally representative portrait of home-based nonparental care providers. Home-based providers are a very heterogeneous group of caregivers and can be challenging to categorize because

of differences in regulation among states. For example, some states regulate providers who care for one or more unrelated children and other states regulate providers when three or more unrelated children are served. Because of this difference, the NSECE categorized home-based providers as "listed," meaning that they appear on some type of state-sanctioned list (e.g., child care licensing, state registered), or "unlisted," meaning they do not appear on any state list. Further, some home-based providers report being paid for their caregiving while many others are unpaid.

Preliminary analyses of NSECE data suggest that home-based child care providers are already serving a significant number of young children with disabilities. Providers were asked to self-report if they serve any children who have an emotional, developmental, or behavioral condition that affects the way the provider cares for them. Of providers that serve at least one child from birth to age 5, data suggest that approximately 22% of listed providers report serving at least one child with a disability compared with 20% of unlisted paid providers and 10% of unlisted, unpaid providers. These findings suggest that families are already accessing home-based care for their young children with disabilities (Hooper, Shaw, & Hallam, 2016).

Some research has considered the participation rates of children with disabilities in specific programs, such as Early Head Start or Head Start. However, little is known about the number or percentage of children with disabilities who participate in child care settings. Parish, Cloud, Huh, and Henning (2005) used data from the National Survey of America's Families to examine the use of child care among low-income preschool children with disabilities compared with typically developing children. They found that participation rates in child care, both center-based and home-based care, were similar regardless of disability status. This suggests that there may be many children with disabilities attending nonparental child care.

Why Do Families Select Home-Based Care?

There are a number of key reasons that families select home-based care. Home-based providers typically offer more flexible programs that accommodate the needs of families with young children. For example, home-based providers are much more likely than center-based providers to care for children during nonstandard hours and to allow families to use flexible schedules (NSECE Project Team, 2015a). Therefore, home-based child care is often the only nonparental care option for families who need evening, overnight, or weekend child care. In addition to the flexibility that home-based child care allows, families of young children often select home-based care because it is both accessible and convenient. Home-based providers often serve multiage groups of children, which allows siblings to be cared for together in one setting. Further, home-based settings are often in a family's neighborhood (Fuller, Kagan, Loeb, & Chang, 2004) and may allow families access to caregivers who speak their home language (Hirshberg, Huang, & Fuller, 2005). Additionally, families using informal care arrangements such as relative care may believe a caregiver who has a prior relationship with the family will be able to best meet the child's specific needs (Booth-LaForce & Kelly, 2004).

Other reasons parents, especially parents of infants and toddlers, select home-based care include the homelike environment (Laughlin, 2013; NICHD Early Child Care Research Network, 2004). Because the provider-child ratios tend to be lower, children also can receive more individualized attention and support in home-based settings (Layzer & Goodson, 2006). Home-based care, especially informal care arrangements, are often less expensive than center-based care (Booth-LaForce & Kelly, 2004; NSECE Project Team, 2015a). This may be especially important to families of children with disabilities because of the additional expenses they may incur related to a child's disability.

Because the provider-child ratios tend to be lower, children also can receive more individualized attention and support in home-based settings.

Are Home-Based Providers Prepared to Serve Young Children With Disabilities?

In comparison to center-based early education programs, little research has been conducted on home-based child care as it relates to serving young children with disabilities. However, caregivers' training and support is important to increasing their skills and knowledge around providing enriching early experiences to children with disabilities and supporting inclusion (Odom, 2000). Past research has demonstrated that home-based providers who have taken some coursework on inclusion are more likely to serve children with disabilities in an inclusive setting (Essa et al., 2008). Mulvihill, Shearer, and Van Horn (2002) found through a survey of child care providers that center-based providers had more positive views of inclusion than home-based providers and were more likely to report serving children with disabilities. However, when home-based providers have had personal experiences with children with disabilities, they are more likely to provide inclusive care. This is in contrast to center-based providers, who tend to view inclusion positively whether or not they have previous experience with children with disabilities (Buell, Gamel-McCormick, & Hallam, 1999; Dinnebell, McInerney, Fox, & Juchartz-Pendry, 1998; Stoneman, 2001). Home-based providers report that their lack of knowledge, fear that a child with a disability may affect the care of other children, and the need to purchase special equipment can serve as barriers to inclusion (Buell et al., 1999). Because home-based child care providers often work alone, they may perceive caring for a child with a disability as more challenging than center-based providers.

Devore and Hanley-Maxwell (2000) completed case studies of six child care providers—four of them home-based—caring for a child with a disability. The providers in this study had begun caring for a child with a disability either because the child was a sibling of children for whom they already provided care or because the provider agreed to serve the child before the parents revealed the child had a disability. These providers reported that they learned to care for children with disabilities from their own experiences rather than through specific training about inclusive care. Based on their findings, the authors suggest that five factors contribute to providers' success in caring for children with disabilities: their willingness to make inclusion work, their ability to balance resources and needs, their problem-solving with parents, their access to social support and technical assistance, and their access to other community supports.

What Are Strengths of the Home-Based Environment?

The literature suggests that home-based settings have strengths that are important to the implementation of the Environment recommended practices. In particular, home-based providers often develop close relationships and communicate frequently with the families they serve (Coley, Chase-Lansdale, & Li-Grining, 2001; Porter & Rice, 2000). Indeed, home-based care providers often see their role as serving both children *and* families, and this perspective influences how they approach their work. Strong relationships and communication between providers and families serve as the foundation for adapting and modifying the learning environment to promote optimal participation. Further, research suggests that family, friends, and neighbors often "go the extra mile" to accommodate and adapt services to meet child and family needs (Porter, Rice, & Mabon, 2003; Porter & Vuong, 2008). This willingness to partner with families can create the foundation for effective collaborative planning and implementation of inclusive educational services. This strength in family partnerships found in home-based child care aligns with the DEC Environment recommended practices E3, E4, and E5. For example, family-provider communication and collaboration are essential to E3, which focuses on how practitioners and families jointly consider and implement environmental modifications to support children's access and participation in learning environments.

Another important feature of home-based child care is the consistency and

> When home-based providers have had personal experiences with children with disabilities, they are more likely to provide inclusive care.

stability this type of setting can provide. Children in home-based care often stay with the same provider for multiple years rather than transitioning between classrooms, as is often the case in center-based care settings (Whitebook et al., 2004). Educational services in home-based settings typically offer a level of stability and continuity not achievable in center-based programs. This type of continuity can be particularly important for young children with disabilities who may struggle with transition and/or benefit from a small group of caregivers who are able to competently and consistently perform adaptations, interventions, etc. Recommended practice E1 highlights the importance of effective services and supports situated to promote children's participation in daily routines and activities. A high-quality home-based setting with a caregiver who receives timely and effective supports can create a predictable, stable caregiving environment and effectively engage children in daily routines.

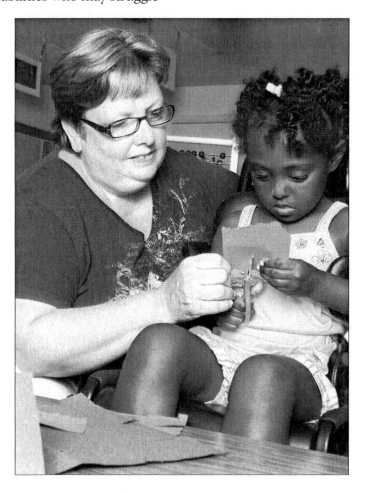

Home-based settings are typically mixed-age and encourage interaction among children of different ages and abilities. This type of environment can serve as an ideal context for inclusion as both the caregiver and children are accustomed to modification in daily routines and activities that allow participation for all ages and abilities. Some research suggests that children with disabilities in mixed-age groupings participated in more conversations with peers, showed increased motor and physical development (Bailey, Burchinal, & McWilliam, 1993; Roberts, Burchinal, & Bailey, 1994), and engaged in more advanced play (Blasco, Bailey, & Burchinal, 1993; Skinner, Buysse, & Bailey, 2004).

How Can We Promote Inclusion in Home-Based Settings?

Building on the strengths of home-based care providers, local communities can enhance the capacity of home-based providers to provide high-quality inclusive environments for young children with disabilities. The research literature points to several key areas to focus on when collaborating with home-based care providers. Research suggests areas of practices that have emerged that may need attention. Table 1 depicts a listing of these areas, possible questions to pose to home-based providers, and strategies and resources. Each issue is discussed in more detail below.

Social Support

Home-based care providers often work in isolation, and this lack of professional contact can become a stressor for the provider and a barrier to quality

Table 1
Strategies to Support Home-Based Providers

Common Concerns	Questions to the Provider	Strategies and Resources
Social support	• Do you have other family child care providers you can talk to? • Who can you talk to when things become stressful?	• Family child care provider networks or professional learning communities • Family child care professional associations • Child Care Resource & Referral Agencies
Itinerant services	• What strategies have you used to accommodate visitors coming into your program? • How do you feel about other service providers coming into your home?	• Coordination of service providers • Use of transdisciplinary models of service • Integration with home-based daily schedule
Community partnerships	• Have you developed relationships with other programs (e.g., schools or libraries)?	• Sharing of resource guides and contacts • Incorporate home-based providers into existing community networks
Technology and materials	• What types of materials or technology are needed in your program? • How comfortable do you feel using technology?	• QRIS and other state and regional funds for materials and equipment

practice. A variety of studies have demonstrated the significance of social support among home-based providers (Bromer, Van Haitsma, Daley, & Modigliani, 2008; Doherty, Forer, Lero, Goelman, & LaGrange, 2006; Kontos, Howes, Shinn, & Galinsky, 1995). Providers who engage in some type of professional networking often cite a multitude of benefits ranging from improved social support to enhanced educational practices (Bromer et al., 2008; McGaha, Snow, & Teleki, 2001; Peterson & Weber, 2010; Rusby, 2002; Taylor, Dunster, & Pollard, 1999). In many communities, provider networks already exist, and these can be enhanced to incorporate relevant content around inclusive practices. In some instances, providers can launch their own groups with like-minded providers, or groups can be facilitated by outside entities, such as the Quality Rating and Improvement System, state resource and referral agencies, and/or public schools (Cortes & Hallam, in press; Gerdes & Jefferson, 2015).

Cora is part of a family child care provider network in her county. The network meets monthly and discusses the benefits and challenges of their work. Recently, a group of providers from the network decided to complete a series of professional development sessions on outdoor play together. The group of six providers attends the professional development sessions, which allow them to jointly problem-solve issues that arise in their practice. During the sessions, they discuss their struggles with creating outdoor environments that promote physical activity and wellness as outlined in recommended practice E6. These conversations, along with support from the state, led to additional technical assistance provided to family child care providers on how to maximize small spaces for outdoor games and activities for young children as well as a resource page on portable activities for mixed-age groups in outdoor environments that is freely available to providers.

Itinerant Services

Home-based providers commonly interact with a range of external entities that come into their homes, such as child care licensing, Child and Adult Care Food Program, and health and nutrition consultants. The inclusion of a child with a disability into a home-based setting will often require additional visits from outside entities. Research on home-based providers suggests that too many or uncoordinated visits by outside entities can be a barrier for sustained engagement of home-based providers in quality initiatives (Hallam, Bargreen, Hooper, Buell, & Han, 2015). Providers report that frequent outside visitors can be intrusive and disruptive to children's daily routines. Thus, it is important for visits to a provider's home be as coordinated, respectful, and limited as possible.

Community Partnerships

The practice of home-based providers can be enhanced via collaboration with other formal entities in the community. Providers may not be able to initiate these partnerships or participate in more traditional partnership activities (e.g., attendance at daytime meetings) because of the caregiving demands in their home. However, agencies and entities that are able to be responsive to home-based providers often develop productive partnerships. Examples of such partnerships include the provision of books and prop boxes by public libraries, dual enrollment of infants and toddlers via Early Head Start and child care partnerships, healthy food deliveries from farmers markets or community-supported agricultural organizations, and school readiness outreach efforts by local school districts. Facilitation and attention to such innovative partnerships allow home-based providers to access a range of supports that facilitate inclusive environments.

Technology and Materials

Studies suggest that home-based settings may have lower global quality than their center-based counterparts (Coley et al., 2001; Dowsett, Huston, Imes, & Gennetian, 2008). An important component to this distinction is the availability of materials, which is often a large portion of global quality assessment (Hofer, 2010; Layzer & Goodson, 2006). In partnering with home-based providers, it is important to keep in mind the mixed-age environment that is often typical in this setting. Some providers may need assistance with accessing and/or organizing materials for particular age ranges or for particular groups of children.

In partnering with home-based providers, it is important to keep in mind the mixed-age environment that is often typical in this setting. Some providers may need assistance with accessing and/or organizing materials for particular age ranges.

Technical assistance and/or coordinated professional development in this area can be particularly fruitful, with past research noting substantive changes in global quality when targeted assistance and/or professional development was provided (Boller, Blair, Del Grosso, & Paulsell, 2010; Hallam, Bargreen, & Ridgley, 2013). Moreover, specialized supports in the area of technology and assistive technology may be needed to address recommended practice E4, using assistive technology to ensure all children can participate in learning activities. Some initiatives have found that home-based providers often use technology tools to

improve their practice when resources are made available to them (Taylor et al., 1999; Weigel, Weiser, Bales, & Moyses, 2012).

Maria cares for two infants, one toddler and two preschoolers, five days a week. Miguel, a 2-year-old in Maria's care, has recently been identified as needing early intervention services. Now, Miguel has a teacher named Laura who comes to the program weekly to assist Maria in modifying her environment and routines to better meet Miguel's educational and developmental needs. This week, Laura brought an iPad to the program and introduced e-books and an app that allows the children to make their own stories. The children loved it! Maria has now applied for a local grant to purchase an iPad for her program.

These types of supports at the local level can facilitate the building of a network of home-based providers to serve young children with disabilities and their families. Much of what happens at the local level can be greatly enhanced by strategic policy decisions made at the state and regional levels.

Building State-Level Infrastructure to Support Inclusive Care in Home-Based Settings

Early care and education policy is in a time of great change with significant investments being made to improve the quality of care provided for all young children. During this dynamic time, it is important that issues of inclusion and home-based care be included in discussions of early childhood program quality. Leveraging state resources to address home-based care and inclusive practice could increase investment in strategies to enhance environmental practices in these settings. Specifically, the design and implementation of Quality Rating and Improvement Systems (QRIS) and statewide professional development systems are key opportunities that can be influenced to promote inclusive practice in home-based care.

Quality Rating and Improvement Systems

QRIS initiatives are designed both to rate and improve program quality across differing types of child care settings. Most QRIS include licensed family child care programs, and some states are exploring the incorporation of other types of unlicensed care because of the recent reauthorization of the Child Care Development and Block Grant (Matthews, Schulman, Vogtman, Johnson-Staub, & Blank, 2015). However, family child care providers typically participate in such systems at much lower rates than center-based programs (Tout, Starr, Isner, et al., 2011). These systems provide opportunity to direct resources to home-based providers to address some of the needs addressed in the above section. For example, QRIS efforts commonly include additional financial incentives and grants for materials and supplies (Child Trends, 2014). More importantly, QRIS initiatives set standards for practice that can guide technical assistance and other types of supports. The integration of the DEC Environment recommended practices into QRIS standards and quality improvement efforts would assist providers in accessing the resources and gaining the needed capacities to implement inclusive services.

Professional Development Systems

Statewide professional development systems typically offer and provide quality assurance for professional development offerings in early care and education. However, home-based providers often report that professional development content is geared toward center-based providers (Hamm, Gault, & Jones-De-Weever, 2005). Advocating for content in professional development systems that address early childhood special education content geared toward family child care providers could enable home-based care providers a mechanism to access ongoing training in this area.

In sum, home-based child care offers the potential for an expanded delivery of inclusive care options for young children with disabilities and their families. Building on the strengths of this sector, implementation of the DEC Environment recommended practices is possible and can be fostered with careful consideration of how systems of support can be designed and/or refined to respond to the needs of the home-based care community.

> Early care and education policy is in a time of great change with significant investments being made to improve the quality of care provided for all young children.

References

Bailey, D. B., Jr., Burchinal, M. R., & McWilliam, R. A. (1993). Age of peers and early childhood development. *Child Development, 64*, 848–862.

Blasco, P. M., Bailey, D. B., Jr., & Burchinal, M. A. (1993). Dimensions of mastery in same-age and mixed-age integrated classrooms. *Early Childhood Research Quarterly, 8*, 193–206. doi:10.1016/S0885-2006(05)80090-0

Boller, K., Blair, R., Del Grosso, P., & Paulsell, D. (2010, July). *Better beginnings: The seeds to success modified field test. Impact evaluation findings.* Princeton, NJ: Mathematica Policy Research.

Booth-LaForce, C., & Kelly, J. F. (2004). Childcare patterns and issues for families of preschool children with disabilities. *Infants & Young Children, 17*, 5–16.

Bromer, J., Van Haitsma, M., Daley, K., & Modigliani, K. (2008, December). *Staffed support networks and quality in family child care: Findings from the family child care network impact study.* Chicago, IL: Herr Research Center for Children and Social Policy.

Buell, M.J., Gamel-McCormick, M., & Hallam, R. A. (1999). Inclusion in a childcare context: Experiences and attitudes of family childcare providers. *Topics in Early Childhood Special Education, 19,* 217–224. doi:10.1177/027112149901900402

Child Trends. (2014). QRIS *compendium.* Retrieved from http://qriscompendium.org/

Coley, R. L., Chase-Lansdale, P. L., & Li-Grining, C. P. (2001). Child care in the era of welfare reform: Quality, choices, and preferences. *Welfare, Children, and Families: A Three-City Study* (Policy Brief 01–04). Baltimore, MD: Johns Hopkins University.

Cortes, J., & Hallam, R. (in press). QRIS as context for empowering family child care providers as leaders. *Young Children.*

DEC/NAEYC. (2009). *Early childhood inclusion. A joint position statement of the Division for Early Childhood (DEC) and the National Association for the Education of Young Children (NAEYC).* Chapel Hill: The University of North Carolina, FPG Child Development Institute.

Devore, S., & Hanley-Maxwell, C. (2000). "I wanted to see if we could make it work": Perspectives on inclusive childcare. *Exceptional Children, 66,* 241–255. doi:10.1177/001440290006600208

Dinnebell, L. A., McInerney, W., Fox, C., & Juchartz-Pendry, K. (1998). An analysis of the perceptions and characteristics of childcare personnel regarding inclusion of young children with special needs in community-based programs. *Topics in Early Childhood Special Education, 18,* 118–128. doi:10.1177/027112149801800207

Division for Early Childhood. (2014). *DEC recommended practices in early intervention/early childhood special education 2014.* Retrieved from http://www.dec-sped.org/recommendedpractices

Doherty, G., Forer, B., Lero, D. S., Goelman, H., & LaGrange, A. (2006). Predictors of quality in family child care. *Early Childhood Research Quarterly, 21,* 296–312. doi:10.1016/j.ecresq.2006.07.006

Dowsett, C. J., Huston, A. C., Imes, A. E., & Gennetian, L. (2008). Structural and process features in three types of child care for children from high and low income families. *Early Childhood Research Quarterly, 23,* 69–93. doi:10.1016/j.ecresq.2007.06.003

Essa, E. L., Bennett, P. R., Burnham, M. M., Martin, S. S., Bingham, A., & Allred, K. (2008). Do variables associated with quality child care programs predict the inclusion of children with disabilities? *Topics in Early Childhood Special Education, 28,* 171–180. doi:10.1177/0271121408324447

Fuller, B., Kagan, S. L., Loeb, S., & Chang, Y.-W. (2004). Child care quality: Centers and home settings that serve poor families. *Early Childhood Research Quarterly, 19,* 505–527. doi:10.1016/j.ecresq.2004.10.006

Gerdes, J., & Jefferson, T. (2015). How a professional learning community changed a family child care provider's beliefs and practices. *Young Children, 70*(5), 8–13.

Hallam, R., Bargreen, K., Hooper, A., Buell, M., & Han, M. (2015). Family child care participation in QRIS: A mixed methods analysis. Poster presented at 2015 NAEYC Professional Development Institute, New Orleans, LA.

Hallam, R. A., Bargreen, K. N., & Ridgley, R. (2013). Quality in family child care settings: The relationship between provider educational experiences and global quality scores in a statewide quality rating and improvement system. *Journal of Research in Childhood Education, 27*, 393–406. doi:10.1080/0256 8543.2013.822950

Hamm, K., Gault, B., & Jones-DeWeever, A. (2005, August). *In our own backyards: Local and state strategies to improve the quality of family child care.* Washington, DC: Institute for Women's Policy Research (IWPR).

Hirshberg, D., Huang, D. S.-C., & Fuller, B. (2005). Which low-income parents select child-care? Family demand and neighborhood organizations. *Children and Youth Services Review, 27*, 1119–1148. doi:10.1016/j.childyouth.2004.12.029

Hofer, K. G. (2010). How measurement characteristics can affect ECERS-R scores and program funding. *Contemporary Issues in Early Childhood, 11*, 175–191. doi:10.2304/ciec.2010.11.2.175

Hooper, A., Shaw, S. & Hallam, R. (2016). Non-parental care arrangements utilized by families of children with disabilities. Poster presented at 2016 Conference for Research Innovations in Early Intervention, San Diego, CA.

Kontos, S., Howes, C., Shinn, M., & Galinsky, E. (1995). *Quality in family child care and relative care.* New York, NY: Teachers College Press.

Laughlin, L. (2013, April). *Who's minding the kids? Child care arrangements: Spring 2011* (P70-135). Washington, DC: U.S. Census Bureau.

Layzer, J. I., & Goodson, B. D. (2006). The "quality" of early care and education settings: Definitional and measurement issues. *Evaluation Review, 30*, 556–576. doi:10.1177/0193841X06291524

Matthews, H., Schulman, K., Vogtman, J., Johnson-Staub, C., & Blank, H. (2015). *Implementing the Child Care and Development Block Grant reauthorization: A guide for states.* Washington, DC: National Women's Law Center.

McGaha, C. G., Snow, C. W., & Teleki, J. K. (2001). Family child care in the United States: A comparative analysis of 1981 and 1998 state regulations. *Early Childhood Education Journal, 28*, 251–255. doi:10.1023/A:1009503127712

Mulvihill, B. A., Shearer, D., & Van Horn, M. L. (2002). Training, experience, and child care providers' perceptions of inclusion. *Early Childhood Research Quarterly, 17*, 197–215. doi:10.1016/S0885-2006(02)00145-X

National Survey of Early Care and Education Project Team. (2015a, April). *Fact sheet: Provision of early care and education during non-standard hours* (OPRE Report No. 2015-44). Washington, DC: Office of Planning, Research and Evaluation, Administration for Children and Families, U.S. Department of Health and Human Services.

National Survey of Early Care and Education Project Team. (2015b, April). *Fact sheet: Who is providing home-based early care and education?* (OPRE Report

No. 2015-43). Washington DC: Office of Planning, Research and Evaluation, Administration for Children and Families, U.S. Department of Health and Human Services.

NICHD Early Child Care Research Network. (2004). Type of child care and children's development at 54 months. *Early Childhood Research Quarterly, 19,* 203–230. doi:10.1016/j.ecresq.2004.04.002

Odom, S. L. (2000). Preschool inclusion: What we know and where we go from here. *Topics in Early Childhood Special Education, 20,* 20–27. doi:10.1177/027112140002000104

Parish, S. L., Cloud, J. M., Huh, J., & Henning, A. N. (2005). Child care, disability, and family structure: Use and quality in a population-based sample of low-income preschool children. *Children and Youth Services Review, 27,* 905–919. doi:10.1016/j.childyouth.2004.12.007

Peterson, S., M. & Weber, M. (2010, December). *Partners in family child care 2009–2010 year 2 report.* Rochester, NY: Children's Institute. Retrieved from https://www.childrensinstitute.net/sites/default/files/documents/T10-007.pdf

Porter, T., & Rice, R. (2000, March). *Lessons learned: Strategies for working with kith and kin caregivers.* New York, NY: Bank Street College of Education.

Porter, T., Rice, R., & Mabon, S. (2003, December). *Doting on kids: Understanding quality in kith and kin child care.* New York, NY: Bank Street College of Education.

Porter, T., & Vuong, L. (2008, July). *Tūtū and me: Assessing the effects of a family interaction program on parents and grandparents.* New York, NY: Bank Street College of Education.

Roberts, J. E., Burchinal, M. R., & Bailey, D. B. (1994). Communication among preschoolers with and without disabilities in same-age and mixed-age classes. *American Journal on Mental Retardation, 99,* 231–249.

Rusby, J. C. (2002). Training needs and challenges of family child care providers. *Child & Youth Care Forum, 31,* 281–293. doi:10.1023/A:1016822526497

Skinner, M. L., Buysse, V., & Bailey, D. B. (2004). Effects of age and developmental status of partners on play of preschoolers with disabilities. *Journal of Early Intervention, 26,* 194–203. doi:10.1177/105381510402600303

Stoneman, Z. (2001). Supporting positive sibling relationships during childhood. *Mental Retardation and Developmental Disabilities Research Reviews, 7,* 134–142. doi:10.1002/mrdd.1019

Taylor, A. R., Dunster, L., & Pollard, J. (1999). . . . And this helps me how? Family child care providers discuss training. *Early Childhood Research Quarterly, 14,* 285–312. doi:10.1016/S0885-2006(99)00020-4

Tout, K., Starr, R., Isner, T., Cleveland, J., Albertson-Junkans, L., Soli, M., & Quinn, K. (2011, December). *Evaluation of Parent Aware: Minnesota's quality rating and improvement system pilot* (Final evaluation report). Minneapolis, MN: Child Trends.

Weigel, D. J., Weiser, D. A., Bales, D. W., & Moyses, K. J. (2012). Identifying online preferences and needs of early childhood professionals. *Early Childhood Research & Practice, 14*(2). Retrieved from http://ecrp.illinois.edu/v14n2/weigel.html

Whitebook, M., Phillips, D., Bellm, D., Crowell, N., Almaraz, M., & Jo, J. Y. (2004). *Two years in early care and education: A community portrait of quality and workforce stability.* Berkeley, CA: Center for the Study of Child Care Employment.

8

'Where Are the Kids Like Me?'
Classroom Environments That Help Create a Sense of Belonging

SeonYeong Yu
University of Massachusetts Amherst

Michaelene M. Ostrosky
University of Illinois at Urbana-Champaign

Paddy C. Favazza
University of Massachusetts Boston

Lori E. Meyer
University of Vermont

As Ms. Tina looked around her preschool classroom after one month of school, she realized that Braelen's comment that "there are no books with kids like me in them" was absolutely correct. The classroom library did not contain any books that included children in wheelchairs like the one Braelen used, or, for that matter, any books at all that represented an inclusive society. As Ms. Tina thought more about this and spoke with her colleagues, she realized that none of the posters in her building included sign language or Braille, and her curriculum was relatively weak in exposing her young, impressionable students to individuals with a range of abilities. She began to consider the role of the school environment in creating a sense of belonging.

The Individuals With Disabilities Education Act (IDEA, 2004) and federally funded early childhood programs (e.g., Head Start) have supported the provision of educational services for young children with disabilities in general education classrooms with typically developing peers (Barton & Smith, 2015). National guidelines such as the Division for Early Childhood (DEC)/ National Association for the Education of Young Children (NAEYC) joint position statement on inclusion (2009), the DEC Recommended Practices (2014), and the policy statement on the inclusion of children with disabilities in early childhood programs (U.S. Department of Health and Human Services/U.S. Department of Education, 2015) also have stressed the need and importance for serving children with disabilities in inclusive educational settings. Recent data from the U.S. Department of Education Office of Special Education Programs (2012) revealed that across all states, approximately half of children with disabilities aged 3 to 5 years received special education and related services in regular early childhood settings.

In inclusive classrooms, young children learn, play, and engage with a diverse group of adults and peers. Classroom environments include interrelated physical (e.g., space, materials), social (e.g., interactions with peers and adults), and temporal (e.g., length of routines and activities) features (Division for Early Childhood, 2014). These environmental features can either facilitate or inhibit opportunities for young children to learn and develop (Catalino & Meyer, 2015). Thus, the DEC Recommended Practices (2014) suggest that practitioners provide support in natural and inclusive environments during daily routines and activities to promote young children's access to and participation in learning experiences.

One of the first steps in supporting children's learning and participation in inclusive settings is for teachers to create a welcoming and accepting classroom

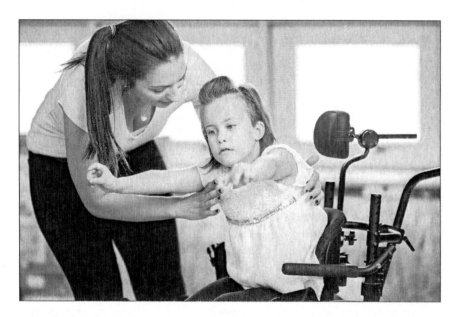

environment for every child (Favazza, 1998). A classroom is not just a physical place that provides educational programs, it is a place that also conveys messages, albeit positive, neutral, or negative ones. Therefore, teachers and families need to consider the messages that children are receiving from their classrooms (Mendoza & Reese, 2001). They need to consider whether adults are modeling inclusive practices and demonstrating support for all individuals in the environment (Murray & O'Doherty, 2001). Children also explore classroom environments in various ways, and through these explorations and interactions with the environment they learn about themselves and their peers. Classroom materials mirror or reflect a child in his/her environment, and materials also provide a window into the lives of others (Ellis, 2015; Style, 1988). In other words, materials such as books, posters, and toys that positively reflect a child in a wheelchair act as a mirror for the child who uses a wheelchair. He gains an understanding of himself by seeing himself in relation to the world and to others. Materials also serve as a window into the diversity (e.g., human differences) in the world. As peers see children with disabilities positively reflected in the materials in their school environment, they learn about human differences. Thus, all children need to see themselves in the environment around them because this positively impacts children's sense of belonging, self-esteem, and understanding of self and others (Ellis, 2015; Favazza, Ostrosky, Meyer, Yu, & Mouzourou, in press).

In the opening vignette, Ms. Tina looked at her classroom and realized the truth behind Braelen's comment that "there are no books with kids like me in them." Ms. Tina's classroom is not atypical; researchers have observed the limited representation of people with disabilities in early childhood classes. For example, Favazza, La Roe, Phillipsen, and Kumar (2000) evaluated the representation of individuals with disabilities in 92 classrooms using Favazza and Odom's (1999) inventory of disability representation (IDR) survey. Results revealed the majority of classes had little to no representation of materials that depicted individuals with disabilities. The teachers also indicated three challenges related to the absence of materials: lack of funds for materials, lack of knowledge of where to obtain materials, and lack of knowledge about how to select and use materials with disability content. Thus, administrative support and professional development are needed to help teachers identify resources, evaluate materials, and embed materials in their curriculum. It also is important to address this topic during preservice education so future teachers receive information about representing children with disabilities and promoting acceptance of diverse abilities in their classrooms.

When children with disabilities do not see themselves reflected in classroom materials, they may inadvertently receive messages such as "I do not belong," "I am not important," or "this is not my world." These messages also can influence typically developing children, who may think "I belong here but she does not belong" or "this is our world, not yours." Thus, the lack of representation within classroom environments may negatively impact the self-concept of children with disabilities and their sense of belonging (Favazza, La Roe, et al., 2000). Also, images in classroom environments (or the lack of images) can influence typically developing children's perceptions, which lay the foundation for attitude formation (Favazza, Ostrosky, Meyer, et al., in press).

Intentionally infusing environments with materials that positively depict individuals with disabilities is the first step in setting the stage for all children to experience a sense of belonging, which is one of the core elements of inclusion. Given the importance of representing children with disabilities in inclusive classroom environments, the purpose of this article is to highlight strategies that early childhood teachers can implement to create high-quality inclusive classrooms wherein all children develop a sense of belonging and better understand and accept each other. Five strategies are described as we use Ms. Tina's classroom as an example for making positive environmental changes. The strategies that promote young children's access and participation, broadly defined as feeling welcome and accepted, are: (1) classroom materials, (2) classroom curriculum (classroom activities, routines, and lesson foci/content), (3) classroom languages, (4) schoolwide environments, and (5) family collaboration.

Intentionally infusing environments with materials that positively depict individuals with disabilities is the first step in setting the stage for all children to experience a sense of belonging, which is one of the core elements of inclusion.

Classroom Materials

Teachers should evaluate classroom books, posters, and dramatic play materials to see if they represent the children in their setting as well as the broader community. While research has shown that there continues to be limited representation of children with disabilities in today's early childhood programs (Favazza, Ostrosky, Meyer, et al., in press), there are steps teachers can take to positively shape program environments.

By critically reviewing storybooks using guidelines such as those developed by Nasatir and Horn (2003), teachers can ensure that the storylines and illustrations promote acceptance of individuals with disabilities and can avoid perpetuating negative or unrealistic portrayals of children with disabilities. By making available classroom and school library books that include children with disabilities portrayed in a positive manner, early childhood educators promote acceptance (Ostrosky, Mouzourou, Dorsey, Favazza, & Leboeuf, 2015).

On her "wish list" at the school's yearly book fair, Ms. Tina decided to suggest three books that parents might purchase for her classroom: All Kinds of Friends, Even Green *(Senisi, 2002),* Can You Hear a Rainbow *(Heelan & Simmonds, 2002), and* Susan Laughs *(Willis & Ross, 2000). By adding these books, Ms. Tina hoped to start expanding her classroom library to include books that positively portray individuals with disabilities.*

By making available classroom and school library books that include children with disabilities portrayed in a positive manner, early childhood educators promote acceptance.

Teachers should carefully evaluate books available in their community libraries before bringing them into their classrooms. Research has shown that some books available at community libraries contain stereotypic language, an imbalance of roles between characters with and without disabilities, and tokenism (Price, Ostrosky, & Mouzourou, 2015). Additionally, providing access to "tools" used by individuals with disabilities (e.g., a doll in a wheelchair in the dramatic play area, small plastic people with walkers in the block area) helps young children become comfortable with disabilities and learn related vocabulary (i.e., wheels, brakes, crutches, ramps). As these materials are made available, children feel more at ease asking questions and engaging in discussions regarding similarities and differences (Favazza, Ostrosky, & Mouzourou, 2016).

When a notification arrived on her desk advertising small grants for teachers, Ms. Tina and another preschool teacher applied for funding and were each awarded a $300 grant to strengthen their array of classroom materials that represent diverse abilities. By sharing materials with one another, Ms. Tina and her colleague had access to a wider variety of resources to strengthen their focus on portraying an inclusive society.

Classroom Curriculum

The term *curriculum* can be used in many ways, but in general, it refers to the "what" of children's learning and may include experiences, activities, routines, and materials that are provided to children within classroom environments (Bredekamp, 2014). In some instances, the curriculum in early childhood classrooms is severely lacking in regards to representing individuals with disabilities. Consider curricular units or topics that many early childhood teachers address, such as occupations, inventors, and community helpers, and the images (or lack thereof) of individuals with disabilities within and across these units. With access to digital images at one's fingertips, it is relatively easy for teachers to enhance these units with additional images or information. For example, within these units teachers could add reference to or highlight individuals with disabilities such as Paralympian Jean Driscoll, the physicist Stephen Hawking, or local community helpers with disabilities (i.e., a bank manager with a prosthetic arm, a preschool teacher who has a cochlear implant). Additionally, there might be individuals within the community who have disabilities that teachers can invite in as storybook readers, volunteers, and special guests in the same vein that one might invite parents and grandparents into the classroom. These guests might even include a student's relative who uses sign language or a fellow teacher who uses a wheelchair.

Once individuals with disabilities have been added to curriculum units, teachers can use these opportunities to discuss how we are more alike than different. "We all communicate, let's learn another way to communicate using sign language! We all use tools and equipment in everyday life! What tools do you use?" (i.e., visual and auditory signals to safely cross the street, glasses to see, GPS to assist in driving). In doing so, children are introduced to individuals with disabilities in natural conversations while placing emphasis on what we all have in common.

As noted earlier, adding books to a classroom library is one way to expose children to materials that represent our diverse world. Additionally, during group time teachers can read books that include characters with disabilities and engage children in discussions around the book content with a focus on similarities.

Ms. Tina decided to start reading one book a week that included a character with disabilities. During the first week, after she preread The Night Search *(Chamberlin & Yoder, 1997) and developed questions to ask her students, Ms. Tina was surprised by the lively discussion that followed. The children were eager to share their own stories of getting lost and the emotions they felt when they could not find someone they knew. They also shared information about why individuals might use canes, and many children talked about family members and friends who were blind. The emphasis on how Ms. Tina's students were similar to the book's main character in terms of their fondness for camping, their experiences getting lost, and family pets left Ms. Tina feeling good about the new direction her curriculum would take and also her ability to answer children's questions at their developmental level.*

Purposefully arranging cooperative learning groups that include children with a range of abilities is another curricular component that can create a sense of belonging and community (Ostrosky, Favazza, van Luling, Mouzourou, & Mustari, 2015; Piercy, Wilton, & Townsend, 2002). Children begin to develop relationships as they work together to complete tasks, such as creating group posters of handprints or determining what objects sink in a container of water and documenting their results before and after testing the items. Semi-structured inclusive learning groups that remain consistent over some period of time help children better understand peers with differing abilities, learn how to collaborate with peers, and solve problems that might occur during group activities. Participation in inclusive learning group activities can increase interactions between children who might not otherwise engage with one another (Yu, Meyer, & Ostrosky, 2013).

Classroom Languages

Another area that needs thoughtful consideration is the examination of languages used in classroom environments. As Ms. Tina pointed out after carefully considering her own class, there was an absence of language diversity. In other words, while she had children who spoke different languages and some who used alternative ways to communicate (sign language), these variances were not reflected in the class environment. One of the first steps in addressing this aspect of the environment is to step back and consider all the ways in which children, teachers, and families communicate with one another.

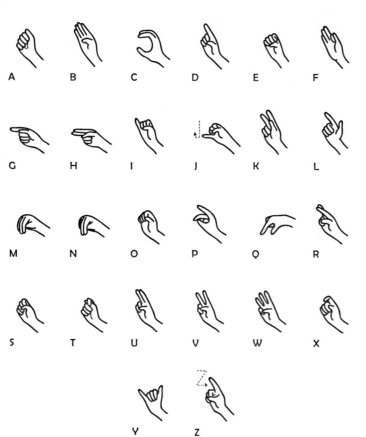

Ms. Tina generated a communication and language list that included several languages and forms of communication used by her students and their families. The list included four different languages (English, Spanish, Russian, Chinese), sign language, and augmentative and alternative communication (AAC) systems.

After identifying all of the languages and types of communication systems used in the classroom, Ms. Tina generated ideas on how to integrate these languages and forms of communication into the classroom setting. Several strategies are described next.

Teachers' creativity can be inspired as they begin to consider ways to embed children's home languages into classroom environments such as on posters and charts as well as in common displays of the alphabet and numbers. In classes with computers, teachers can share child-friendly links to sites that show the alphabet and numbers in sign language and voice output to enable children to both see *and* hear the words for signs, similar to seeing and hearing words when learning a new language (i.e., Spanish, French). In this way, access to other languages is presented using multiple modalities as a strategy for learning the languages used by all children in a class.

Another strategy to embed children's languages into classroom environments is to teach simple signs for games, songs, transitions, and/or everyday expressions (e.g., please, thank you, you're welcome, hello, goodbye, how are you) and common responses (e.g., happy, sad, thirsty, hot, sick). This strategy encourages children not only to see multiple languages represented in the environment, but it supports them in using the languages throughout the school day. Further, teachers can examine materials that are used daily (i.e., job chart, attendance list) and routine activities (i.e., hello/goodbye songs, cleanup songs) to create ongoing opportunities to see and use other languages. For example, after identifying a material such as the job chart, which is used each day during morning circle time, the teacher could embed other languages into job-related conversations, model the new language, and provide questions that prompt children to use the new words or phrases (i.e., line leader, turn on/off lights). By including multiple languages across routines, children have numerous opportunities throughout the school day to learn a new language. It also is important to identify and support children's needs for assistive technology and/or AAC to promote their access to and participation in learning experiences. When addressing this need, it is critical that children be introduced to the assistive technology and AAC used by peers to ensure that all children have access to social and communication exchanges with one another (Favazza, Ostrosky, & Mouzourou, 2016)

Language serves as a powerful connector among people from diverse cultures and communities. Seeing, hearing, and using words, phrases, signs, and symbols that reflect other cultures as well as the strengths and needs of individual students sends the message that each language and culture is important and that all children and families are respected and accepted. Therefore, using diverse languages and modes of communication in a classroom may serve as one of many factors that facilitate full participation and inclusion, connecting children to one another. Because of language differences, challenges in communicating, or misunderstandings related to language and communication, children might not "connect" with one another in inclusive settings. Using multiple forms of communication sends the message that "all belong" and supports children's access to and participation in learning and social experiences (Bratanić, 2007; Chick, 1996; Eisenchlas, Schalley, & Guillemin, 2013; Nemeth, 2009).

> Seeing, hearing, and using words, phrases, signs, and symbols that reflect other cultures as well as the strengths and needs of individual students sends the message that each language and culture is important and that all children and families are respected and accepted.

Schoolwide Environment

Because a child's school environment does not end at the classroom door, there are aspects of the school that should be examined to foster a sense of belonging for all children. For example, children with and without disabilities engage in activities that are held in the larger school context such as in the library, playground, office, and even on the school bus. Therefore, it is important to think about spaces in the school and activities within those spaces, ensuring the use of materials, activities, and programs that promote and encourage interactions between children with and without disabilities. One step is providing schoolwide opportunities to see Braille and picture symbols alongside other spoken languages (e.g., Spanish) by labeling rooms such as the bathroom, library, or office (el baño, biblioteca, oficina; Duran & Santos, 2011). Pairing multiple languages together in everyday settings is a simple visible strategy that serves to both "normalize" their co-existence and broaden the world for all who enter the setting. Such environmental strategies send the message that "some of us speak Spanish, some of us use picture symbols, some of us use both!" This sends a strong message that everyone belongs.

Another aspect of the school that could be examined is use of evidence-based programs to promote interactions between children with and without disabilities. First Step to Success (Walker, Severson, Feil, Stiller, & Golly, 1998) is

a schoolwide program that focuses on specific supports for children with challenging behaviors. Parents and teachers work together to address antisocial behaviors that lead to negative social outcomes for children with disabilities. The Making Friends Program (Favazza, Ostrosky, & Mouzourou, 2016) addresses underlying attitudes of teachers and children about individuals with disabilities by providing concrete strategies for teachers and parents to use with young children to promote greater acceptance of human differences. Both programs have demonstrated success in addressing two persistent and widespread challenges that interfere with inclusion: challenging behaviors and negative attitudes. Extending professional development opportunities to key school staff using resources such as these widens the circle of inclusive practices within the school environment and raises the visibility of children with diverse abilities, making inclusion a schoolwide priority. However, these efforts are inadequate if family members are not included in efforts to create inclusive environments.

Family Collaboration

Families are the first circle of inclusion for children, and yet we sometimes neglect to include them in the next circle of inclusion, the school environment. The DEC Recommended Practices (2014) suggest that practitioners work with families and other adults to modify and adapt the physical, social, and temporal environments to promote each child's access to and participation in learning experiences.

Following a school-sponsored family night, Ms. Tina remarked, "I can honestly say, I have never met a parent who did not want his or her child to feel accepted and included within a school and classroom."

There are many ways to engage families that support the school while at the same time create a sense of community. For example, parents can be given a list of carefully selected books that promote understanding and acceptance of human differences. They can be encouraged to obtain books from the local library and use teacher-created discussion guides to facilitate conversations with their children (Favazza, Ostrosky, & Mouzourou, 2016; Price et al., 2015). Researchers found that after using such books and guided discussion bookmarks, parents reported that both they and their children learned a variety of new concepts related to disabilities through their shared-book reading experiences (Meyer et al., 2015).

Families of children with disabilities can help increase understanding of disabilities and disability representation in classrooms.

A mother in Ms. Tina's class made ankle-foot orthotics (AFO) for her son's stuffed animal because he wanted his toy to have a pair like his. She also made AFOs for other stuffed toys in the preschool classroom and extended it further by offering to make AFOs for children with and without disabilities who then wanted AFOs for their stuffed animals at home. In another preschool class, a mom made a blanket that included pictures of all of the classmates and T-shirts with a class picture on it. Still another parent volunteered to partner with the occupational therapist (OT) to personalize the visual supports used in the class and school. After obtaining parents' permission, the OT included photographs of children with and without disabilities in many of the images depicted in the visual supports used at school. Parents also volunteered to record books on tape for Ms. Tina's classroom library.

All of these low-cost strategies can help raise the visibility of individuals with disabilities and increase interactions and personalize the collaborations among family members, students, teachers, and other school personnel, leading to a greater sense of belonging for all.

Conclusion

While increasing numbers of young children with disabilities are taught alongside their typically developing peers in inclusive settings, one of the challenges that teachers and parents face is to create accepting, inclusive environments where all students and families feel a sense of belonging (Connor 2011; Ellis, 2015). The lack of representation of individuals with disabilities may reinforce children's feelings of being invisible to their classmates and to the world. Thus, high-quality inclusive classrooms need to include representation of individuals with disabilities because this is strongly related to the development of self-esteem, a sense of self, a feeling of belonging, and positive attitude formation. Carefully examining the breadth and depth of disability representation within school environments is an important first step to conveying the core message of each and every inclusive setting: that *we all belong.*

High-quality inclusive classrooms need to include representation of individuals with disabilities because this is strongly related to the development of self-esteem, a sense of self, a feeling of belonging, and positive attitude formation.

References

Barton, E. E., & Smith, B. J. (2015). Advancing high-quality preschool inclusion: A discussion and recommendations for the field. *Topics in Early Childhood Special Education, 35*, 69–78. doi:10.1177/0271121415583048

Bratanić, M. (2007). Nonverbal communication as a factor in linguistic and cultural miscommunication. In A. Esposito, M. Brantanić, E. Keller, & M. Marinaro (Eds.), *Fundamentals of verbal and nonverbal communication and the biometric issue* (pp. 82–91). Amsterdam, Netherlands: IOS Press.

Bredekamp, S. (2014). *Effective practices in early childhood education: Building a foundation* (2nd ed.). Upper Saddle River, NJ: Pearson.

Catalino, T., & Meyer, L. E. (2015). Improving access and participation. In *DEC recommended practices: Enhancing services for young children with disabilities and their families* (DEC Recommended Practices Monograph Series No. 1; pp. 53–63). Los Angeles, CA: Division for Early Childhood.

Chamberlin, K., & Yoder, D. (1997). *The night search.* Holidaysburg, PA: Jason and Nordic.

Chick, J. K. (1996). Intercultural miscommunication. In S. L. McKay & N. H. Hornberger (Eds.), *Sociolinguistics and language teaching* (pp. 329–348). New York, NY: Cambridge University Press.

Connor, D. J. (2011). Questioning "normal": Seeing children first and labels second. *School Talk: National Council of Teachers of English, 16*(2), 1–6.

Division for Early Childhood. (2014). *DEC recommended practices in early intervention/early childhood special education 2014.* Retrieved from http://www.dec-sped.org/recommendedpractices

Division for Early Childhood & National Association for the Education of Young Children (2009, April). *Early childhood inclusion* (Joint position statement). Chapel Hill: The University of North Carolina, FPG Child Development Institute.

Duran, L., & Santos, R. M. (2011). *NCQTL inventory of practices to support the language and communication development of young children who are dual language learners* [Unpublished document]. The National Center on Quality Teaching and Learning (NCQTL), University of Washington, Seattle.

Eisenchlas, S. A., Schalley, A. C., & Guillemin, D. (2013). The importance of literacy in home language: The view from Australia. *Open SAGE.* doi:10.1177/2158244013507270

Ellis, K. (2015). *Disability and popular culture: Focusing passion, creating community and expressing defiance.* Burlington, VT: Ashgate.

Favazza, P. C. (1998). Preparing for children with disabilities in early childhood classrooms. *Early Childhood Education Journal, 25*, 255–258. doi:10.1023/A:1025650922587

Favazza, P. C., La Roe, J., Phillipsen, L., & Kumar, P. (2000). Representing young children with disabilities in classroom environments. *Young Exceptional Children, 3*(3), 2–8. doi:10.1177/109625060000300301

Favazza, P. C. & Odom, S. L. (1999). Inventory of disability representation. In P. Favazza, J. La Roe, & S. Odom (Eds.), *Special friends: A manual for creating accepting environments* (pp. 62–64). Boulder, CO: Roots and Wings.

Favazza, P. C., Ostrosky, M. M., Meyer, L. E., Yu, S., & Mouzourou, C. (in press). Limited representation of individuals with disabilities in early childhood classes: Alarming or status quo? *International Journal of Inclusive Education.*

Favazza, P. C., Ostrosky, M. M., & Mouzourou, C. (2016). *The making friends program: Supporting acceptance in your K–2 classroom.* Baltimore, MD: Paul H. Brookes.

Heelan, J. R., & Simmonds, N. (2002). *Can you hear a rainbow? The story of a deaf boy named Chris.* Atlanta, GA: Peachtree.

Individuals With Disabilities Education Act, 20 U.S.C. § 1400 (2004).

Mendoza, J., & Reese, D. (2001). Examining multicultural picture books for the early childhood classroom: Possibilities and pitfalls. *Early Childhood Research & Practice, 3*(2). Retrieved from http://ecrp.uiuc.edu/v3n2/mendoza.html

Meyer, L. E., Ostrosky, M. M., Yu, S., Favazza, P. C., Mouzourou, C., van Luling, L., & Park, H. (2015). Parents' responses to a kindergarten-classroom lending-library component designed to support shared reading at home. *Journal of Early Childhood Literacy.* Advance online publication. doi:10.1177/1468798415577870

Murray, C., & O'Doherty, A. (2001). *Éist: Respecting diversity in early childhood care, education and training.* Dublin, Ireland: Pavee Point.

Nasatir, D., & Horn, E. (2003). Addressing disability as a part of diversity. *Young Exceptional Children, 6*(4), 2–10. doi:10.1177/109625060300600401

Nemeth, K. N. (2009). *Many languages, one classroom: Teaching dual and English language learners.* Beltsville, MD: Gryphon House.

Ostrosky, M. M., Mouzourou, C., Dorsey, E. A., Favazza, P. C., & Leboeuf, L. M. (2015). Pick a book, any book: Using children's books to support positive attitudes toward peers with disabilities. *Young Exceptional Children, 18*(1), 30–43. doi:10.1177/1096250613512666

Ostrosky, M. M., Favazza, P. C., van Luling, L. M., Mouzourou, C., & Mustari, E. (2015). *Acceptance of children with disabilities: The impact of a multi-component intervention.* Manuscript submitted for publication.

Piercy, M., Wilton, K., & Townsend, M. (2002). Promoting the social acceptance of young children with moderate-severe intellectual disabilities using cooperative-learning techniques. *American Journal on Mental Retardation, 107,* 352–360.

Price, C. L., Ostrosky, M. M., & Mouzourou, C. (2015). Exploring representations of characters with disabilities in library books. *Early Childhood Education Journal.* Advance online publication. doi:10.1007/s10643-015-0740-3

Senisi, E. B. (2002). *All kinds of friends, even green!* Bethesda, MD: Woodbine House.

Style, E. (1988). *Curriculum as window and mirror. The National SEED Project.* Retrieved from http://nationalseedproject.org/about-us/timeline/26-latest-articles/41-curriculum-as-window-and-mirror

U.S. Department of Education. (2012). *Annual report to Congress on the implementation of the Individuals With Disabilities Act.* Washington, DC: Author.

U.S. Department of Health and Human Services/U.S. Department of Education. (2015, September 14). *Policy statement on inclusion of children with disabilities in early childhood programs.* Retrieved from http://www2.ed.gov/policy/speced/guid/earlylearning/joint-statement-full-text.pdf

Walker, H. M., Severson, H. H., Feil, E. G., Stiller, B., & Golly, A. (1998). First step to success: Intervening at the point of school entry to prevent antisocial behavior patterns. *Psychology in the Schools, 35,* 259–269. doi:10.1002/(SICI)1520-6807(199807)35:3<259::AID-PITS6>3.0.CO;2-I

Willis, J., & Ross, T. (2000). *Susan laughs.* New York, NY: Henry Holt.

Yu, S., Meyer, L. E., & Ostrosky, M. M. (2013). Creating accepting classroom environments: Promoting positive attitudes toward peers with challenging behaviors. In M. M. Ostrosky & S. R. Sandall (Eds.), *YEC monograph series No. 15: Addressing young children's challenging behaviors* (pp. 14–28). Missoula, MT: Division for Early Childhood.

9

Pick, Present, Play
Promoting Young Children's Communication

HEDDA MEADAN
University of Illinois at Urbana-Champaign

MAUREEN ANGELL
Illinois State University

Mrs. Greco has been teaching for more than 20 years at the Hillside School. Many teachers at the school praise her for the success of her students. During a parent-teacher conference with Mr. and Mrs. Bryer, the parents of Luke, who is 4 years old and has autism, Mrs. Greco describes Luke's improvement on using the word "more" when asking for his snack. His parents are very surprised, stating that when at home during mealtimes or when playing with his favorite toys and activities they have not heard Luke communicate in that way. This prompts Mrs. Greco to explain and teach strategies for arranging the environment at home to foster Luke's communication. As she begins to explain, Mrs. Greco struggles to think of a quick and easy way to teach the parents how to implement these strategies.

* * *

That same week, Mrs. Greco is organizing her classroom after school when a first-year teacher, Ms. Mendez, comes in asking for advice on how to encourage communication among her students during play. Mrs. Greco is eager to help this new teacher and begins describing how to arrange the classroom more adequately for the students. When Ms. Mendez asks for a specific example of a communication opportunity she could provide, Mrs. Greco tries to think of a quick strategy she could give that could be easy for the new teacher to remember and implement.

Many young children who have been identified with developmental delays or disabilities, including intellectual disabilities, Down syndrome, and autism spectrum disorders (ASD), exhibit speech-language delays along with other impairments inherent in their diagnosed disabilities. These impairments include deficits in social-pragmatic communication skills (Sigafoos, Arthur-Kelly, & Butterfield, 2006). Early development and use of appropriate social-pragmatic communication skills (i.e., the skills that allow the child to interact with others in different settings) are important to maximizing the quality of life of children with developmental delays or disabilities and their families because appropriate communicative interactions among family members and peers are critical for developing meaningful relationships. In addition, communication and language deficits at a young age could influence a child's development and, in some cases, are related to later learning disabilities, challenging behavior, and deficits in academic performance and outcomes (Walker, Bigelow, & Harjusola-Webb, 2008). Sigafoos et al. (2006) noted that in almost all cases, there is a need for communication partners to implement systematic and ongoing intervention to further develop the communication abilities of individuals with disabilities.

Naturalistic teaching and systematic instructional strategies are grounded in behavioral principles such as prompting, reinforcing, modeling, and shaping new language. There is a strong research base supporting the effectiveness of naturalistic strategies in enhancing communication skills of children with diverse abilities and needs, including children who use verbal communication and children who are nonverbal or require augmentative and alternative communication (AAC) systems. Hancock and Kaiser (2006) noted that naturalistic teaching strategies have been used since the mid-1970s (Hart & Risley, 1975; Hart & Rogers-Warren, 1978) with a wide range of children in the early stages of communication development who presented with developmental delays (e.g., Hancock, Kaiser, & Delaney, 2002; Hemmeter & Kaiser, 1994; McDuffie et al., 2013; Meadan, Angell, Stoner, & Daczewitz, 2014; Peterson, Carta, & Greenwood, 2005), ASD (e.g., Christensen-Sandfort & Whinnery , 2013; Harjusola-Webb & Robbins, 2012; Kaiser, Hancock, & Nietfeld, 2000; Mancil, Conroy, & Haydon, 2009; Meadan et al., 2016; Olive et al., 2007), specific language impairments (Alpert & Kaiser, 1992; Mobayed, Collins, Strangis, Schuster, & Hemmeter, 2000), or severe multiple disabilities (Douglas, McNaughton, & Light, 2013; Halle, Marshall, & Spradin, 1979; Kaiser & Goetz, 1993; Yoder & Warren, 2002).

Naturalistic milieu teaching may be described as a conversation-based model of early language intervention that uses child interest and initiations as opportunities to model and prompt language use in natural contexts (Hancock & Kaiser, 2006; Hart & Rogers-Warren, 1978). Hancock and Kaiser (2006) explained the use of enhanced milieu teaching (EMT) as emphasizing the reciprocity, turn taking, and use of feedback and modeling when interacting with children, in addition to following the child's lead in play and conversation.

Naturalistic teaching strategies have been referred to with different names, including incidental teaching, naturalistic interventions, milieu teaching, embedded teaching, responsive education, and prelinguistic milieu teaching. Wong et al. (2014) described naturalistic intervention as

> a collection of practices including environmental arrangement, interaction techniques, and strategies based on applied behavior analysis principles. These practices are designed to encourage specific target behaviors based on learners' interests by building more complex skills

---

> Naturalistic teaching and systematic instructional strategies are grounded in behavioral principles such as prompting, reinforcing, modeling, and shaping new language.

that are naturally reinforcing and appropriate to the interaction. Naturalistic intervention occurs within typical settings, activities, and/or routines in which the learner participates. (p. 67)

An important goal in the field of special education has been to ensure that families and children are provided with supports and services that are supported by scientific evidence. Interventions that researchers have shown to be effective are called evidence-based practices (EBPs). Evidence-based practice includes a combination of the best available scientific evidence, professional expertise, and understanding of child and family characteristics, priorities, and preferences. Naturalistic interventions were identified as EBP by the National Standards Project (NSP), the Centers for Medicare and Medicaid Services (CMMS), the National Autism Center (NAC), and the National Professional Development Center on ASD (NPDC) for infants through high school students.

Environmental Arrangement

One frequently used naturalistic strategy is environmental arrangement. Environmental arrangement refers to the intentional altering of space, materials (toys, books), equipment, routines, schedule, and activities by families, teachers, and service providers to support each child's learning across developmental domains (Davis & Fox, 1999; Division for Early Childhood [DEC], 2014; McEvoy, Fox, & Rosenberg, 1991; Walker et al., 2008). The Environment recommended practice we focus on is E3: "Practitioners work with the family and other adults to modify and adapt the physical, social, and temporal environments to promote each child's access to and participation in learning experiences" (DEC, 2014, p. 8). More specifically, we discuss environmental practices that enhance communication and set up opportunities for communication among children (peers and siblings) and adults (parents, teachers, and service providers). The goal of this type of environmental practice is to "increase the children's interest in the environment as an occasion for communication. The environment is managed to promote requests and comments by children and to support language teaching efforts by adults" (Ostrosky & Kaiser, 1991, p. 7). The environmental practices included in the DEC Recommended Practices (2014) encompass the physical environment, the social environment, and the temporal environment.

Physical environment practices include structuring and organizing the environment (e.g., space, equipment, and materials) in the home, child care, and classroom to increase motivation for communication and promote opportunities for children to communicate more frequently throughout the day. For example, an adult can place a preferred item in view, but out of reach, in the home or give access to activities and items that children enjoy playing in pairs or groups (i.e., social toys) in the environment. Social environment practices include arranging the people in the environment (e.g., peers, siblings, teachers, and parents) to promote social interaction and provide opportunities for social engagement and communication among children and adults. For example, adults can group children in different ways, such as pairing children with different communication abilities and needs. Temporal environment practices include following routines and activities that are familiar to the children and promote initiations and social interaction. For example, adults can use predictable schedules and activities and intentionally sequence activities and routines.

Pick, Present, Play

> The Pick, Present, Play strategies are easy to use and are designed to help children improve their communication skills. By using them, adults create more chances for children to practice using communication while they are motivated to communicate to get what they really want or need.

Environmental arrangement practices that promote communication development include a variety of strategies to set up the physical, social, and temporal environments to create many chances for communication among children and adults, both at home and in preschool and child care settings. We describe three different easy and clear ways to arrange the environment to encourage children to communicate. It is important to keep in mind that the key to successfully arranging the environment is to use children's favorite items or activities, or items or activities that are new, or novel, and exciting to the children.

The first way to use environmental arrangement to encourage communication is to *pick* toys, activities, foods, or materials that the child is interested in and give the child a reason to communicate. Picking favorite or interesting items and activities will enhance the child's motivation to communicate. Another strategy is to *present* the toys, activities, foods, or materials in a way that increases the probability that the child will communicate. For example, the adult can put the child's favorite cereal in a clear container that the child cannot open independently and will, therefore, need to communicate with his AAC system for help in accessing the cereal. Finally, the adult can also *play* with an item or activity the child likes in a way that will require the child to communicate. For example, a teacher can give the child a puzzle with a missing piece so the child has to communicate with the teacher to get the piece. Or, a father can push the child only once in the swing or stop the swing so his child has to ask (e.g., verbalize, sign, use AAC device) for "more."

The Pick, Present, Play strategies are easy to use and are designed to help children improve their communication skills. By using them, adults create more chances for children to practice using communication while they are motivated to communicate to get what they really want or need. This creates a pattern of ongoing communication that will set children up to successfully respond, initiate, and communicate more often with others. Adults can use all three strategies in the same activity or routine, but this is not required. For example, a teacher can give a child a spoonful of goldfish snack crackers during snack time (pick child's favorite snack) and put the goldfish box next to her, out of the child's reach, so the child will need to ask for more goldfish when she has eaten the small portion of snacks she received (present food out of reach). In this situation, the teacher is using the pick and present strategies and not the play strategy.

Parents can use each strategy alone or together. Pick, Present, Play strategies align well with the environmental strategies described above (physical, social, and temporal). For example, a parent can give her child access to favorite train track pieces (pick/physical environment), split the pieces between the child and his brother (present/social environment), and ask them to take turns in completing the whole train track (play/temporal environment).

Figure 1
Pick, Present, Play Strategies Flowchart

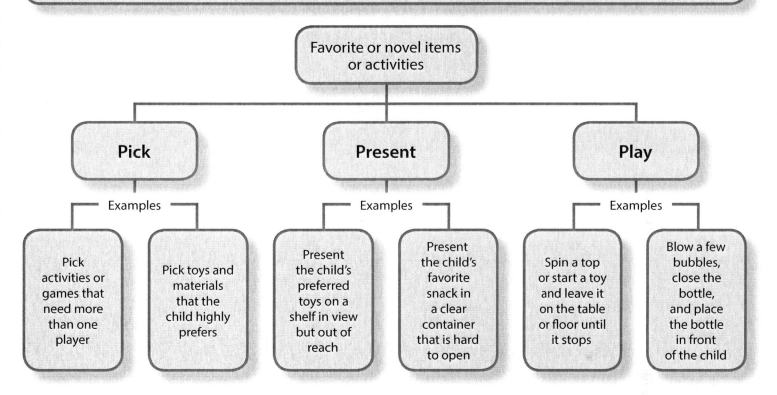

Guiding Parents and Professionals

Environmental arrangement is a naturalistic strategy that requires intentional planning of the physical, social, and temporal environments. Environmental arrangement strategies could be considered *prerequisite* for using many of the other naturalistic teaching communication strategies. Using environmental arrangement strategies enhances children's motivation to communicate, and, therefore, creates opportunities for adults to enhance and promote the children's communication skills. For example, when a father pushes his son on a swing and then stops the swing knowing that his son loves to swing and wants to be pushed again (i.e., environmental arrangement), he creates an opportunity to use another strategy. The father can mand (e.g., ask the child "what do you want?") or model (e.g., the dad can say or sign "swing" and wait for the child to imitate him). In another situation, a teacher can give a child who prefers to color during free playtime only a white piece of paper and leave the colored pencils on a high shelf (e.g., environmental arrangement). In this situation the teacher can use time delay and look expectantly at the child until the child initiates communication by

Table 1
Action Plan Form

What	Activity or Routine	Target Word or Sign	Action Steps	Materials or Resources
How	In what routine or activity are you going to use the strategy?	What word do you want the child to communicate? Do you want him to speak or sign?	What would using this strategy look like during the activity you have chosen?	What will you need to use this strategy during the activity?
Example for a parent	Bath time	Say "toy"	*Pick* child's favorite bath toys. Put (*present*) the bath toys slightly out of reach but still visible. *Play* with a toy a couple times, then put it back out of reach.	Favorite bath toys
Example for a teacher	Free play	Sign "more"	*Pick* child's favorite activity, such as top spinning. Put (*present*) the top in a clear container and close container. Spin (*play*) the top a couple times, then put it on the table.	Tops

saying, signing, or using the AAC device "colors, please."

Many of the naturalistic teaching strategies that aim at promoting and enhancing communication skills of young children include specific steps adults need to complete to implement the strategies effectively. For example, to effectively use the modeling strategy, the adult needs to (a) establish joint attention by focusing attention on the child's specific interest; (b) present a verbal model, sign model, or gestural model that is related to the child's interest; (c) wait 2–3 seconds for the child to respond; and (d) respond to the child's behavior by providing verbal feedback, repeating the model, or using the mand-model strategy (Meadan et al., 2016). In another example, for an adult to effectively use the mand-model strategy, he or she needs to (a) establish joint attention by focusing attention on the child's specific interest; (b) present a verbal prompt in the form of a question, a choice, or a mand; (c) wait 2–3 seconds for the child to respond; and (d) respond to the child's behavior by providing verbal feedback, repeating the mand-model, or using the modeling strategy.

The DEC Recommended Practices emphasize the need for practitioners to work with family members and other adults to modify and adapt the physical, social, and temporal environments to promote each child's learning (E3). However, because environmental arrangement strategies vary and do not include clear guidelines, similar to the ones described for modeling and mand-model, and require intentional planning for arrangement of the environment, parents and professionals could have a difficult time consistently implementing these strategies. To guide and support parents and professionals, practitioners can teach the Pick, Present, Play strategies using a handout similar to Appendix A or a flowchart similar to Figure 1. To support the parents and professionals in planning and implementing the strategies, the practitioners could help them complete an action plan (see Table 1) that includes information about the activity or routine in which the strategy will be used, the target words or signs to practice during the activity, the action steps that need to be taken to implement the strategy, and the materials and resources needed. It is important to note that the Pick, Present, Play strategies are related to DEC Recommended Practices from different topic areas (e.g., family, interaction, instruction) in addition to Environment recommended practices (e.g., E1, E3).

The following week Mrs. Greco plans a time to meet with Mrs. Bryer after school to talk more about environmental arrangement. Mrs. Greco gives the mother the handout and flowchart outlining the elements of Pick, Present, Play as well as the action plan that lays out how to plan and prepare for using the Pick, Present, Play strategies. Mrs. Greco explains how to use the action plan, and together they practice a possible scenario. Mrs. Bryer reports that Luke loves to pop bubbles and decides to target the word "more." She completes the action plan with the support of Ms. Greco. She will pick bubbles, one of her son's favorite activities. She will present the bubbles in the container with the lid closed so Luke has to ask her to make him more bubbles. Then, when he says "more," she will play with the bubbles by blowing one wand-full of bubbles and then put the lid back on so Luke has to communicate again to get more. Ms. Greco uses the same handout, flowchart, and action plan form to help Ms. Mendez understand and implement the Pick, Present, Play strategies.

Meadan and colleagues have used the Pick, Present, Play strategies to guide parents in a series of studies (Meadan et al., 2014; Meadan et al., 2016). The findings consistently demonstrated that parents were able to quickly learn how to use these strategies and were satisfied with the procedures used to teach the strategies and the outcomes. One parent reported that

> the Pick, Present, Play [environmental arrangement] just seems to happen now, kind of the way our house is set up now . . . her toys are put in the toy box at night so she has to ask in the morning and the snacks aren't where she can reach them all the time anymore so she has to ask, and I think they will just continue just because it's the way things are set up now naturally.

Many young children with developmental delays or disabilities, from diverse cultural and linguistic backgrounds, could benefit from strategies such as the

Many of the naturalistic teaching strategies that aim at promoting and enhancing communication skills of young children include specific steps adults need to complete to implement the strategies effectively.

Pick, Present, Play that aim to provide opportunities for the child to practice and enhance his or her communication skills. The Pick, Present, Play strategies are clear and easy to implement in the natural environment.

References

Alpert, C. L., & Kaiser, A. P. (1992). Training parents as milieu language teachers. *Journal of Early Intervention, 16*, 31–52. doi:10.1177/105381519201600104

Christensen-Sandfort, R. J., & Whinnery, S. B. (2013). Impact of milieu teaching on communication skills of young children with autism spectrum disorder. *Topics in Early Childhood Special Education, 32*, 211–222. doi:10.1177/0271121411404930

Davis, C. A., & Fox, J. (1999). Evaluating environmental arrangement as setting events: Review and implications for measurement. *Journal of Behavioral Education, 9*, 77–96. doi:10.1023/A:1022884816219

Division for Early Childhood. (2014). *DEC recommended practices in early intervention/early childhood special education 2014.* Retrieved from http://www.dec-sped.org/recommendedpractices

Douglas, S. N., McNaughton, D., & Light, J. (2013). Online training for paraeducators to support the communication of young children. *Journal of Early Intervention, 35*, 223–242. doi:10.1177/1053815114526782

Halle, J. W., Marshall, A. M., & Spradlin, J. E. (1979). Time delay: A technique to increase language use and facilitate generalization in retarded children. *Journal of Applied Behavior Analysis, 12*, 431–439. doi:10.1901/jaba.1979.12-431

Hancock, T. B., & Kaiser, A. P. (2006). Enhanced milieu teaching. In R. J. McCauley & M. E. Fey (Eds.), *Treatment of language disorders in children* (pp. 203–236). Baltimore, MD: Paul H. Brookes.

Hancock, T. B., Kaiser, A. P., & Delaney, E. M. (2002). Teaching parents of preschoolers at high risk: Strategies to support language and positive behavior. *Topics in Early Childhood Special Education, 22*, 191–212. doi:10.1177/02711214020220040z

Harjusola-Webb, S., & Robbins, S. H. (2012). The effects of teacher-implemented naturalistic intervention on the communication of preschoolers with autism. *Topics in Early Childhood Special Education, 32*, 99–110. doi:10.1177/0271121410397060

Hart, B., & Risley, T. R. (1975). Incidental teaching of language in the preschool. *Journal of Applied Behavior Analysis, 8*, 411–420. doi:10.1901/jaba.1975.8-411

Hart, B., & Rogers-Warren, A. (1978). A milieu approach to teaching language. In R. L. Schiefelbusch (Ed.), *Language intervention strategies* (Vol. 2, pp. 193–235). Baltimore, MD: University Park Press

Hemmeter, M. L., & Kaiser, A. P. (1994). Enhanced milieu teaching: Effects of parent-implemented language intervention. *Journal of Early Intervention, 18*, 269–289. doi:10.1177/105381519401800303

Kaiser, A. P., & Goetz, L. (1993). Enhancing communication with persons labeled severely disabled. *Research and Practice for Persons with Severe Disabilities, 18*, 137–142. doi:10.1177/154079699301800301

Kaiser, A. P., Hancock, T. B., & Nietfeld, J. P. (2000). The effects of parent-implemented enhanced milieu teaching on the social communication of children who have autism. *Early Education and Development, 11*, 423–446. doi:10.1207/s15566935eed1104_4

Mancil, G. R., Conroy, M. A., & Haydon, T. F. (2009). Effects of a modified milieu therapy intervention on the social communicative behaviors of young children with autism spectrum disorders. *Journal of Autism and Developmental Disorders, 39*, 149–163. doi:10.1007/s10803-008-0613-3

McDuffie, A., Machalicek, W., Oakes, A., Haebig, E., Weismer, S. E., & Abbeduto, L. (2013). Distance video-teleconferencing in early intervention: Pilot study of a naturalistic parent-implemented language intervention. *Topics in Early Childhood Special Education, 33*, 172–185. doi:10.1177/0271121413476348

McEvoy, M. A., Fox, J. J., & Rosenberg, M. S. (1991). Organizing preschool environments: Suggestions for enhancing the development/learning of preschool children with handicaps. *Topics in Early Childhood Special Education, 11*, 18–28. doi:10.1177/027112149101100204

Meadan, H., Angell, M. E., Stoner, J. B., & Daczewitz, M. (2014). Parent-implemented social-pragmatic communication intervention: A pilot study. *Focus on Autism and Other Developmental Disabilities, 29*, 95–110. doi:10.1177/1088357613517504

Meadan, H., Snodgrass, M. R., Meyer, L. E., Fisher, K. W., Chung, M. Y., & Halle, J. W. (2016). Internet-based parent-implemented intervention for young children with autism: A pilot study. *Journal of Early Intervention, 38*, 3–23. doi:10.1177/1053815116630327

Mobayed, K. L., Collins, B. C., Strangis, D. F., Schuster, J. W., & Hemmeter, M. L. (2000). Teaching parents to employ mand-model procedures to teach their children requesting. *Journal of Early Intervention, 23*, 165–179. doi:10.1177/105381510002300601

Olive, M. L., de la Cruz, B., Davis, T. N., Chan, J. M., Lang, R. B., O'Reilly, M. F., & Dickson, S. M. (2007). The effects of enhanced milieu teaching and a voice output communication aid on the requesting of three children with autism. *Journal of Autism and Developmental Disorders, 37*, 1505–1513. doi:10.1007/s10803-006-0243-6

Ostrosky, M. M., & Kaiser, A. P. (1991). Preschool classroom environments that promote communication. *Teaching Exceptional Children, 23*(4), 6–10. doi:10.1177/004005999102300403

Peterson, P., Carta, J. J., & Greenwood, C. (2005). Teaching enhanced milieu language teaching skills to parents in multiple risk families. *Journal of Early Intervention, 27*, 94–109. doi:10.1177/10538151050270205

Sigafoos, J., Arthur-Kelly, M., & Butterfield, N. (2006). *Enhancing everyday communication for children with disabilities.* Baltimore, MD: Paul H. Brookes.

Walker, D., Bigelow, K. M., & Harjusola-Webb, S. (2008). Increasing communication and language-learning opportunities for infants and toddlers. In C. A. Peterson, L. Fox, & P. M. Blasco (Eds.), *Early intervention for infants and toddlers and their families: Practices and outcomes* (Young Exceptional Children Monograph Series No. 10, pp. 105–121). Missoula, MT: Division for Early Childhood.

Wong, C., Odom, S. L., Hume, K., Cox, A. W., Fettig, A., Kucharczyk, S., ... Schultz, T. R. (2014). *Evidence-based practices for children, youth, and young adults with autism spectrum disorder.* Chapel Hill: The University of North Carolina, Frank Porter Graham Child Development Institute, Autism Evidence-Based Practice Review Group.

Yoder, P. J., & Warren, S. F. (2002). Effects of prelinguistic milieu teaching and parent responsivity education on dyads involving children with intellectual disabilities. *Journal of Speech, Language, and Hearing Research, 45,* 1158–1174. doi:10.1044/1092-4388(2002/094)

Appendix A

Pick, Present, Play Environmental Arrangement Handout

Environmental arrangement includes a variety of strategies that set up opportunities for communication between you and the child. You can *pick* toys and materials that are of interest to the child and provide a reason for the child to communicate, *present* the materials and toys in a way that increases the probability that the child will communicate (e.g., put a preferred toy in sight, but out of reach), and *play* with the materials in a way that will require the child to communicate (e.g., give the child a puzzle with a missing piece).

Examples

Pick materials/toys/activities that will motivate the child to communicate.
- Toys/materials/activities that are highly preferred by the child
- Activities/games that require more than one player

Present the materials/toys/activities in a way that will increase the likelihood the child will communicate.
- Place the child's preferred toys on a shelf that is in view, but out-of-reach.
- Place the child's favorite snack in a clear container that is difficult to open.
- Provide the child with only a few of the materials needed to complete a task.

Play with the materials/toys/activities in a way that will increase the likelihood the child will communicate.
- Blow a few bubbles, close the bottle, and place the bottle in front of the child.
- Activate a toy and leave it on the table or floor until the motion stops, with the assumption that the child cannot reactivate the toy by himself.

Add examples

_____

_____

_____

_____

10

Using Modified Ride-On Toy Cars to Provide Accessible, Early Social Mobility

KENDRA GAGNON
SUSAN HOHENADEL
Rockhurst University

ANDRINA SABET
Cleveland State University

JENNIFER TUCKER
University of Central Florida

JAMES COLE GALLOWAY
University of Delaware

Landon is a 4-year-old boy with diagnoses of Down syndrome and cerebral palsy. He began attending school in an early childhood special education classroom a few months after his third birthday. At that time, Landon had limited ability to crawl and scoot on the floor in his classroom. Given the difficulty of moving, he was not motivated to move in the classroom or on the playground. He had a gait trainer and was able to stand and take a few steps with assistance and verbal cues. His teacher, Mrs. Clark, and his family were concerned that Landon was so dependent on others for his mobility—either pushed in a stroller, pulled in a wagon, or carried—and wanted to increase his environmental exploration and independence.

A few weeks after Landon started school, his physical therapist, Kendra, suggested that a power ride-on toy car may provide an immediate, low-tech mobility solution for him. His special education team agreed to try a seated power ride-on car with an activation button on the steering wheel. On his first trial with the car, Landon was able to activate the car to move independently in the school hallway, follow stop and go commands, and stop when approaching obstacles. Kendra worked closely with Mrs. Clark and Landon's special education team to work on a school mobility plan that provided Landon with a variety of self-directed mobility options at school, including driving his power car, walking in his walker, and/or crawling/scooting on the floor. Landon's teachers and caregivers were encouraged to let Landon use any or all of these mobility options during the school day—letting Landon choose as much as possible—to amass the highest frequency of self-directed movement opportunities possible.

Within three months, Landon was able to drive his power car throughout the school, stopping, starting, and steering independently. He was also able to walk over 175 feet forward using his walker. In addition to his improved mobility, Mrs. Clark noted more social interactions with his peers and more communication with his teachers. These new interactions included some age-appropriate "defiant" behaviors, including saying "no" often and moving in the opposite direction of his teachers' requests. By the end of the school year, Landon was able to drive his power car throughout the school, including the playground. Interestingly, he was also able to use his walker, which he now steered independently, to move throughout the school building and on the playground. When moving in the school, Mrs. Clark let him choose whether he wanted to walk or drive, and he typically did both at some point during the school day.

Landon riding his "standing car," a 12-volt ATV-style ride-on quad car with customized side rails and a button in the seat that is wired to make the car "go" when he stands up.

After Landon turned 4 and began to outgrow his original ride-on car, Kendra suggested progressing him to a "standing car," an ATV-style ride-on quad car with a button in the seat. The wiring was reversed so that when Landon was sitting on the button, the car would stop and when Landon stood up and released the button, the car would go. The team agreed this would be an optimal solution for Landon to promote upright balance and posture while providing him with mobility and participation opportunities with his peers and teachers. The first day Landon drove his standing car, he was able to independently drive in the school and on the playground, steering around obstacles.

Landon is now almost 5 years old and is independent with his walker and his standing car in all school environments, including the playground. He is no longer limited in his walking distance and can walk up and down inclines, through doors, and even climb up the playground structure to go down the slide on his own. He continues to work on improving the speed of his walking so that he can keep up with his peers, but he and his teachers can choose to use his power car when speed is a priority. He now chooses walking more often than he chooses to drive, but he continues to enjoy a variety of options for self-directed mobility in his preschool environment. One key to Landon's mobility success story is the use of modified ride-on toy cars to support his early mobility, which meets if not exceeds the DEC Recommended Practices for assistive technology.

Introduction

There are many ways in which providers may use assistive technology to help children with mobility impairments move, live, and play. Providers and families may assume that assistive technology is expensive and complex and must be specifically designed for children with disabilities. However, with small modifications, everyday objects and toys may be used just as effectively as expensive technologies to achieve mobility goals. The primary purpose of this manuscript is to describe how one such example of "low tech" assistive technology—modified ride-on toy cars—is being used by early childhood professionals across the country to implement the Division of Early Childhood (DEC) Recommended Practices (2004) related to assistive technology.

The DEC Recommended Practices were developed to bridge the gap between research and practice, providing early childhood professionals with evidence-based strategies that can be implemented in practice to achieve better outcomes for children who have or who are at risk for developmental disabilities (DEC, 2014). The recommended practices are broadly categorized into eight topic areas. One of these areas is Environment, which include practices that may address the child's social, physical, and/or temporal environment. Recommended practices E4, E5, and E6 recognize the importance of assistive technology for providing children with opportunities to live, play, and interact with peers and families in natural environments.

E4. Practitioners work with families and other adults to identify each child's needs for assistive technology to promote access to and participation in learning experiences.

For Landon, it was important for his special education team—including therapists and teachers—to work with his family to identify his unique needs to increase participation in the school environment. The team chose assistive technology to support his environment and routines, not the other way around.

E5. Practitioners work with families and other adults to acquire or create appropriate assistive technology to promote each child's access to and participation in learning experiences.

Once the decision was made that self-directed movement and independence should be the primary focus for mobility for Landon, the school team worked with Landon's family to choose a modified ride-on toy car because of the low cost, speed of acquisition, and lack of social stigma attached to using a toy versus a specialized piece of medical equipment. The physical therapist attended a workshop to learn how to modify toy cars and brought back what she learned to Landon and the team.

E6. Practitioners create environments that provide opportunities for movement and regular physical activity to maintain or improve fitness, wellness, and development across domains.

For Landon, the modified toy ride-on cars he used provided him with a fun way to move throughout the school environment with his peers. Landon's power car was just one of many mobility options that he was able to choose from throughout the day, with the overall goal of "more movement" rather than emphasizing a specific type or quality of movement. This resulted in not only more movement but also improved social interactions, such as "chasing" his friends on the playground and exploring boundaries with teachers and caregivers. As Landon's mobility improved, he started to use a "standing car" so that he could maintain the ability to move freely and independently while still working on improved strength, posture,

> With small modifications, everyday objects and toys may be used just as effectively as expensive technologies to achieve mobility goals.

and endurance. This variety and flexibility was key to helping Landon improve development across domains via more opportunities for social mobility.

For Landon, modified ride-on toy cars were examples of assistive technology used by his providers to implement the DEC Environmental Practices, allowing him to experience early mobility, engage in his environment, and participate in routines. In this article, we will provide a brief overview of the ride-on toy car movement (widely known in the rehabilitation community as GoBabyGo!), review the literature supporting the use of modified ride-on toy cars, and describe how three different GoBabyGo! "chapters" are structured to help provide modified ride-on toy cars in their communities. A secondary purpose is to give interested providers the necessary background and suggested framework to start a modified ride-on toy car program in their community as well as inspiration to explore other "low tech" or "light tech" assistive technology options for mobility.

The Importance of Early Mobility

Movement is a crucial component of social interaction and participation in the world. For children with medical conditions and/or developmental disabilities such as cerebral palsy, spina bifida, and Down syndrome, impaired or slowed mobility not only affects physical development, it also impacts social interactions and the development of meaningful relationships. Most children with typical development begin to move and explore their world independently, usually through rolling or crawling, by 6–8 months of age (WHO Multicentre Growth Reference Study Group, 2006). However, children with mobility impairments take much longer than that, and those with severe impairments may never achieve independent mobility. The benefits of early self-directed locomotion are well documented and include improvements in cognitive skills, memory and spatial abilities, and social interactions with peers and caregivers (Anderson et al., 2013; Bai & Bertenthal, 1992; Biringen, Emde, Campos, & Appelbaum, 1995; Bottos, Bolcati, Sciuto, Ruggeri, & Feliciangeli, 2001; Butler, 2009; Campos et al., 2000; Deitz, Swinth, & White, 2002; Gustafson, 1984; Livingstone, 2011; Ragonesi & Galloway, 2012; Tefft, Guerette, & Furumasu, 2011; Uchiyama et al., 2008). The importance of motor behaviors to influence and be influenced by cognitive, language, and social abilities has given rise to the mantra "moving to learn, learning to move!" It is important to note that the developmental benefits of mobility do not rely on the use of walking as the primary mode of locomotion (Butler, 2009; Wiart & Darrah, 2002).

Children with impaired mobility traditionally do not receive power mobility (usually via traditional power wheelchairs) until at least school age and many not at all (Butler, 2009; Chen, Ragonesi, Galloway, & Agrawal, 2011). This is especially disturbing given that the benefits of mobility are seen in equal measure in children who develop self-directed locomotion through crawling, cruising, and walking as in children who experience self-directed walking via assistive technology such as a walker or powered mobility device (Anderson et al., 2013; Campos et al., 2000; Gustafson, 1984; Ragonesi & Galloway, 2012; Uchiyama et al., 2008). This begs the question: Why must children with mobility impairments endure

The benefits of early self-directed locomotion are well documented and include improvements in cognitive skills, memory and spatial abilities, and social interactions with peers and caregivers.

a passive life until they are 5 or older when they are deemed by caregivers as "ready" to receive their first assisted mobility devices?

There are multiple explanations for the delay in access to powered mobility, including the cost and size of a power wheelchair as well as perceptions of child and family "readiness"(Bottos et al., 2001; Furumasu, Guerette, & Tefft, 2004; Home & Ham, 2003; Livingstone, 2011; Wiart, Darrah, Hollis, Cook, & May, 2010). Current research suggests that children as young as 7 months old can successfully use power mobility to explore their environment and participate in daily life (Agrawal, Chen, Ragonesi, & Galloway, 2012; Livingstone, 2011; Lynch, Ryu, Agrawal, & Galloway, 2009). Emerging principles of assistive technology for children emphasize encouraging early mobility, creating mobile learning environments, making mobility fun and feasible in everyday life, and providing several mobility options (i.e., walker and wheeled mobility) that can be used together to provide the child choices for mobility and amass a higher overall frequency and duration of use (Clarke, 1988; Galloway, Ryu, & Agrawal, 2008; Logan, Feldner, Galloway, & Huang, 2016; Logan, Huang, Stahlin, & Galloway, 2014; Lynch et al., 2009).

In this modified ride-on toy car, the foot pedal has been removed and replaced with a large "go" button attached to the steering wheel.

Using Modified Ride-On Toy Cars to Promote Early Mobility: GoBabyGo!

In response to these emerging principles of assistive technology, providers and families have begun exploring the use of modified ride-on toy cars for early mobility, a movement widely known in the rehabilitation community as GoBabyGo! (GBG). The original GBG program was developed at the University of Delaware and has expanded to sites around the country and the world. The GBG mission is "to advance technologies so all people can create their world via independent mobility" (GoBabyGo! [University of Delaware], n.d.). A major goal of GBG is to provide low-tech, developmentally inspired assistive technology to infants and young children by modifying inexpensive, commercially available ride-on toy cars (Huang & Galloway, 2012; Huang, Ragonesi, Stoner, Peffley, & Galloway, 2014). A simple modification of a toy car may include rewiring a foot pedal to a large switch and mounting it on the steering wheel so a child without leg strength or fine-motor control may easily activate the switch to drive the car (Huang & Galloway, 2012; Huang et al., 2014). A more advanced modification may involve reverse-wiring a switch and mounting it to the car's seat so the car accelerates when the child stands and releases the switch, effectively creating a standing car or power walker. Items found in most local hardware stores—PVC pipe, pool noodles, swimming kickboards, and Velcro—can be used to provide modifications to ensure the child is supported, safe, and successful in driving the car.

The children who receive modified toy cars have a range of abilities, from children with moderately delayed development who will eventually walk independently to those with significant disability who will always be dependent on transportation or require power mobility for participation in daily life. For children across a range of abilities, providing early power mobility promotes learning, exploration, and socialization (Anderson et al., 2013; Bai & Bertenthal, 1992; Home & Ham, 2003; Ragonesi, Chen, Agrawal, & Galloway, 2011). Contrary to concerns that providing power mobility will decrease a child's motivation to move independently, early power mobility may actually increase a child's motivation to explore other forms of movement (Livingstone, 2011). Using modified ride-on cars allows families and teachers to unlock this motivation and get a child moving "right now," often for less than $200, without waiting for insurance approvals or specially equipped vehicles and ramps. Research has shown that children with a variety of abilities may successfully use modified ride-on cars for power mobility, resulting in increased movement, socialization, and reported enjoyment (Huang & Galloway, 2012; Huang et al., 2014; Logan, Feldner, et al., 2016; Logan, Huang, et al., 2014).

Development of Local Programs to Modify Ride-On Cars: GoBabyGo! Chapters

A basic premise of GBG is to modify cars for the particular needs of each child and family in their environment(s). Individuals who best understand those needs and contexts are those who live and work in the communities with the children and families they want to help. Although anyone may modify ride-on toy cars, many providers find that connecting with GBG—often through social media and via local workshops—provides valuable information, instruction, resources, and relationships. This has led to the emergence of GBG "chapters" across the nation and around the world. These local GBG chapters are led by parents, therapists, and organizations that understand the unique needs of children with disabilities in their communities. To date, there are approximately 60 chapters that have modified more than 4,000 cars for children and families planetwide. There is no formal organizational structure for GBG or process or cost associated with starting a chapter. Anyone who is interested in the GBG movement and sees a need in their community for modified ride-on toy cars can start modifying cars or even start their own GBG chapter any time. It is important to note that GoBabyGo! is not a product or corporation, nor is it trademarked. Rather, GBG refers to the movement toward using ride-on toy cars for early mobility and describes a network of individuals around the world who share experiences and resources related to modifying ride-on toy cars.

To help individuals start modifying ride-on toy cars in their communities, the University of Delaware GBG team has a number of resources posted on its website (www.udel.edu/gobabygo). This includes an FAQ section with links to a manual, a YouTube channel, and an active Facebook page as well as a list of contacts for GBG chapters and suggestions for how to start a program. The open-source, collaborative nature of GBG has created a network of individuals who are actively sharing information and resources on modifying ride-on toy

Contrary to concerns that providing power mobility will decrease a child's motivation to move independently, early power mobility may actually increase a child's motivation to explore other forms of movement.

Figure 1

Organizational Structure for Typical Variety KC GoBabyGo Build Event

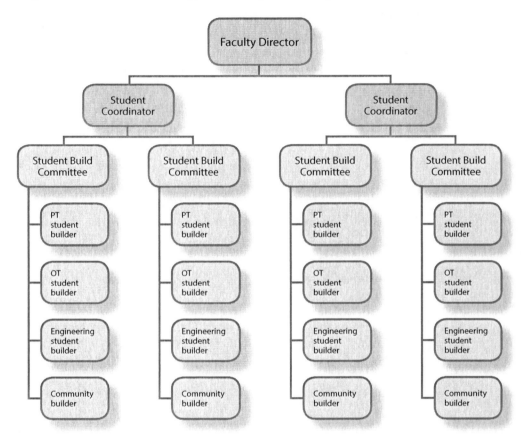

cars. GBG chapters are united in the common purpose to provide early mobility for children with disabilities, but each local chapter has its unique structure and goals. To provide a framework for structuring a program to modify ride-on toy cars, we will describe the structure and processes underlying three GoBabyGo! "super chapters" at Rockhurst University, the University of Central Florida, and Cleveland State University.

Variety KC GoBabyGo at Rockhurst University

Variety KC GoBabyGo at Rockhurst University was developed in February 2015 and is directed by two faculty members, one from the physical therapy program and the other from the engineering and computing program. Variety KC GBG is a student-led organization, and its core members come from the physical therapy, occupational therapy, and engineering programs. The program is led by two student coordinators, who are paid through work study positions to devote up to five hours each per week to the program. The student coordinators lead a GBG student committee, which consists of 8–12 student volunteers, to organize each build event. The student coordinators and committee are responsible for processing applications, contacting families and their therapists to schedule and complete an assessment for a ride-on car, developing a supplies list for build events, organizing supplies, and directing builders during build events.

Physical and occupational therapy students have the opportunity to participate in the program as nonrequired service. Engineering students participate in the program as a required portion of a course, then have the opportunity to continue their involvement on a volunteer basis. Variety KC GBG committee members and student coordinators hold a meeting at the beginning of each academic semester to set a build schedule for the semester and begin coordinating assessments. Typically, the organization hosts at least three build days per semester, where 20–30 students come together to modify four to six cars. Special build events, workshops, and presentations may also be held throughout the semester. The primary goal of Variety KC GBG is to provide modified ride-on cars for children who need them in the Kansas City community. The secondary goal is to provide physical therapy, occupational therapy, and engineering students the opportunity to experience authentic learning in interprofessional teams.

One of these cars has been modified for a child who requires only a seat belt for support. The other uses a swimming kick board and industrial-strength Velcro for a higher backrest and chest strapping. PVC pipe and pool noodles provide additional support.

Student builders provide most of the manpower needed for Variety KC GoBabyGo, but community partnerships are essential to the program's success. Variety KC GoBabyGo is funded by Variety Children's Charity of Kansas City (Variety KC), a local nonprofit organization. In addition to fundraising for the GBG program, Variety Children's Charity hosts an online application system for the program and coordinates almost all public relations and media outreach efforts. Through its website, Facebook page, and media, Variety KC GBG reaches out to community therapists and agencies, including school districts, hospitals, clinics, and early learning centers, to identify children who may benefit from a power ride-on car. This three-pronged approach—Rockhurst University builders, Variety Children's Charity funding and outreach, and community therapists and agencies—has resulted in a successful and sustainable program in the Kansas City community.

GoBabyGo Cleveland

GBG Cleveland began in 2014 and is co-directed by a physical therapist researcher and a faculty member from the Cleveland State University (CSU) physical therapy program. This chapter has its roots in the medical model of pediatric care, but it has evolved to incorporate a strong community network and a funded research component. GBG Cleveland started in the Seating and Mobility Clinic at Cleveland Clinic Children's Hospital for Rehabilitation, when health care professionals began using the adapted cars for the introduction of powered mobility for children of all abilities who were referred to the clinic.

Figure 2

Key Components of GoBabyGo Cleveland and Its Initiatives

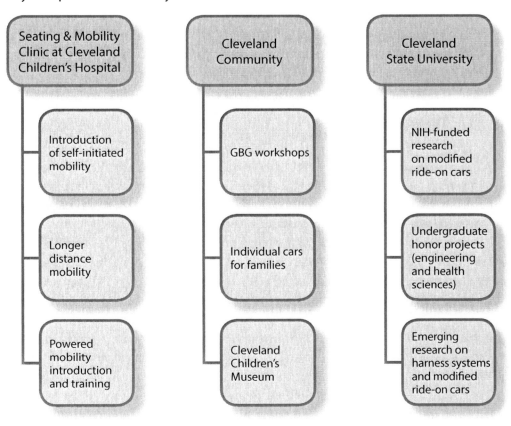

To expand the reach of this technology outside the clinic and into the Cleveland community, Cleveland Clinic Children's Hospital partnered with United Cerebral Palsy, students at CSU, and a local business, National Interstate Insurance, to host a large-scale community workshop. This workshop launched an additional community partnership with Replay for Kids. Replay for Kids is well established in the Cleveland community for adapting toys for children with varied abilities. Replay for Kids supports GBG Cleveland by assisting with workshops and supporting individual families with performing their ride-on car modifications outside of workshops. In addition, CSU has created a partnership with the Cleveland Children's Museum. This interactive program incorporates CSU physical, occupational, and speech therapy students using the adapted cars and body weight–supported harness systems to allow children with varying levels of ability to explore and engage with the museum's programming and exhibits.

On the academic side, GBG Cleveland is actively engaged in NIH-funded research at the Center for Innovative Medical Professions at CSU. It is currently examining the effects of modified ride-on cars on development in infants with Down syndrome who begin to use the cars at 7 months of age. Future studies, pending funding, will incorporate use of body weight–supported harnesses, in addition to the modified cars, to promote early mobility.

Figure 2 depicts the three primary components of GBG Cleveland and describes the initiatives and key partners involved in each of these components. GBG Cleveland identifies need through the Seating and Mobility Clinic and the NICU developmental follow-up clinic, and it has a network of community partners to provide manpower needed to modify ride-on toy cars for children and families. The program is supported financially by a combination of NIH funding and corporate and individual donations. GBG Cleveland continues to explore ways to create additional resources for sustainability and future growth.

University of Central Florida GoBabyGo!

The University of Central Florida (UCF) identifies itself as America's partnership university. Central Florida is rich with opportunities for clinical and research collaborations to address the needs and improve the quality of life for children with or at risk for developmental disabilities and their families. In this spirit, UCF GBG was developed in March 2015 and is directed by a UCF faculty member from the doctor of physical therapy program. Initial development included meetings with UCF and community stakeholders as well as investigation of community need and resources. A preliminary infrastructure was established for UCF GBG with the director, an academic coordinator for administrative needs, and a community ambassador. In May 2015, UCF GBG held its first build workshop with support of the UCF College of Health and Public Affairs and the Down Syndrome Association of Central Florida. The workshop was met with tremendous enthusiasm from the community and clinicians, who saw UCF GBG as a natural partner for addressing community outreach, research, and advocacy for children with motor impairments.

Immediately following the initial workshop, UCF stakeholders worked to establish a more permanent and sustainable structure for UCF GBG. The UCF College of Health and Public Affairs provided start-up funds for modified car supplies. The UCF GBG director, an academic faculty member, receives protected time to devote to development and implementation of UCF GBG initiatives. The academic coordinator assists with program development and community outreach and provides administrative support to the director. In addition, a graduate research assistant was funded by the UCF College of Health and Public Affairs and the doctor of physical therapy program to assist the UCF GBG director. The community ambassador, a clinician from one of the local children's hospitals with extensive seating experience, assists with planning UCF GBG initiatives and coordinates onsite clinical supervision of volunteers at build events.

UCF GBG is working to create a network of student volunteers. A student special interest group that includes physical therapy and engineering students has formed. The student group holds smaller build events (two to three cars) throughout the academic year under the direction of a faculty advisor who reviews the applications of children to determine appropriate recipients and provides on-site clinical expertise regarding seating modifications for the individual children. The UCF GBG student interest group hopes to grow in the future to include interprofessional teams of students from other programs, including medicine, exceptional education, and communication sciences.

Through strong university support as well as strategic partnerships with

Through strong university support as well as strategic partnerships with community clinicians, University of Central Florida GoBabyGo! is able to meet its mission to provide innovative, accessible, and practical options to improve the lives of individuals with limited mobility.

Figure 3

Personnel Structure for GoBabyGo! at the University of Central Florida

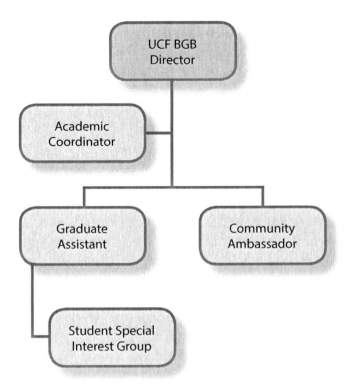

community clinicians, UCF GBG is able to meet its mission to provide innovative, accessible, and practical options to improve the lives of individuals with limited mobility. UCF GBG has received financial support through community donors, including local businesses, organizations, and individuals. UCF GBG has grown tremendously during its first year and has identified many new opportunities for projects to support early mobility for children with or at risk for developmental disabilities and their families. Next steps for UCF GBG include strategic planning for long-term sustainability, collaborative research with other chapters, and further development of community partnerships.

Key Themes and Outcomes

Although each GBG chapter described has its own goals, structure, and processes, there are some overarching themes that consistently arise. We will focus on three critical components of all GBG chapters: identifying community need, securing personnel, and accessing additional resources, including funding and space.

Identifying Community Need

Each chapter's primary goal is to provide early social mobility opportunities for local children with disabilities. This requires collaboration with local stakeholders, including families, therapists, and organizations that live and work with

Starting a GBG Chapter in Your Community

- **Identify a leader.** This can be anyone who is interested in modifying ride-on cars for children in your community.

- **Recruit volunteer builders.** Anyone can participate, but your group should include at least one electrician or electrical engineer (or someone with a similar background) to provide oversight and ensure all modifications are done correctly and safely. Physical and/or occupational therapists may help problem-solve postural supports and more complex physical adaptations.

- **Identify community partners.** They may be able to identify car recipients but may also be able to help access funding and/or secure space.

- **Plan a workshop.** Contact the University of Delaware GBG chapter, or any of the three "super chapters," for more information on bringing a national speaker to your site.

children with disabilities. Although each of these three chapters is situated within a university, there are many modified ride-on toy car programs that are housed in clinics, schools, hospitals, and even community organizations. All GBG chapters have strong community ties. Each chapter has a variety of communication channels and multiple partnerships in place to identify community needs. A key component for each chapter is the focus on collaborating with the family when modifying a car, which provides an empowering experience for families. This is unique compared with traditional provision of assistive technology, where the family's unique needs and routines are often not fully considered by the medical or school team.

Securing Personnel

Each chapter must also have access to personnel to coordinate and carry out various GBG initiatives. A successful chapter must have a director with sufficient time and resources to develop the program. Administrative support, volunteers, and/or paid student assistants may assist with community outreach, manage social media, and coordinate day-to-day tasks such as managing and reviewing applications and securing and organizing supplies. GBG chapters also require manpower to modify cars to meet the needs of the community. The GBG chapters described in this article use community volunteers, clinicians, and student volunteers in a variety of disciplines. Whether students or community volunteers, or both, participate, a key feature of a successful GBG chapter is interprofessional teaming. When building teams include a diverse representation of disciplines and stakeholders, including the family, it provides a greater opportunity to create a product that will be fun and functional for the child and family in daily routines. It is also important to note that, although GBG chapters are often led by physical or occupational therapists, there is no specific professional or personal background required to start a chapter. Engineering oversight is necessary to "sign off" on a car to ensure its safety, but anyone can direct and/or participate in a GBG chapter.

Accessing Funding and Space

Finally, funding is a key need for a successful GBG chapter. Relative to other pieces of pediatric assistive technology, modified ride-on cars are relatively low cost. At the time of this writing, an average modification costs $200–300, including approximately $100–150 for the car itself and an additional $100–150 for materials. However, most GBG chapters describe high levels of response and enthusiasm from the community when they begin, which often results in high numbers of children and families who would like support for a modified car. GBG chapters may partner with outside agencies or donors to raise funds, secure grants, conduct workshops for a fee, or even require that the recipient secure materials and/or funding for the modification. Space to store equipment and conduct build workshops and events may be provided by the home GBG institution, or it may be accessed via community partners.

Conclusion and Next Steps

Modifying ride-on toy cars provides an opportunity for low-tech and low-cost power mobility for young children with mobility impairments and their families. When children cannot roll, scoot, crawl, or walk, the cars provide novel opportunities for self-initiated movement. Children who have some limited mobility, such as crawling or rolling on the floor in their home, find that ride-on cars provide a fun way to move longer distances to engage in outdoor community play and activities. For children who may benefit from longer-term use of wheeled mobility, ride-on toy cars are an approachable training ground, providing a light-tech way to introduce the concept of powered mobility where the focus can simply be on a fun way to learn how to move.

Most importantly, for all the adults in the room, the cars provide insight into the abilities and interests of a child. When a child has physical disabilities that limit movement, it is easy to make assumptions about their likes and dislikes because they cannot move to pick out their toys and peers. Mobility puts children in the driver's seat to make their own choices. In these ways, modifying ride-on toy cars for children with mobility impairments is an effective strategy to implement the DEC Environment recommended practices, providing children and families with assistive technology that helps them engage with their environment and participate in routines to promote mobility, sociability, and inclusion.

- **Secure funding.** Each modified car will cost about $200. Funding for your first build workshop may be secured by private donations, via grants, or through registration fees paid by workshop participants.

- **Get the word out.** Start a Facebook page for your chapter. Use your Facebook page and other social media channels to spread the word.

- **Hold your workshop.** Be sure to have recipients "test drive" at the end of the workshop and invite local media to cover the event. You may need to prepare photo/media release forms for recipients, participants, and families.

- **Make a plan to keep going!** Once the word gets out, you may get offers for donations, requests for recipients, and community members who want to build. Be ready to manage these requests and start planning the next build.

References

Agrawal, S. K., Chen, X., Ragonesi, C., & Galloway, J. C. (2012). Training toddlers seated on mobile robots to steer using force-feedback joystick. *IEEE Transactions on Haptics, 5*, 376–383. doi:10.1109/TOH.2011.67

Anderson, D. I., Campos, J. J., Witherington, D. C., Dahl, A., Rivera, M., He, M., . . . Barbu-Roth, M. (2013). The role of locomotion in psychological development. *Frontiers in Psychology, 4*(440). doi:10.3389/fpsyg.2013.00440

Bai, D. L., & Bertenthal, B. I. (1992). Locomotor status and the development of spatial search skills. *Child Development, 63*, 215–226. doi:10.1111/j.1467-8624.1992.tb03608.x

Biringen, Z., Emde, R. N., Campos, J. J., & Appelbaum, M. I. (1995). Affective reorganization in the infant, the mother, and the dyad: The role of upright locomotion and its timing. *Child Development, 66*, 499–514. doi:10.1111/j.1467-8624.1995.tb00886.x

Bottos, M., Bolcati, C., Sciuto, L., Ruggeri, C., & Feliciangeli, A. (2001). Powered wheelchairs and independence in young children with tetraplegia. *Developmental Medicine and Child Neurology, 43*, 769–777. doi:10.1111/j.1469-8749.2001.tb00159.x

Butler, C. (2009). *Effective mobility for children with motor disabilities.* Seattle, WA: Global Help.

Campos, J. J., Anderson, D. I., Barbu-Roth, M. A., Hubbard, E. M., Hertenstein, M. J., & Witherington, D. (2000). Travel broadens the mind. *Infancy, 1*, 149–219. doi:10.1207/S15327078IN0102_1

Chen, X., Ragonesi, C., Galloway, J. C., & Agrawal, S. K. (2011). Training toddlers seated on mobile robots to drive indoors amidst obstacles. *IEEE Transactions on Neural Systems and Rehabilitation Engineering, 19,* 271–279. doi:10.1109/TNSRE.2011.2114370

Clarke, K. L. (1988). Barriers or enablers? Mobility devices for visually impaired and multihandicapped infants and preschoolers. *Education of the Visually Handicapped, 20*(3), 115–132.

Deitz, J., Swinth, Y., & White, O. (2002). Powered mobility and preschoolers with complex developmental delays. *The American Journal of Occupational Therapy, 56,* 86–96. doi:10.5014/ajot.56.1.86

Division for Early Childhood. (2014). *DEC recommended practices in early intervention/early childhood special education 2014.* Retrieved from http://www.dec-sped.org/recommendedpractices

Furumasu, J., Guerette, P., & Tefft, D. (2004). Relevance of the pediatric powered wheelchair screening test for children with cerebral palsy. *Developmental Medicine & Child Neurology, 46,* 468–474. doi:10.1111/j.1469-8749.2004.tb00507.x

Galloway, J. C., Ryu, J.-C., & Agrawal, S. K. (2008). Babies driving robots: Self-generated mobility in very young infants. *Intelligent Service Robotics, 1,* 123–134. doi:10.1007/s11370-007-0011-2

GoBabyGo at CSU [Cleveland State University]. (n.d.). Retrieved from https://www.csuohio.edu/sciences/health-sciences/gobabygo-csu

GoBabyGo! [Rockhurst University]. (n.d.). Retrieved from http://ww2.rockhurst.edu/gobabygo

GoBabyGo! [University of Delaware]. (n.d.). Retrieved from http://www.udel.edu/gobabygo/

Gustafson, G. E. (1984). Effects of the ability to locomote on infants' social and exploratory behaviors: An experimental study. *Developmental Psychology, 20,* 397–405.

Home, A. M., & Ham, R. (2003). Provision of powered mobility equipment to young children: The Whizz-Kidz experience. *British Journal of Therapy and Rehabilitation, 10,* 511–517. doi:10.12968/bjtr.2003.10.11.13462

Huang, H.-H., & Galloway, J. C. (2012). Modified ride-on toy cars for early power mobility: A technical report. *Pediatric Physical Therapy, 24,* 149–154. doi:10.1097/PEP.0b013e31824d73f9

Huang, H.-H., Ragonesi, C. B., Stoner, T., Peffley, T., & Galloway, J. C. (2014). Modified toy cars for mobility and socialization: Case report of a child with cerebral palsy. *Pediatric Physical Therapy, 26,* 76–84. doi:10.1097/PEP.0000000000000001

Livingstone, R. (2011, November). *Power mobility for infants and preschool children.* Child Development & Rehabilitation . Retrieved from www.child-development.ca

Logan, S., Feldner, H. A., Galloway, J. C., & Huang, H.-H. (2016). Modified ride-on car use by children with complex medical needs. *Pediatric Physical Therapy, 28,* 100–107. doi:10.1097/PEP.0000000000000210

Logan, S., Huang, H.-H., Stahlin, K., & Galloway, J. C. (2014). Modified ride-on car for mobility and socialization: Single-case study of an infant with

Down syndrome. *Pediatric Physical Therapy*, *26*, 418–426. doi:10.1097/PEP.0000000000000070

Lynch, A., Ryu, J.-C., Agrawal, S., & Galloway, J. C. (2009). Power mobility training for a 7-month-old infant with spina bifida. *Pediatric Physical Therapy*, *21*, 362–368. doi:10.1097/PEP.0b013e3181bfae4c

Ragonesi, C. B., Chen, X., Agrawal, S., & Galloway, J. C. (2011). Power mobility and socialization in preschool: Follow-up case study of a child with cerebral palsy. *Pediatric Physical Therapy*, *23*, 399–406. doi:10.1097/PEP.0b013e318235266a

Ragonesi, C. B., & Galloway, J. C. (2012). Short-term, early intensive power mobility training: Case report of an infant at risk for cerebral palsy. *Pediatric Physical Therapy*, *24*, 141–148. doi:10.1097/PEP.0b013e31824c764b

Tefft, D., Guerette, P., & Furumasu, J. (2011). The impact of early powered mobility on parental stress, negative emotions, and family social interactions. *Physical & Occupational Therapy in Pediatrics*, *31*, 4–15. doi:10.3109/01942638.2010.529005

UCF GoBabyGo. (n.d.). Retrieved from http://www.ucfgobabygo.org/

Uchiyama, I., Anderson, D. I., Campos, J. J., Witherington, D., Frankel, C. B., Lejeune, L., & Barbu-Roth, M. (2008). Locomotor experience affects self and emotion. *Developmental Psychology*, *44*, 1225–1231. doi:10.1037/a0013224

WHO Multicentre Growth Reference Study Group. (2006). WHO Motor Development Study: Windows of achievement and gross motor development milestones. *Acta Paediatrica, Supplement S450*, 86–95. doi:10.1111/j.1651-2227.2006.tb02379.x

Wiart, L., & Darrah, J. (2002). Changing philosophical perspectives on the management of children with physical disabilities—their effect on the use of powered mobility. *Disability and Rehabilitation*, *24*, 492–498. doi:10.1080/09638280110105240

Wiart, L., Darrah, J., Hollis, V., Cook, A., & May, L. (2010). Mothers' perceptions of their children's use of powered mobility. *Physical & Occupational Therapy In Pediatrics*, *24*(4), 3–21. doi:10.1300/J006v24n04_02

11

RESOURCES WITHIN REASON

Resources to Support Environmental Practices

CAMILLE CATLETT
Frank Porter Graham Child Development Institute
University of North Carolina at Chapel Hill

ENVIRONMENTAL PRACTICES, AS DESCRIBED IN THE 2014 DEC RECOMmended Practices, "refer to aspects of the space, materials (toys, books, etc.), equipment, routines, and activities that practitioners and families can intentionally alter to support each child's learning across developmental domains" (p. 8). Environmental practices "encompass the physical environment (e.g., space, equipment, and materials), the social environment (e.g., interactions with peers, siblings, family members), and the temporal environment (e.g., sequence and length of routines and activities)" (p. 8). They relate not only to supporting the child's access to learning opportunities but also ensuring their safety. Here are some resources for promoting nurturing and responsive interactions within environments that can foster each child's learning and development.

This annotated collection of resources is organized in categories that align with the major components of this aspect of recommended practice. It starts with general resources—information about and tools for implementing the Environment recommended practices. This is followed by resources for supporting the use of the recommended practices in natural and inclusive environments, physical environments, and learning environments. All resources are available online at no cost.

General Resources

Environment Checklists

Five checklists are currently available to support practitioners and families to learn about and incorporate recommended environmental practices.

- **Natural Environments Learning Opportunities Checklist** includes the types of environmental arrangement and adult (parent or practitioner) practices that can be used to engage children in everyday activities to encourage and sustain child learning while engaged in the activities.
- **Environment Arrangements Checklist** includes practices for encouraging child physical activity using environmental arrangements and active child play opportunities as part of everyday learning.
- **Child Physical Activity Checklist** includes practices for encouraging child physical activity and active child play opportunities as part of everyday learning.
- **Environmental Adaptations Checklist** includes procedures for determining the types of environmental adaptations (physical, social, temporal, etc.) that can be used to promote child participation in learning activities to enhance child competence.
- **Assistive Technology Checklist** includes procedures for identifying and using assistive technology (AT) to promote child participation in learning activities to enhance child competence.

Each checklist is downloadable for use as a self-assessment tool and to plan for effective ways to use environmental practices to support each child.

http://ectacenter.org/decrp/topic-environment.asp

Environment Practice Guides for Practitioners

Each practice guide features a recommended practice, describes how to do the practice, offers an illustrative vignette and a short video of the practice, and lists suggestions for additional resources. These practice guides are available in web and mobile device formats.

http://ectacenter.org/decrp/topic-environment.asp

Environment Practice Guides for Families

Each practice guide features a recommended practice, describes how to do the practice, offers an illustrative vignette and a short video of the practice, and lists suggestions for additional resources. These practice guides are available in web and mobile device formats.

http://ectacenter.org/decrp/topic-environment.asp

Natural and Inclusive Environments

Differentiated Instruction

Tracey Hall's paper offers a model through which teachers can be flexible in their approach to teaching and adjusting environments, the curriculum, and presentation of information to learners rather than expecting students to modify themselves.

> http://teachingcommons.cdl.edu/education/_media/documents/
> NCACDifferentiatedInstructionPaper.doc

Early Childhood Inclusion: A Joint Position Statement of the Division for Early Childhood (DEC) and the National Association for the Education of Young Children (NAEYC)

The position statement contains a definition of early childhood inclusion and provides recommendations for families and professionals for improving inclusive early childhood services and policies.

> http://npdci.fpg.unc.edu/resources/articles/Early_Childhood_Inclusion

Early Intervention Services in Natural Environments

This page contains links to documents outlining key principles and practices when providing high-quality early intervention services in natural environments. Other resources include approaches for service delivery, position statements, a list of state resources, and laws on natural environment.

> http://ectacenter.org/topics/eiservices/eiservices.asp

Fabulous and Free: Resources to Support High-Quality Inclusion

In March 2016, DEC sponsored a webinar on inclusion resources. The handout, developed by Camille Catlett, features high-quality, no cost resources in four categories: evidence sources (e.g., position statements, research), print resources (e.g., articles, chapters), audiovisual resources (e.g., videos, PowerPoints, recorded webinars), and online resources (e.g., websites, modules).

> http://fpg.unc.edu/presentations/dec-pd-sig-webinar

Head Start Center for Inclusion

The goal of the Head Start Center for Inclusion is to "increase the competence, confidence, and effectiveness of personnel in Head Start programs to include children with disabilities." However, the available resources hosted on its website could be helpful for all practitioners seeking to support the access and participation of children with disabilities in inclusive classrooms.

> https://depts.washington.edu/hscenter/

IFSP Process: Planning and Implementing Family-Centered Services in Natural Environments

This webpage gives an overview of the Individualized Family Service Plan process and contains links to various resources about developing quality IFSPs.

http://ectacenter.org/topics/ifsp/ifspprocess.asp

Including Children With Disabilities in State Pre-K Programs

This policy brief provides an overview of the law and sets forth a list of policy recommendations that can help ensure that children with disabilities receive an appropriate public education in the least restrictive environment.

http://www.edlawcenter.org/assets/files/pdfs/publications/PreKPolicyBrief_InclusionChildrenWithDisabilities.pdf

Inclusion in Least Restrictive Environments

This is a collection of resources on inclusion in early childhood, ranging from laws and policies to evidence-based practices.

http://www.ectacenter.org/topics/inclusion/default.asp

Policy Statement on Inclusion of Children With Disabilities in Early Childhood Programs

In September 2015, the U.S. Departments of Education and Health and Human Services released this joint policy statement. In addition to a federal definition, it provides recommendations for action by states in areas that range from policy development to professional development to support the full participation of young children of diverse abilities.

http://www2.ed.gov/about/inits/ed/earlylearning/inclusion/index.html

Quality Inclusive Practices Checklist

This instrument was designed to assess quality inclusive practices within early childhood environments. The features used to define high-quality, inclusive practices are organized by access, participation, and (systemic) supports, the three defining features of inclusion delineated in the joint DEC/NAEYC position statement.

http://www.heartland.edu/documents/heip/faculty/QualityInclusivePracticesChecklist.pdf

Team Lydia Rose: Supporting Inclusion Every Day in Every Way

This video illustrates how inclusive practices should begin as early as possible. In the first part, Janelle describes her 2-year-old daughter's birth, early weeks in the NICU, and her stroke at 4 months old. In the second part, Janelle is joined by Lydia Rose's child development center teacher and her early interventionist as they discuss and illustrate a range of topics including inclusion, collaboration, and early intervention in natural environments.

https://vimeo.com/118072510

Understanding LRE

This module is designed for families and professionals to learn about least restrictive environment (LRE) and inclusion in preschool years. The module covers defining LRE and inclusion and why inclusive education is important for young children. Also discussed is how inclusive services look and how to successfully implement them.

http://www.eclre.org/good-to-know/understanding-lre.aspx

Physical Environments

Academy of Pediatric Physical Therapy Fact Sheets and Resources

The Academy of Pediatric Physical Therapy of the American Physical Therapy Association publishes several open access fact sheets for practitioners and consumers to promote participation for children with disabilities and their families. Fact sheet topics include natural environments, assistive technology, and fitness for young children, to name a few.

https://pediatricapta.org/fact-sheets/

ADA Accessibility Guidelines for Play Areas

These are the final accessibility guidelines to serve as the basis for standards to be adopted by the Department of Justice for new construction and alterations of play areas covered by the Americans With Disabilities Act (ADA). The guidelines include scoping and technical provisions for ground level and elevated play components, accessible routes, ramps and transfer systems, ground surfaces, and soft contained play structures. The guidelines will ensure that newly constructed and altered play areas meet the requirements of the ADA and are readily accessible to and usable by individuals with disabilities.

https://www.access-board.gov/guidelines-and-standards/buildings-and-sites/about-the-ada-standards/background/ada-accessibility-guidelines-for-play-areas

Henry Gets Around

This clip shows how a child with physical disabilities is able to participate fully in all the activities inside and outside the classroom. He walks, runs, climbs, and jumps while being supported by his ankle-foot orthosis and sometimes gets around by using a wheelchair.

http://www2.cde.state.co.us/media/resultsmatter/RMSeries/HenryGetsAround.asp

Physical Activity in the Child Care Setting

This video clip discusses the importance of physical activity for young children and offers suggestions on implementing activities in child care settings. It also includes considerations for children with disabilities.

> http://www.youtube.com/watch?v=F-mcKvLKNtk

Power Mobility for Infants and Preschool Children

This document contains a brief overview of information regarding the use and introduction of power mobility for infants and preschool children with disabilities. It is intended to provide clinicians with relevant background information and to describe the current best level of evidence.

> http://www.childdevelopment.ca/Libraries/Evidence_for_Practice/Power_
> Mobility_for_Infants_Preschoolers_2012.sflb.ashx

Promoting the Health, Safety, and Well-Being of Young Children With Disabilities and Developmental Delays

This 2013 position statement from DEC elaborates on six recommendations for promoting the health, safety, and well-being of young children with disabilities and developmental delays within early learning and development environments.

> http://dec.membershipsoftware.org/files/Position%20Statement%20and%20
> Papers/Health%20Position%20Statement.pdf

Social and Environmental Factors Associated with Preschoolers' Non-Sedentary Physical Activity

The two-fold purpose of this study was to (1) describe with direct observation data the physical activity behaviors and the accompanying social and environmental events of those behaviors for children in preschools and (2) determine which contextual conditions were predictors of moderate-to-vigorous physical activity (MVPA) and nonsedentary physical activity (i.e., light activity + MVPA) for 3-, 4-, and 5-year-old children during their outdoor play.

> http://www.ncbi.nlm.nih.gov/pmc/articles/PMC2648129/

Learning Environments, Including Universal Design for Learning and Assistive Technology

About Universal Design for Learning

This multimedia resource highlights how Universal Design for Learning (UDL) can be used as a framework to improve and optimize teaching and learning for all people based on scientific insights into how humans learn.

> http://www.cast.org/our-work/about-udl.html#.Vxz0BmO8k9S

Accessible Environments: Toward Universal Design

This compilation from North Carolina State University's Center for Universal Design offers insights to the history and applications of Universal Design for Learning to support children of diverse abilities.

https://www.ncsu.edu/ncsu/design/cud/pubs_p/docs/ACC%20Environments.pdf

Center on Technology and Disability (CTD)

OSEP's Center on Technology and Disability (CTD) helps educators, families, and organizations to implement effective assistive and instructional technology. The CTD provides information and technical assistance on assistive and instructional technology for children and youth with disabilities. You can subscribe to receive e-mail updates about upcoming CTD events and activities.

http://www.ctdinstitute.org/

Early Childhood Inclusion/Universal Design for Learning Checklist

Universally Designed Learning (UDL) environments ensure equitable access and meaningful participation through flexible, engaging, and creative approaches within a developmentally appropriate setting. This checklist was developed to guide early childhood observations through the lens of Universal Design for Learning. The outcomes identified from using this tool can be reviewed to create greater UDL awareness, highlight currently used UDL practices, and acknowledge areas to strengthen UDL policies and strategies within the learning environment.

https://www.pakeys.org/uploadedcontent/docs/Higher%20Ed/CunconanLahr%20Kennedy%20Stifel%20Universal%20Design%20for%20Learning%20handout%202.pdf#page=5

Integrating Principles of Universal Design Into the Early Childhood Curriculum

The authors offer examples and recommendations for how teachers of young children can support each young learner in diverse early learning settings by using Universal Design for Learning.

http://www.southernearlychildhood.org/upload/pdf/Dimensions_Vol41_1_Dinnebeil.pdf

Promoting Positive Outcomes for Children With Disabilities: Recommendations for Curriculum, Assessment, and Program Evaluation

This DEC position statement includes a section on Universal Design for Learning.

https://www.naeyc.org/files/naeyc/file/positions/PrmtgPositiveOutcomes.pdf

So Many Ways to Learn

Set to music, this video illustrates the many ways that young children learn. It's good for highlighting the effectiveness of Universal Design for Learning.

http://www2.cde.state.co.us/media/ResultsMatter/RMSeries/SoManyWaysToLearn_SA.asp

Strategies for Including Children With Disabilities in Classroom Activities

As this video demonstrates, interacting with materials and with others creates a rich learning environment for everyone. Some strategies assure positive experiences, such as sensory activities, group table activities, verbal prompts, and simple questions and positive feedback to answers.

https://eclkc.ohs.acf.hhs.gov/hslc/tta-system/teaching/Disabilities/program%20planning/accessibility/StrategiesforIn1.htm

Teaching Tools for Young Children With Challenging Behavior

The teaching tools provide (1) easily accessible ideas and materials such as handouts, worksheets, techniques, strategies, and visuals to support children in the classroom and other learning environments; and (2) ideas of effective intervention approaches for children who do not need a functional assessment to learn about a child's persistent challenging behavior.

http://challengingbehavior.fmhi.usf.edu/do/resources/teaching_tools/ttyc.htm

Universal Design for Learning and Assistive Technology

This webpage provides a brief introduction to Universal Design for Learning (UDL) and how assistive technology (AT) complements this approach.

http://ectacenter.org/topics/atech/udl.asp

Universal Design for Learning Guidelines Version 2.0

The UDL Guidelines, an articulation of the UDL framework, can assist anyone who plans lessons/units of study or develops curricula (goals, methods, materials, and assessments) to reduce barriers, as well as optimize levels of challenge and support, to meet the needs of all learners from the start.

http://www.udlcenter.org/aboutudl/udlguidelines

The Universal Design of Early Education: Moving Forward for All Children

This article explains the rationale behind the Universal Design for Learning and how it can support children with disabilities as well as typically developing children. It contains a chart outlining the seven principles of the Universal Design for Learning and their corresponding educational applications.

http://journal.naeyc.org/btj/200609/ConnPowersBTJ.pdf

References

Division for Early Childhood. (2014). *DEC recommended practices in early intervention/early childhood special education 2014.* Retrieved from http://www.dec-sped.org/recommendedpractices

12

Editorial Team

Editors

Tricia Catalino, *Touro University Nevada*
Lori E. Meyer, *University of Vermont*

Resources Within Reason

Camille Catlett, *Frank Porter Graham Child Development Institute, University of North Carolina at Chapel Hill*

Managing Editors

Winnie Looby and Beth Peloquin, *University of Vermont*

Reviewers

Yusuf Akamoglu, *University of Illinois at Urbana-Champaign*
Katherine Ancell, *Southern Illinois University*
Amanda Arevalo, *Arevalo Physical Therapy*
Karyn Aspden, *Massey University*
Betsy Ayankoya, *University of North Carolina at Chapel Hill*
Sheresa Blanchard, *East Carolina University*
Teresa Byington, *University of Nevada, Reno*
Sandra Cameron, *Barre Supervisory Union*
Jessica Caron, *Pennsylvania State University*
Greg Cheatham, *University of Kansas*
Paula Cox, *physical therapy consultant/trainer*
Natalie Danner, *Western Oregon University*
Lindsay Diamond, *University of Nevada, Las Vegas*
Laurie Dinnebeil, *University of Toledo*
Emily Dorsey, *University of Nebraska–Lincoln*
Melinda Ely, *University of Illinois at Urbana-Champaign*
Leslie Ermolovich, *University of Vermont*
Ashley Fecht, *Touro University Nevada*
Angel Fettig, *University of Massachusetts Boston*
Michelle Gatmaitan, *Kent State University*
Rita Guthrie, *Medina County Board of Developmental Disabilities*
Shana Haines, *University of Vermont*
Jessica Hardy, *Vanderbilt University*
Mary Louise Hemmeter, *Vanderbilt University*

Index